GETTING INTO THE BUSINESS OF COMICS

by Lurene Haines

Published by Stabur Press

Cover art by David Dorman and Lurene Haines © 1994 by David Dorman and Lurene Haines

Baker Street © 1989 Gary Reed and Guy Davis
Batman #508 by Doug Moench, Mike Manley and Joe Rubinstein © 1994 DC Comics. All Rights Reserved
Batman: Red Rain by Doug Moench, Kelley Jones, Malcolm Jones III and Les Dorscheid © 1994 DC Comics.
          All Rights Reserved
Caligula © 1994 Topper Helmers and Rod Underhill
Concrete © 1994 Paul Chadwick
Creepsville © 1994 Frank Kurtz
Edge © 1993 David Dorman
Elfquest © 1993 Warp Graphics
Feud © 1993 Mark A. Nelson and Mike Baron
George White cartoon art © 1994 Coleen Duran
Ghostdancing #1 by Jamie Delano and Richard Case © 1994 Jamie Delano and Richard Case. All Rights Reserved
Ginger Fox art © 1986 Mitch O'Connell
Good Taste Gone Bad © 1993 Mitch O'Connell
Heat © 1994 David Dorman
Hellboy © 1993 Mike Mignola
I.K. Don art © 1993 Mitch O'Connell
Johnny Dynamite ™ & © 1994 Max Allan Collins and Terry Beatty
Justice League America #69 by Dan Jurgens and Rick Burchett © 1992 DC Comics. All Rights Reserved.
Justice League International #65 by Gerard Jones, Chuck Wojtkiewcz and Bob Dvorak © 1994 DC Comics.
          All Rights Reserved.
Prime™ is trademark and © 1993 Malibu Comics Entertainment, Inc. All Rights Reserved.
The Power of Shazam! by Jerry Ordway © 1994 DC Comics. All Rights Reserved.
Radical Dreamer © 1994 Mark Wheatley
Roadkill © 1993 David Dorman
Rockorc © 1993 Les Dorscheid
Rune™ is trademark and © 1993 Malibu Comics Entertainment, Inc. All Rights Reserved.
Sandman art by Marc Hempel © 1993 DC Comics. All Rights Reserved.
Sandman #19 by Neil Gaiman and Charles Vess © 1990 DC Comics. All Rights Reserved.
Sean Taggart cartoon art © 1994 Sean Taggart
Star Slammers © 1994 Walter Simonson
Adventures of Superman #511 by Karl Kesel, Barry Kitson and James Pascoe © 1994 DC Comics. All Rights Reserved
Thumbscrew: "I'll Wait For You" art © 1993 Lurene Haines
Time Cop © 1994 Dark Horse Comics, Inc. and Mark Verheiden. Time Cop created by
          Mike Richardson and Mark Verheiden
Top Dog logo © & ™ 1994 Top Dog Marketing and George White
Understanding Minicomics © 1993 Matt Feazell
Upturned Stone © 1993 Scott Hampton
Vampire art © 1994 Tim Bradstreet
Warstrike™ is trademark and © 1993 Malibu Comics Entertainment, Inc. All Rights Reserved.
Wizard art © 1988 Michael Kaluta

Library of Congress Catalog Card Number: 94-66262

ISBN: 0941613-48-8

Production and design by Lurene Haines © 1994 Lurene Haines

*For David, who makes my life
wonderfully fascinating, amazingly exciting and
incredibly happy.*

Acknowledgements

I would like to thank every one of people who helped me with this project. Without your assistance, not only would this book never have been published, but many readers would have lost out on your valuable advice and expertise.

First, I would like to thank the gang at Arena Magazine; publisher Bob Hickey, editor Joe Martin, and master bookkeeper Mike Hickey. On seeing my proposal for this feature as a monthly column, these fine fellows jumped at the opportunity and as a result are largely responsible for the 'birth' of this book.

I would also like to thank Gary Reed of Caliber Press and Stabur Corporation. Gary recognized the value of this material, and supported the project even before he was economically involved. I admire his forthrightness, honesty and business sense.

I would also like to thank Scott Hampton. This fine professional provided me with invaluable support, advice, insight and encouragement.

I think the fact that both Gary and Scott are so ready to support newcomers to the field readily demonstrates their consummate professionalism. I'm proud to call them both my friends.

I would also like to thank Del Stone Jr., editor extraordinaire. Despite tight deadlines and a profound lack of compensation, Del came through. Now that's a bud!

Also, special thanks to my lawyer, Bruce McDonald. In addition to cranking out my contract under an unexpectedly tight deadline, he also provided invaluable help with the section on copyright notices and trademarks. I'm sure aspiring and established professionals alike will benefit from the information he supplied.

No acknowledgment would be complete without a thank you to my husband and professional associate, David Dorman. Through every project I undertake - and particularly this one - David has made my life a whole lot easier. He is supportive, caring, compassionate, and an excellent source of critique and feedback. My life wouldn't be the same without him.

Finally, I would also like to thank each and every professional who took time out of their valuable workday to talk with me about the business side of comics. (You know who you are - check the bios at the back of the book, if you must!) For many of you, addressing the nitty-gritty issues of business is a less than tasteful job. However, each and every one of you gave me your fullest support, superb advice, and much laughter.

For all of this I thank everyone most sincerely.

Table of Contents

Chapter Seven - The Legal Business of the Biz 85

How legal and business affairs affect you as a professional and how to master these skills. ■ Rules and guidelines dictating business conduct. ■ Notable business practices - negotiations, contracts, standardized forms. ■ Copyright rules. ■ Ownership of original works. ■ Reproduction rights. ■ Licensing and merchandising. ■ Bookkeeping and taxes.

Chapter Eight - You Got The Job: Keeping Your Humility, Pursuing More Work and Fans 106

Professional business practices and behaviors. ■ Social and business interactions with peers and employers. ■ Methods for securing more work. ■ Behaviors for dealing with customers and fans.

Chapter Nine - You Got The Job: How To Be A Good Businessman 120

Communication skills. ■ Organization. ■ Financial management. ■ Business responsibilities.

Chapter Ten - Special Cases and Related Fields or "Creators Aren't The Only Working Stiffs" 144

Areas outside the freelancer arena where career and job opportunities exist. ■ General structure of a publishing house. ■ Review of other comic industry positions. ■ Industries related to comics. ■ Unrelated fields.

Conclusion 165

Appendices

Contributor Biographies 207
Index 216

Welcome to a new kind of book
about breaking into the comic industry!

You might be saying, "Oh, no! Not another '*How To Draw The Superhero Way*' book!" Well, relax. This book has little to do with the art of *creating*. There are many books and articles out there that will help you refine your skills as a creator. Many will instruct you in basic drawing or writing techniques. Some are more specific, detailing the methods approved by a particular company. But, not one of them provides you with the *business information* you need to successfully approach a career in the comic industry.

That's where this book comes in.

Getting Into The Business Of Comics is a broad guide to the specific business practices and techniques used by professionals, to assure the smooth success of their careers. Many of these skills may seem overly simple or obvious to you, but rest assured, they are skills that are indispensable in ensuring your status as a professional. Many of these methods may also seem very familiar to you. That is because these are basic business methods used by many professions - not just the comic industry! That alone should be one indicator of why these techniques are so successful.

In this book I hope to provide you with the basic tools you need to get started. I will take the approach here that you have achieved a level of creative expertise you feel is sufficient to get you a professional comic industry job. I am not here to offer creative advice on improving your skills. I'm here, with the help of many of our industry's finest professionals, to offer suggestions on the business skills you should master and ultimately practice. Once you've taken this first step, the rest should be simple.

If you discover along the way that this doesn't seem to be **nearly** as much fun as you thought comics would be, then perhaps another business would be more appropriate for you. Just keep one thing in mind; comics may be entertainment, but when all is said and done, *this is a business*.

Many young professionals have come to me in a panic for advice on salvaging a business arrangement that has gone bad. Almost without fail the problems resulted from negligence in following common-sense business procedure.

But bad decisions are not restricted to newcomers. Frequently an experienced, long-established professional finds himself in a bad work situation. Again, it's most often due to a poor business decision - deals on a handshake, failure to nail down pertinent details in writing, or lack of information about the parties involved. Nobody's immune; both creators and publishers have been burned by bad business dealings.

This book is your opportunity to find out these crucial bits of preventative info **before** it's too late. If you pay close attention and try out the suggestions, you'll have a great shot at getting your "dream job."

Each chapter of this book will deal with one particular aspect of getting into comics, and conducting yourself as a professional. In addition there are ten appendices which will provide you with useful information and excellent reference material. This book provides the keys to open the door to your future success as a comic professional. It's up to you to use them properly.

So, without further ado, let's get started on Getting Into the Business of Comics!

Chapter One
An Overview of the Industry

*"I've **always** wanted to draw comics..."*
*"So just how did **you** get to work on comics?"*
"I've got this comic some friends and I drew in school. Do you think you might like to publish it?"
"You know, I can draw as good as (fill in big name of your choice) so how come nobody will hire me?"
*"Gee, how do **I** get into comics?"*

The list of pleas, bizarre queries and strange comments goes on and on. Any professional in this strange business we call 'the comic book industry' can give you a list as long as their arm of the thoughtless, thoughtful and thought-provoking remarks made by aspiring comic professionals.

Basically this all boils down to one thing; they haven't taken the time to truly investigate what is involved in getting into the business of comics. And they just don't know where to start.

What Is The Business of Comics?

The comic book industry has been an active part of our culture for more than 50 years. Although in the past the comic book was primarily a form of entertainment for kids, it has since evolved into a more diverse form of entertainment, appealing to young and old alike, and has generated a highly successful collectors market. All that aside, what the comic book represents for many in our culture is an alternate form of expression and creativity.

That means out there, somewhere, potential artists or writers or editors are just itching to try their hand at generating their own unique interpretation of a comic book. They want to 'break into' the business.

Getting Into The Business

This book is not intended to tell you how to develop the 'talent' you need to get work. Art schools, writing courses and business colleges can do that much more effectively than my limited expertise, space or funds. Instead, I'll offer suggestions and methods for improving your abilities. I will assume that you feel you have reached a skill level adequate to pursue comic book work. I'll propose ways you can find out where you stand ability-wise, and hopefully provide some useful advice on how to deal with critiques and professional feedback. Ultimately, however, we will deal with the *business* of getting work.

I hope to shed some light on a variety of areas crucial for doing business in the comic industry. Or in many cases, **any** industry or business. Much of what I'll discuss will be basic common-sense information. You may find yourself thinking, "Hey! *Everybody* knows that?"

But trust me, they don't.

In the short time I've been a comic professional, I've worked very hard and tried to stay on top of all the latest business and professional information. I attend dozens of conventions and make numerous appearances each year, and at every one, without fail, some eager - though often timid - aspiring professional will come up and ask me what appears to be the silliest question with the most obvious answer.

But if I've learned nothing else, I've learned to respect the courage it took to ask a question that might seem dumb to everyone else. And I always answer them as honestly and fully as I can. And with good humor.

And that's what I hope to do here.

I'll try to break down the different aspects of getting into this crazy business, and the various routes and methods you can utilize to make sure you have the greatest chance of securing your dream career.

Try to work in a retail store. At least learn to understand what is involved in the business. Frankly, it doesn't have to be a comic book store, because what a small store owner or a chain-store manager does - the problems they have, the things they have to deal with - is essentially the same in any product category. Different scales, different priorities, but they all have to deal with the facts of running a business that services customers. The better people see that and the broader their outlook - rather than focusing on just the business of comics - the better they'll understand it's a matter of satisfying lots of customers who want lots of different kinds of things. When they understand the reality that this is an entertainment business, the happier and more successful they'll be.

Bruce Bristow, Vice President of
Sales and Marketing for DC Comics

Becoming A Professional Professional

There are a number of useful methods for understanding and learning how to navigate the tricky waters of the comic industry. You should utilize as many as you can.

Enthusiasm is indispensable. If you truly love what you do, then you'll produce work that you're happy with - sometimes work that will inspire you even further. That enthusiasm can be contagious, too. Other professionals like to deal with someone who clearly enjoys his work. Nothing will put you off a business deal faster than someone who can't

ProFile

Professional: Guy Davis, Illustrator
Credits Include: *Baker Street*, Caliber Press; *Phantom Stranger, Sandman Mystery Theater*, DC Comics
Question: How have the independent publishers affected your comic career?

I worked for the independents for about three years. They *were* my career. They gave me the freedom to go with my own style, to try different things. Right now I'm also doing some work for DC Comics.

My experience with the independents has been mixed. Some was real good, some not so great. Caliber was good, but early on I did some projects with some other small companies and it wasn't too pleasant.

Art from *Baker Street: Honour Among Punks* by **Caliber Press**

share your enthusiasm or excitement for a project. But remember to keep it under control. Hyper-excitement is just as much a put-off as total lethargy!

You should also bring *your own personal work experience* to bear in the comic industry. Being a comic professional isn't the first job I've ever held, and I've found that many business techniques and methods I've used in other jobs have great application here.

Don't be afraid to *ask questions*. People will respect you for wanting to do a good job. But remember, if you can look up the answer, do it! There's nothing that will shake confidence in you faster that the appearance of a professional who seems perpetually confused.

Probably the most important method for improving your chances of getting work, and becoming a true professional is your **ability to listen**. I mean *really* listen.

Every time a business professional gives me advice, I *pay attention*. Often they haven't imparted any startlingly new insight, but they almost always give me a whole new perspective on that information. That always makes a big difference in approaching a business problem the next time around.

Hopefully this book will provide *you* with a whole new perspective as well as a lot of new and useful information.

The independent and small-press markets are very valuable to the newcomer as a source of seeing their work in print. This gives the freelancer an opportunity to see the strengths and weaknesses of their work - how it looks in print - and improve on it, before considering approaching the big publishers. They can also provide you with an opportunity to do creator-owned material. You could think of the smaller publishers as a sort of testing ground.

*Dave Dorman, Illustrator (**Star Wars**, Dark Horse Comics)*

A Look At The Industry

From a professional standpoint, we're very fortunate to have such a wide and diverse comic market in which to work. As a freelancer, this provides a broad source of publishing houses to choose from, adding variety and generating a satisfying degree of competitiveness.

As of October 1, 1992 there were more than 120 different companies actively soliciting published material. Of those publishers, about 25-30 are well-known. These, of course, include the top five publishers (in alphabetical order) D.C. Comics, Dark Horse Comics, Malibu Publishing, Marvel Comics and Valiant.

Where To Begin

Presumably, you have already taken a stab at producing some sort of sample or work. Either you have had classes and are producing material for scholastic requirements and homework, or you've been working on your own, practicing. With your samples in hand, you're ready to start. But where to begin - who should you approach with your beloved work?

Many newcomers look at the market, and see only the big, high profile companies. But it's important to know a few things before you approach a potential publisher. You need to decide if that publisher is willing to publish you and if they can offer you more than 'just getting published.' Established pros are always hearing, "I've always wanted to draw/write (fill in the blank with the comic character of your choice)!"

These naive newcomers are certain that just by appearing in an editor's office, or confronting a professional at a convention or store appearance with samples in hand, will guarantee that they're "discovered."

BZZZZT. I'm sorry, that answer is incorrect.

In actuality, an unsolicited appearance, or putting an editor/professional on the spot is more likely to gain their chagrin. Particularly if the aspiring newcomer fails to follow acceptable form and procedure or if their work is unpolished. And especially, if in combination with those things, the newcomer is an *unproven commodity.*

An *unproven commodity* simply means that the publishers generally want a recognizable **Name** - an established or fan-favorite professional - to help sell their books. Now that's not a bad thing, and it's not exclusively the case. But publishing, as we've already said, is a highly competitive business. The top guns are fiercely competing with each other for market share, so anything that will help draw attention to a new book means more sales and a bigger share. That often means using a **Name**.

Soooo, just how did that professional become a **Name**?

Well, it varies from case to case, and depends upon when the professional got into the business. The way things were done twenty years ago contrasts dramatically with what is now accepted form. Many of our new professionals got their break by working hard as assistants to established pros (as in my case) - a variation of schooling and on-the-job-training. Others started in production or editorial departments and worked their way up. However, not everybody lives in the city of a publisher or working pro. The very nature of our business allows for professionals to live wherever they choose and send in their work.

The Small Press

So given these limitations, how does one get started?

That's where the 'small press' comes in. Many professionals will gladly tell you, almost NOBODY starts at the top. Like anything else in life, there are exceptions to every rule, but very few of these in our own beloved industry. You'll find you're going to have to start humbly and work your way up.

For many folks, humbly means the mailroom at the publisher of your choice. Well, that's all well and good if you're interested in handling mail or if you already happen to live in that publisher's city. However, what humbly means *here* is a willingness to start small and work your way up. Starting small in the comic industry means that sometimes the opportunity to be published by a lesser-known company can provide you with both

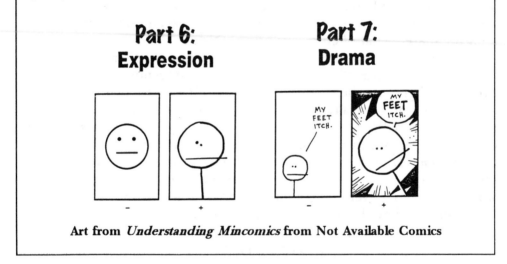
exposure and an opportunity to hone your skills while your work is published (ie., *On The Job Training!*).

Of the 120-plus publishers in our industry, about seventy-five percent of those are small or independent companies. Some got started as vanity press ("I have a comic I want to publish and nobody else wants it, so I'll do it myself!"), some are offshoots of larger companies ("We are pleased to introduce our Alternative Comics line."), some are foreign press ("Those Americans have no taste in comics. Let's show them what *real* comic art looks like - and make some bucks!"), some handle only reprint material ("Well, we've got all these great/lame books around from about _insert time span of your choice here_ years ago. Let's sell them to this new audience") and some just pop up ("I inherited/swindled/borrowed all this money, so I think I'll publish comics.") Whatever the reason for their existence, what they represent is a fertile publishing market, and a great selection of publishers to choose from.

> *Don't try to break into the business at the very top of the industry, at the very top page rates. Try to find an independent publisher, or someone, who's willing to take a chance on you even if it means you won't make big bucks. A published credit is among the most important things you can acquire to use as a sample to get more work.*
>
> Chris Ulm, Editor In Chief for Malibu Comics/Writer
> (**Robotech**, Eternity Comics)

For an unproven newcomer still honing his skills, this is very, very, good. These publishers are generally working from a much smaller budget that the 'big guys'. This means, they generally can't afford to hire a **Name** or many **Names**. From an economic viewpoint, that's not great news for an aspiring (and probably starving) professional. But grit your teeth. With a bit of economic sacrifice these smaller publishers can afford a proving ground, exposure to the industry, and best of all sample tearsheets.

On the other hand, many professionals have nothing but glowing words about their economic arrangements with the independents. Some of these independent publishers offer attractive alternative financial agreements including share of profits and substantial royalties instead of up-front page rates. And best of all, creator rights - something the 'big guys' rarely offer (and most assuredly *not* to an unproven newcomer!) The type of financial arrangement you can live with, whether exposure through publishing with that company will benefit you, how badly you want to keep the rights to characters your create and just how desperately you want to be published should dictate which publisher(s) you approach.

Some of the better known independent companies include Caliber Press, Dark Horse Comics, Eclipse Enterprises, Kitchen Sink Press, Malibu Comics, and Now Comics. There is as much variation in their handling of creators, both in terms of rights and financial arrangements, as there is in the types of material they publish. It is up to you, as an aspiring professional, to inquire into what each company has available should you choose to approach them for work.

The type of material, or genre, published by each company also varies. The two most recognized companies, Marvel and DC Comics, tend toward a lineup of popular superhero material. That's not to say these companies avoid different types of material, however they tend to publish 'alternative' works under a different bannerhead (ie. *Epic Comics* for Marvel, and *Vertigo* and *Piranha Press* for DC Comics.) These lines tend to follow the company policy in terms of financial arrangements, but

ProFile

Professional: Mitch O'Connell, Artist

Credits Include: *The World of Ginger Fox* graphic novel for Comico; *Good Taste Gone Bad: The Art Of Mitch O'Connell* from Good Taste Products; illustration for *Spy Magazine, Playboy Magazine, National Lampoon*; advertising work for *Seven-11, Burger King, MacDonalds Restaurant , Coca-Cola,* and *Kelloggs.*

Question: Do you feel that your work in outside markets, both unrelated and related to comics, has been useful for you obtaining work in the comic industry?

I guess the only way to make a living at drawing comics, is to draw a real hot-selling title off of which you can make royalties. I don't have any interest in drawing a superhero comic or really trying to kill myself doing all the work required to draw thirty pages per month. I don't have any difficulty getting comic work when I want it, not that I'm Mr. Bigshot, but because I basically choose more off-beat, unusual stories. I do maybe seven covers a year. I just do fun projects that I enjoy in comics, because that's not how I expect to make a living. I make a living being a commercial illustrator. I use that to finance doing fun stuff in comics - which does pay some money - and also to do my own work, which hangs in galleries. I probably do four gallery shows a year.

Always be open to anything you can possibly get. In art school, all I wanted to do was draw comics. I was showing my portfolio to comic book editors from when I was 15- to 18-years old, and I never got much of a response. I segued into doing commercial art, and made a living at it for five years, then went back into comics and did a graphic novel.

Advertising art for men's clothing store *I.K. Don*

sometimes offer more attractive creator-rights agreements.

The other companies, or independents, publish product that range from conventional superhero to extremely experimental/cutting edge material. Frequently, this variation from the superhero genre is what most appeals to a newcomer.

> *Don't limit yourself. Don't feel you have to do traditional superhero books. I think the greatest stuff that's ever been done in comics has been brought on the creator's enthusiasm for the subject matter. Now, there have been great superhero comics, and people love that stuff. But great humor, adventure and even romance, is valuable work. There's Carl Barks, and Jeff Smith. For superhero stuff you've got C.C. Beck and Mike Allred. Clive Barker does horror. There's a guy that's very enthusiastic about everything he works on! I think that you should be doing what you like to do because market is always changing. I like to be optimistic, and I hope diversity will win out in the end.*
>
> *Frank Kurtz, Editor for* **Hero Illustrated Magazine***/Artist/Writer*
> *(***Creepsville***, GoGo Comics)*

Now What Do I Do?

With all this information about money, exposure and genre in mind, you should carefully examine the material published by each company. Spend some time in your local comic stores. Don't stick to just one shop, but look around. The store owners are fans, just like you, and they may have a tendency to order material they prefer, or only titles that are guaranteed hot sellers. If you check across a couple of shops, you're bound to see a wider selection of books, and therefore you'll get a much better idea of what's out there, and with who you'd like to do business.

Don't just look, either. Ask questions. Most shop owners are glad to answer questions, and many are very knowledgeable about the business. Also, ask if you can look at their distributor order books.

Distributing companies handle the products produced by the publishers. They are the direct contact between the publishers and the stores. They are responsible for providing order forms, processing the orders and shipping the product. The order books, also called catalogues or solicitations, list all the material that is to be printed by every publisher, for the next sales period. There is often a description of the books, and sometimes some artwork samples. This can provide some very useful research information if your local store doesn't order from the more obscure companies.

Check out the comic industry trade publications too. Our industry plays host to a variety of comics news sources, some of which include the well-known weekly paper **The Comics Buyers Guide**, monthlies **Wizard: The Guide To Comics** and **Heros Illustrated**, and **Comic Shop News**. Each of these publications offers a unique perspective on a variety of areas in the industry, including a good look at what's new from the various publishers. To be a knowledgeable professional (and to give yourself an advantage in doing business in the comics industry) it is in your best interest to read at least a couple of these trade publications regularly.

At this point, you may want to create a record of information on prospective publishers. This can take the form of a notebook, or card file. Just jot down a few pieces of pertinent information about the specific publishers that interest you. Note the company name and address. List some information about the products; the genre they tend to publish, the style of the product (black and white vs. color, monthly book vs. mini-series, comics vs. graphic novels), the recognizability of talent (ie., do they tend to use 'Names,' etc.), who owns the rights to the characters (listed in the indicia), the average cost of their books, and any other information you think would be important in deciding whether that publisher would be interested in your work.

Now You're Ready To Get Started

Now you're armed with valuable information about your potential employers, and you've gotten a truly professional start on your career. You've done some *research*. You know who is publishing material similar to what you have to offer, the caliber of work they're publishing, and the types of professionals they hire. If you're interested in working on superhero books, you now have a record of whom to contact. If you want to pursue a character you've created, but don't want to give up your rights, you know which publisher honors creator-rights.

Your next step is to send out requests for *submission guidelines.*

Submission guidelines are a written guide, produced by the individual publishers, which details the manner and format in which a publisher will consider unsolicited material. Many publishers will not even consider new material unless the samples follow the company guidelines for new submissions. Some companies don't have a structured set of guidelines, so just ask for the editor of new submissions. This way you follow the most efficient company format, and your sample won't sit on a desk at the bottomof somebody's "To Do" pile.

To get the guideline, here's what you do: Request, in a business-like manner, a copy of "*Insert company name here* submission guidelines." Include a self-addressed, stamped envelope (S.A.S.E.) for the reply. Although it's not required, the SASE is a courtesy. Remember, publishers get hundreds of inquiries so set yourself apart as a true professional!

When the guidelines arrive, add the information to your record on the company. This way you have a log of information to draw on when making your actual submissions - and a way to keep track of whom you've

ProFile

Professional: Scott Hampton, Illustrator
Credits Include: *Silverheels* Graphic Novel, and *Pigeons From Hell*, Eclipse Enterprises; *Batman:Nightcries*, DC Comics; *The Upturned Stone*, Kitchen Sink Press
Question: What effect have independent publishers had on your comic career?

     The independent publishers, Pacific Comics and Eclipse mostly, allowed me a venue for my own interests and ideas. I got in early, when they were wide open and Marvel and DC hadn't yet gotten very far into creator-oriented material.

     They often represent a willingness to see you as more than a 'cog in the machine', exclusively aligned with them, and accept you as an independent. They generally respect the idea of being a freelancer a bit more than Marvel and DC, which, because of their size, have to operate like a corporation. However, in recent years Marvel and DC have become much more open to new and experimental ideas, and DC, in particular, has improved creator contracts tremendously.

     My experience with the independents.has been generally very good. In any career that spans 10 years, though, there're bound to be ups and downs. In my experience, the down side was their poor cash-flow situation. The up side was that they were generally more enthusiastic about the work, and frequently less intrusive and controlling.

Art from Hampton's *Upturned Stone* published by Kitchen Sink Press

contacted, how you contacted them, and what the response was.

That's the first step in establishing yourself in the industry; investigating and researching who you think are the best publishers to approach. All of this should be done long before you consider *personally* approaching a potential employer and will help prepare you for setting your best, and most impressive, foot forward.

> *Keep your day job. This may sound harsh, but don't give up your entire life just because you want to follow a dream of working in comics.*
>
> *Chris Ulm, Editor In Chief for Malibu Comics/Writer*
> *(**Dead Clown**, Malibu Comics)*

Summary

To review; you want to *do research* to learn about and know your market, *prepare an organized record* of potential employers, and *send for submissions guidelines* so that you can follow correct procedure when submitting samples. Always remember, the three keys to getting started are research, organization and business procedure.

Chapter Two
Preparing A Professional Portfolio

In this chapter we're going to look at an important and very concrete step on the road to working in the comic industry: preparing a professional portfolio. We're going to look at just what a portfolio is, and why it is important in your search for employment, and all the different factors to consider when you prepare a professional portfolio.

Just What Is A 'Portfolio'?

A portfolio is an organized display of samples of work, published and/or unpublished.

For artists, there are a variety of professional portfolio cases available from art or office supply shops. However, it can take the form of an ordinary binder with page inserts, a scrapbook with copies and originals mounted on the pages, or even a neatly organized sketchbook. The pages can be displayed in loose form, but it is recommended that they be anchored and protected for safety's sake, particularly in the case of original art. The most important aspect being that the work is organized and easy to examine.

For writers, it is important that their written work is brief, concise examples of their writing. A portfolio is not as important for a writer as samples, which I will discuss later in this chapter.

Why Do I Need One?

Many aspiring professionals - and sometimes even established pros - come to conventions or approach publishers and editors with a set of loose originals or samples in hand, hoping to find work by showing their 'wares'. Sometimes they are just looking for critiques. Unfortunately, this method is often one reason these individuals are unable to get work. To an interested editor or publisher, this disorganized rag-tag collection of work represents an inexperienced and unprofessional employee. It would be the same as showing up for a butcher's job with a bag full of miscellaneous pieces of steaks and chops from the last job or practice - pretty weird, and not too impressive.

By taking the simple first step of organizing your work into an easy-to-scan, eye-pleasing display, you make it effortless for potential employers to examine your work and also prove your ability to be organized and professional.

There are a variety of methods for presenting your work, and several different ways that the you can use this portfolio to promote yourself. But one thing is certain; if you are serious about acquiring professional employment then you must *prepare a portfolio right away.* Not later, when you've completed some dreamed of volume or type of work - you'll never achieve it in time, and you'll always be procrastinating. Not after you've reached the level of satisfaction with your work for which you ultimately aim - that's a distant, ever-changing goal you should always be reaching for.

Do it now. Right now.

If you feel your work isn't satisfactory, then now is not the time to approach employers. Continue your education or practicing. When you're more satisfied, *then* prepare your portfolio, and search for employ. Publishers don't hire aspiring professionals on spec, counting on them developing into some massive talent in the distant future. There are lots of other pros out there to choose from. Employers want to see what you can do *now.*

Prepare a portfolio that shows your strengths. Are you trying to be a penciller, an inker or both? Show action and conversation in your work. Have photocopy samples that you can leave with the editor, and keep doing new work

Mark A. Nelson, Illustrator
("Pencils and Inks", **Hero Illustrated Magazine***)*

What Do I Do?

1. Do The Work

Before you can prepare your portfolio, you must first do the work. That may sound simplistic, or obvious, but often professionals are approached by a wanna-be who assures us that they 'have work at home' or that 'the idea is all worked out.' Ultimately they have nothing concrete to show. You must have finished work before you can expect to interest an employer. Or get a professional critique. Only a well-established, proven professional can sell work 'on spec.' Individuals just getting started need to prove themselves first, and that means doing the work.

There are many ways to display your work, depending on a few factors. Some things to consider are: your finances, size and weight of originals, value of originals, your choice of display method, type of work you do, etc. The list can go on and on. Make your own list, and once you have itemized the characteristics and limitations, then select the method you wish to use for display.

2. Choose A Portfolio Type

As I mentioned earlier, there are a variety of portfolio types available. Using your list of characterizations and limitations, you should

ProFile

Professional: Dave Dorman, Illustrator
Credits Include: *The Greatest Batman Stories Ever Told, DC Comics;*
Aliens:Tribes graphic album, *Indiana Jones and the Temple of Doom, Star*
Wars: Dark Empire and *Tales of The Jedi* series' from Dark Horse Comics;
Roadkill, December and *Heat* from Caliber Press; *Malibu Ultraverse Master*
Series painted trading cards from Skybox.
Question: How do you use your portfolio, sample sheets and business cards?

A portfolio is an easy way to show your potential client the style and
variety of work you can do.

I try to include a variety of new pieces mixed with strong, familiar
work. However, I try to tailor samples to the publisher I'm approaching.
That's really important. I don't normally show horror samples to the
superhero publishers! I try to keep my portfolio to a reasonable size. No
point in overwhelming your potential employer. It's best to get in, do your
business and get out.

I personally prefer to show high quality copies or printed samples in
my portfolio. No originals. They're fragile and sometimes unwieldy and I'm
concerned about damage, since they're valuable to me.

Business cards and sample sheets are very important since they're
easy to leave with a potential client, whether they've see my portfolio or not,
and they're very simple for the publisher to keep readily on file.

Cover art for *Roadkill: A Chronicle of the Deadworld* from Caliber Press

make a choice on which type of portfolio will best suit your needs.

If you plan to travel to many shows and interviews, something very portable is best. If you will be flying, consider that it must meet the carry-on luggage requirements. Don't check your portfolio if you can avoid it! There's nothing worse than spending time and money to go to a show or interview looking for work, only to discover that you have no samples to show because Joe Winter's ski pole pierced and tore them, or that they've been rerouted on a tour of the Orient without you!

Make sure it's reasonably light-weight, too. You'll have to haul it back and forth from car, to home, to hotel, to airport, and through long, long airport concourses. No need to show up with your beautiful samples, if the prospective employer can't tear their eyes off your arm looped and piled on the floor because your ten-ton portfolio has turned you into the amazing Elasto!

Consider the display method, too. Some people choose to display their work matted and shrink-wrapped. It looks really great, but can be unwieldy. One of the easiest forms is the binder or portfolio case. Plastic, perforated pages with a sheet of black paper inside. This provides a double-faced page, and a good black setting on which to display your work. It also adds protection. Most importantly, it makes perusal of your samples effortless - as simple as turning the pages of a book.

If you can keep the overall dimensions down to 11" X 17", that will make it even easier for an interested party to set it on the table in front of them or hold in their lap. And if they're not juggling loose pages, struggling to protect their tabletop or hold up an oversized portfolio, they'll be more inclined to spend some time examining your work.

3. Make copies

Many people place great value on their creations - whether dollar or sentimental - and it only makes sense to protect that value by displaying copies of your work. If it's only a copy that is destroyed, damaged, or (heavens forbid, but it happens) stolen, the cost and emotional trauma is much less than if it were the irreplaceable original.

Copies take a variety of forms. If you work in black and white, then a simple, inexpensive (and clean!) photocopy is suitable to display your work. Full size (11" X 17") copies will easily hold a full size page of comic art. Reductions to letter size (8 1/2" X 11") will provide a more portable sample, and will clearly show how the art will look in comic reproduction.

Color copies are a little more complicated, but valuable if you want to pursue work as a colorist, or for fully-painted material (Just remember, that professionals like to see the original drawings as well as the finished painted samples!) To make color copies, you can use photography, expensive color printing, or - thanks to our ever-improving technology - color photocopies. These types of reproductions are a bit more expensive than the black and white. Costs vary depending on equipment availability and the economics of your area. Often you can make an excellent quality color reproduction, however sometimes the match is poor. In those cases consider alternatives, because a poor sample makes you look bad - and apologies and explanations to the prospective employer don't improve their perception of the work. Just *don't* display bad samples.

4. Display originals

If you're brave, or your originals aren't too important to you, or you are continuously creating new work to replace the old, or if you can't get a good reproduction, or time is very short, then feel free to display the original. However, there are a couple of very important considerations here: portability and protection.

If you like to work on 4' X 4' X 3/8" masonite, then there is not much chance you can fit that in a portfolio, let alone carry it around easily. Then again, because of its large size, your only reasonable source of copies would be a photograph. On the other hand, if you work on paper or bristol that is 11" X 17" or smaller then you can very easily display the original art. It is light-weight, and will easily fit in a standard display folder.

> When you're first starting out try and have some consistency in your [artistic] style.
>
> I've seen too many people bring a portfolio in that has a little bit of this, and a little bit of that, and a little bit of the other - showing that they can do all these different styles - but I didn't really see the style that belonged to that individual. If I was an editor, I'd be more inclined to give someone work that was showing a consistent style or identity of their own. The same thing applies to writers - don't mimic someone elses "voice" or writing style.
>
> Richard Case, Illustrator (**Doom Patrol**, DC Comics)

If you make the choice to display originals, then the most important thing to consider is protection. Now this isn't just for you, but also for the recipient of your portfolio.

Here's a scenario. You've approached a pro to check out your stuff. While looking at your unprotected work, a big, unexpected wet sneeze overcomes them. This isn't going to help your originals look better, and the inadvertent victim is going to feel like chopped jerk for damaging your work -and probably will be a bit resentful. I know, I know, that sounds ridiculous! But guilt is an insidious thing, and they may feel that you put them on the spot to look at your work, and that your lack of professional presentation made them responsible for the damage.

Some pros won't even examine unprotected originals for just this sort of reason. Spend a little extra time and a few dollars. Plastic page protectors are pretty inexpensive - at the very least invest in them for your originals.

5. Tearsheets and Published Work

There are some aspiring professionals who have managed to get something published. Sometimes it's not much; a small company might have published it - even one now out of business - but published samples are an excellent inclusion in your portfolio. If they're good. If it's a far cry from your usual caliber of work, mention the credit in your résumé or cover letter, but don't display the work unless the prospective employer asks specifically to see it. If the publisher did a hatchet job in reproducing the work, display it with good, clean copies of the originals alongside so that a comparison can be made.

Published samples are very useful. They indicate to a potential employer that you've made the effort to get work in the past and completed the assignment to that publisher's satisfaction. Granted the experience may not have been a good one - with problems getting paid by the publisher, meeting your deadline, or even getting your original artwork returned - but it helps provide the appearance of professionalism on your part. Make the best of a bad experience. Make it work to your benefit in the future.

Your Portfolio Format

Now that you've decided what type of work to show, it's important that you carefully choose the format for display. For this section, I will use a standard book-style portfolio case, with two-sided plastic pages (you can use a black paper insert to provide backing) for the example.

1. Selecting Work To Display

The most important things to remember when choosing portfolio material is **ALWAYS DISPLAY YOUR BEST AND MOST CURRENT WORK!!!**

I emphasize this point because, without fail, at every show or appearance pros are approached by numerous aspiring creators who qualify their work with "This isn't my best stuff" or "This is older work, I'm much better now." My response is always a gentle "Then why don't you display your best, current stuff?" The reason is, they generally don't have anything else.

I've heard about a creator who got many of his jobs based on a portfolio that contained good work he had done in high school - at least ten years ago. He scored a few professional jobs based on the portfolio before word got around that he was unable to deliver that same quality of work. The portfolio doesn't fool anyone anymore, and his new published credits aren't much of a selling point. Now he has a hard time getting work on his own merit.

The second most important thing to remember is **NEVER MAKE EXCUSES FOR YOUR WORK!!**

There is no excuse. No really, there isn't.

If your stuff is good, it's good, and you have a chance. If it isn't then you won't get hired. Don't apologize or make excuses. Every pro's heard them a dozen times before, in infinite variations. The didn't care about them before, and they don't care about them now. They only want to see what you've got to show them. Right. This. Minute. Offer descriptions if you wish, or describe new work your currently doing, but don't discredit the work you're displaying. You're just giving yourself bad PR, and it sounds really unprofessional.

Your rule of thumb should be: let the work speak for itself.

2. Choosing The Amount Of Work To Display

There is no set rule for what is too much or too little.

Some creators are very quick and prolific, and have a great deal of good work to choose from. Some are much slower and meticulous, and have fewer pieces to show. Whatever your case, make sure to select the best that you have to offer.

Keep in mind portability when you decide how much to display. As a guide, you should consider between three and five double-sided pages. This will allow you to show 6 to 10 of your best pieces of work. Feel free to increase that slightly, but don't go overboard. If all your work looks the same, a prospective employer is going to get tired of it after ten to twelve pages.

ProFile

Professional: Richard Case, Illustrator

Credits Include: *Doom Patrol* from DC Comics; *Dr. Strange* and *Dark Hold* from Marvel Comics; *Ghost Dancing* (penciller and inker) for Vertigo; *Annie Ammo* (writing and drawing) for Axis

Question: What elements do you feel are critical for a professionally prepared portfolio?

Storytelling would be one of the chief elements. It's important to see if they can tell a story well in pictures. Anatomy, whether it is relatively accurate. I would rather see some knowledge of true anatomy. You can usually tell if someone has really *learned* their anatomy, or just picked it up by looking at comic books. Often, when I'm seeing someone's work, I can tell they've just studied comics, because it's so watered-down from looking at so many other comic book artists, that it doesn't really have that professional look to it.

The other thing is the presentation, itself. Pages should be on good stock paper, and not just bound notebook paper. A portfolio case or folder is definitely preferable to a stack of loose pages, although the case itself doesn't really need to be that big a deal. If you want to get into comic books, it's important to include samples that show you can tell a story. I always look for at least six pages. This shows that they can draw various types of scenes, different kinds of camera angles, and shows that they're conscious of these elements. A lot of kids think it's fun to just do the pin-ups. Don't just do pin-ups! It's okay to have a *few* pin-ups, just to show they can do full visual stuff and show their knack for that. But it's really a storytelling medium, and that's how the portfolio samples should be done.

NONE OF YOU HAVE BEEN OUTSIDE. YOU DON'T KNOW HOW IT IS. THE AIR IS BAD OUT THERE, IT HURTS MY LUNGS. THE FOOD IS POISONED IT MAKES ME SICK

**Art from *Ghost Dancing #1*
from Vertigo Press**

3. Determining The Type of Work To Show

The type of work you actively seek should decide the type of work samples you display in your portfolio. If you're interested in superheros, don't display funny animal work. If you're looking for work in the alternative, horror, or science fiction comics, then don't show superhero samples.

The same holds true for which companies you approach. If you just love Marvel's characters then DON'T show them samples featuring D.C. Comics' characters! Big corporations consider employee loyalty an important factor. If it appears, even superficially, that you could be tempted away by another company down the road, that will curb their interest. But more importantly, they want to see how you would handle *their* characters, since that's what they would be hiring you to draw.

So tailor your portfolio to your audience. If you're attending a convention with representatives from more than one company you wish to approach, then feel free to mix and match your display. They will understand.

On a related line, display the type of work you want to do. Don't show color samples, if all you're interested in is pencilling. Also, if you pencil great, but you like to ink your work, though your inking needs practice, then display a copy of the finished pencils alongside the finished inks. Give a potential employer the opportunity to hire you based on your abilities, not just your dreams. Who knows? They may hate your inks, but go nuts for the pencil work! I've seen it happen before.

If you're pitching your own series, have some completed comics to show. Nobody wants to see sketchbooks. Nobody wants to read proposals. They want a comic book story they can read in five minutes. Something my agent suggests to people is, "Plot out the first hundred pages of your saga, then do an eight-page short story that implies all of it and that will stand on its own." There's a logical tendency to start at the beginning - the origin of your character and so on - and such a story probably doesn't have the tone of the overall series. Get it professionally lettered so that it will look professional.

If you're just after inking or pencilling work, there's the standard advice; full size photocopies, no more than twelve samples, drawn to the industry standard (10" X 15" image area). Inkers should have copies of the uninked pencils for comparison.

I would add that a neatly typed coversheet with your address and phone number on it is a good idea. You're going to leave these with people, so have plenty of copies made. Good luck!

*Paul Chadwick, Artist/Writer (**Concrete**, Dark Horse Comics)*

---

4. Your Portfolio Layout

Although there's no set layout, here is a reasonable guide to get you started:

- Make sure you permanently mark your name, address and phone number somewhere in your portfolio, in case of loss or theft. I've been left with sketchbooks that were forgotten, and had no I.D. inside. Fortunately I tracked down the owner. We're not always that lucky.

- Start your first page with a striking piece of work. There is an effect studied in psychology called the *primacy-recency effect*. It simply says that people can remember the first thing and most recent thing they've seen easiest. Start and finish your portfolio with strong pieces. Chances are those will be what the prospective employer remembers. It's also not a bad idea to have a business card or small sign prominently featuring your name and phone number on that front page. Get that subconscious image planted in the their mind.

- Try to find some form of organization for the interior pieces; chronological order, character groupings, color and black&white groups, etc. This makes it a bit easier for the prospective employer to look through. And remember.

- Try to finish with another really strong piece. Remember that primacy-recency effect! You might want to include another card or sign with your name and phone number on it. Make sure these have clear bold lettering on them. You want to be remembered.

Dorman's sample sheet features a vertical format. He has used a professional print shop to produce his samples on a high quality gloss stock. The cost for this type of sample sheet can be quite high.

Lurene Haines

Dave Dorman •
Illustrations

My sample sheet is a simple color photocopy, using photographs for the originals. Although the quality of reproduction is not quite as good as Dorman's, it allows me an inexpensive way to constantly update my sample sheet, and lets me print out as many, or few, as I need.

Little 'Extras' That Can Help

Now that we've got a professional portfolio all laid out and ready to show, there are a couple of things that you should seriously consider as a fixed part of that 'portfolio' - sample sheets and business cards.

Sample Sheets

Sample sheets are reproductions of your artwork, with your name, address and phone number included. It gives you the opportunity to pass on a permanent copy of work from your portfolio to a prospective employer. These are suitable for individuals who have examined your work, and for those that haven't got time or won't be available when you're able to meet with them. In upcoming chapters we'll also discuss their use in contacting potential employers by mail.

Artist sample sheets can take the form of photocopies, photographs, color copies, professionally printed pages and large cards, or good black-and-white copies on lightweight cardstock.

For writers, sample sheets are one form of 'portfolio.' Copies of script pages, prose work, or story proposals can be attached to your contact information. This is ideal to leave with a prospective client.

One thing to keep in mind, for both artists and writers: make sure you have a good supply of sample sheets on hand. Don't use your last sheet, only to discover that the next person would have been an invaluable contact that you've missed out on. Frequently you can get a price break on volume copying too.

Chuck Wojtkiewicz
Illustration • Graphic Art

Address and Phone
Information Go Here

■ *Artist* **Chuck Wojtkiewicz** *(pronounced Voyt-kev-itch) made a two-sided, top-fold business card. He put his contact information on the outside front and a gorgeous sample of his work on the inside, making a sort of mini-sample sheet.*

■ *Look for Chuck's work in* **Justice League International.** *from DC Comics.*

Business Cards

No matter how unimportant business cards may seem to you, they are invaluable, and fairly inexpensive for simple black and whites. Again, you can usually get a price break if you order larger amounts.

Business cards are indispensable. Keep a few in your pockets and wallet or bag. Slip extras into your portfolio. Always keep them handy.

When you meet a prospective employer, or another professional, you speak volumes about your level of professionalism and business acumen if you can say "Oh, here's my card."

Always hand a card to any prospect that looks at your portfolio. Include one when you hand out your sample sheets. For artists, use the business card as an opportunity to showcase your work. It's almost like a little billboard! People like to look at business card art. Make yours stand out, and they'll remember you.

Writers, don't think it won't help you, too! A good friend of mine, and aspiring prose writer, finally took my advice and had some really nice cards made up before attending a large convention. He was stunned by the response and said he could kick himself for waiting so long. He made some excellent work connections - and even got a few lunch invites from editors!

Summary

You now know just what a portfolio is, and why it is important in your search for employment. Always remember to keep in mind the wide variety of factors you must consider when preparing a professional portfolio. You must *choose the type of portfolio* display case best suited to your needs, decide whether you will *use copies or originals* in your display, include *tearsheets* or any copies of *published work* you may have done, carefully *select the right genre* of work to display (ie., superhero vs. horror), decide the *number of pages* you will show, what *type of work* you want to get (ie. pencilling vs. painted), *select a layout* that most impressively displays your work.

And finally, don't forget *sample sheets* and *business cards*, those little extras that show your professionalism and give you the edge over the other newcomers.

Chapter Three
Approaching Potential Employers Part 1:
Conventions, Feedback and Making Introductions

There are a variety of ways to approach potential employers. These can include sending in samples by mail, hitting the pavement in search of a personal interview with the publisher/editor of choice, and attending conventions.

In this chapter we'll concentrate on making use of conventions in the search for work. I'll discuss introducing yourself to publishers and editors, the business etiquette involved in showing your work, and how to use their feedback to improve your chances. To get started, however, it is imperative to understand the importance of attending conventions, and how they can benefit your burgeoning career.

The Convention Circuit

In our industry we are fortunate to have an extensive convention circuit. By convention circuit, I mean a variety of events, featuring comic content, held throughout the year and around the country (and the world!) A local sponsor organizes a show of comics (and comic-related material), the sellers, the publishers and the creators. These shows are open to the public and frequented by fans of the genre, collectors, and curiosity-seekers. The convention sponsors charge a range of entrance fees for attending these events contingent on a variety of factors. These can include size, duration, numbers of retailers and professionals attending, and the level of 'stardom' of the guest professionals.

Conventions are held everywhere and range dramatically in size. For the purposes of simplicity I will concentrate on information specific to the United States.

Your town or city may be the site of many different conventions throughout the year, or they may be held only occasionally. In the U.S. there are a variety of well-known conventions held each year. Some of the larger, more established conventions include HerosCon held in Charlotte, North Carolina twice a year; Great Eastern's New York show in the winter; and Wondercon held in Oakland, California every spring. The Chicago Comicon (held in Chicago every July) and the San Diego Comicon (which usually runs in August) are the two largest shows in the U.S. in terms of attending professionals. In addition, there are shows in many other major cities, including Atlanta and Dallas. As you can see by this list, there are major conventions representing most geographic areas of the country.

The Anatomy of a Convention

Most conventions are structured similarly, despite any special events that may be scheduled. There are usually four main components to any convention; the dealer/retailers room, the publisher's area, the guest area/artists alley, and panels and displays.

1. The Retailers

There is usually an area designated for retailers (the guys who sell the goods). These are important people. They represent the customers who will ultimately buy your product. It is vital to keep in mind that they are a crucial component in your employment. They ultimately decide which product to order from the distributors and publishers. Cultivating a positive and friendly relationship with the retailer ensures that your latest project will be remembered when ordering time rolls around.

2. The Publishers

Depending on the size of the function, there may be representatives from a few, or most of the comic publishers in our industry. The Publishers set up display areas to promote their latest properties, and provide sneak previews of upcoming projects. They also structure their convention time to consider work from newcomers, and often will be on the lookout for new talent while attending a show.

In the case of our largest convention, the San Diego Comicon, it is unusual for a publisher to *not* attend. For that reason the larger shows, despite their greater cost to attend, are often the best places to search out employment.

> *Develop some sort of relationship with other comic professionals. Join a professional society like CAPS (Cartoon Artist's Professional Society - originally founded by Mark Evanier) in Los Angeles, or whatever is available in your local area. There are scores of comic professionals that meet monthly. This way you can share information with more experienced people.*
>
> Rod Underhill, Attorney/Computer Fine Artist/Writer
> (**The Forbidden Airlock**, Eclectus)

3. The Creators

Most shows use a 'name' creator as a drawing card for the public. Sometimes they bring in guests who are the latest hot talent, and sometimes the guest is a popular favorite who's been around for years. Depending on the size of the function, there can be one or two main guests or, in the case of the much larger shows like Chicago and San Diego, there may be a whole flotilla of big names present. Some will be guests of the show, and some

ProFiles

Professional: Walter Simonson, Artist/Writer
Credits Include: *Thor* from Marvel; *Manhunter, Legends of The World's Finest* (writer) from DC Comics; *Star Slammers* for Malibu's Bravura line
Question: How important a role do you feel conventions play for an aspiring professional, and what advice would you give on attending?

The role of conventions has certainly changed since I started in comics. When I started out, conventions were *not* very important, especially in a business way. And there weren't that many of them - a big one in New York, but not a lot else. So in my early experience conventions were irrelevant. Now it's probably your best shot at getting a hold of editors and assistant editors - the people that can actually look at your work and give you feedback on it. Because of the competition these days, that's really important. There are a lot more people out there trying to get into comics than there used to be. Not only that, but there are now schools that crank out students. I teach at the School of Visual Arts myself, so I'm helping that floodtide of new folks!

At conventions you have a chance to talk to professionals and get their opinions. You can also get to talk to the people - the editors and assistants - who actually assign projects and sign your vouchers. Whatever opinions you get from professional freelancers, it's always worth remembering that these aren't the guys who sign your checks! So, even though you should listen to what they have to say - their feedback can be really valuable - what you really want is to nail down some of the official company people as well.

It's not always easy at conventions, because there are so many people who go there with the same idea in mind. I think most big cons now do things like portfolio reviews where they give out tickets, so that at least you're guaranteed a slot to see somebody. I think that, especially when you're

'Rojas'character design from
***Star Slammers* from**
Malibu's Bravura Line

starting out, your eye isn't trained (of course I'm referring to artists here, not writers) and it's very difficult to judge your own work. A convention really offers you a chance to get some direct face-to-face feedback. *I* certainly found that was very valuable. Mail feedback is great, but the conventions give you a much better chance to see people.

Also, if your work is good enough to take copies and give to people, it's a chance for other people to begin to know who you are. Because there really *are* so many people trying to get into the business, it's really useful to tag your face and your name to your work. The conventions do offer you a chance to do that. The key word here, cliché though it may be, is 'networking'.

The major conventions of course are the ones where you have both the opportunity to meet various professionals - staff as well as freelancers - as well as check out your competition. Like the conventions in San Diego, Chicago and New York. A ton of people show up for those. The show in Philadelphia is still new, and it's a bit early to say whether it'll continue to be as big as the others. The smaller cons - I don't go to that many of them myself, so I'm not sure what your chances are there - might be more difficult to get work at because you may not meet that many people who are actually company staff. But you will meet some professionals, and I think that kind of feedback is really important.

will simply be appearing as part of their own self-promotion and to maintain contact with their readers.

Creators can offer some very valuable insights into the business. Long-established pros have a wealth of useful information and valuable advice. Their input can be very helpful to a newcomer.

4. Panel Discussions and Displays

Many conventions offer a variety of programming events. Some conventions combine sports memorabilia, science fiction/horror, gaming, or media (ie., movies, T.V., video, genre magazines) as part of their presentation. Whatever the content, many cons offer programming in the form of *panel discussions.* These generally feature authorities (and I use this term loosely!) on the topic of discussion, who present information, discuss it among themselves, and answer questions from the audience. Panel members can include publishers, editors, creators, and knowledgeable fans. Panels are valuable tools for the newcomer. Since topics range anywhere from entertainment to the business of the business, they can be a precious source of information and insight. They can also provide an open forum for questioning individuals who might not otherwise be accessible. Learn to listen carefully; much useful information is available at a panel discussion.

Displays at conventions can mean a variety of things. They can take the form of an art gallery displaying originals from attending and non-attending professionals. It can mean an exhibit of memorabilia. It can also mean a demonstration by a creator. Check out what is offered by the convention programming and don't spend your whole time dogging the heels of a potential employer. There's a lot to be learned on the road to becoming a professional, and the more useful information you can find, the better you'll be at your job.

No matter the size, frequency or structure of conventions in your area, one thing is abundantly clear: **attending a convention is one of the most important methods of securing work in the comic industry.**

Many established professionals will tell you just how critical attending industry shows can be. A friend of mine - a relative newcomer to the field of professional inking - for many years resisted attending any large convention because he balked at the cost of travel. He was having a lot of trouble acquiring work in the industry despite an aggressive strategy of sending samples to the publishers. Finally after much nagging and convincing, he relented and decided to attend the San Diego Comicon. It was the best decision he could have made. Within the first day of displaying his work at the show, and shopping it around to various publishers, he had scored one of the biggest jobs of his (or any other pro's) career! Many of his established contemporaries were jealous of his coup, but one thing is certain: he would have never gotten the job if he hadn't been at the convention, in person, promoting his work.

For many aspiring professionals, it's also not feasible to make the trip to a publisher, let alone trying to secure an appointment time to show your work. Because of the way editors structure their time at conventions, this provides an ideal opportunity to show your work. It can save you the expense of an
unannounced (and likely wasted) trip to the publisher's city, or the aggravation of being on a 'wait list' for a portfolio review time. Plus, it provides the opportunity to approach more than one publisher at a time. Besides showing your work, a convention provides another critical element to getting work in the industry: *networking*. Forgive the 'biz-speak,' but networking is the best way to describe this all-important function conventions provide. This is the opportunity to socialize, make contacts, introduce yourself and, finally, familiarize yourself with the way things are done in the industry. The more knowledgeable you are as a newcomer, the more respect you'll gain, and the more likely you'll be considered for work over other newcomers.

Attending the Convention

The first consideration before you attend a convention is to ensure that your portfolio is prepared and that you are well stocked with sample sheets and business cards. Then, before you head out, prepare a strategy. Consider the length of the show, which potential employers will be

31

attending, whom you would like to approach for work consideration, which professionals you'd like to meet and talk with, and any programming events you are interested in attending. Don't plan to spend the whole time chasing down one elusive lead. Set aside time - keeping in mind the schedules of the publishers and editors - to pursue prospective work, and then use the rest of the time for looking, listening and 'networking' (also called 'schmoozing' in more casual circles).

A good strategy is to take a little extra time to look through the program book, if possible, before the convention begins. This will help you organize your time more effectively. Once the doors are opened, try to avoid that big rush to the most popular location. The crowds will thin out a bit as time passes, and you can have a more leisurely conversation with your target employer or pro. Then, consider following these steps:

1. Find out Portfolio Review Times

Your first stop should be to check with each publisher to see when they have scheduled portfolio reviews. Introduce yourself, explain who you are (briefly!), leave a sample sheet and business card if permitted, and then plan to come back during the scheduled review time.

Whatever you do, **DON'T, DON'T, DON'T!** expect that publisher to make a special exception for you, no matter how friendly they may seem. Portfolio reviews are scheduled for two reasons: 1) to allow the publisher time to do their usual business - promoting books, lining up new projects, and meeting the readership - while still taking time to consider newcomers, and 2) to ensure that the publisher will have time to consider your portfolio seriously without extraneous interruptions or distractions. It's in your best interests to make use of this uninterrupted time to guarantee that the publisher can concentrate on your portfolio.

If the publisher has not scheduled a portfolio review time, and doesn't seem too busy, then ask if you can show your work. If everything goes well, you can display your portfolio and make inquiries about prospective employment. If the publisher puts you off, try to politely pin them down on a specific time - at their convenience! - to return for a review. If they are still vague or noncommittal, take the time to check back regularly (but not obsessively or annoyingly) during the show until they *can* make time.

If the publisher appears interested, but seems swamped with interruptions and distractions, ask for a specific time to show your work, when you can talk uninterrupted. If they are receptive, suggest lunch, coffee, or just a five minute break away from the melee at their booth or table. If the publisher is agreeable, you're in luck. But try not to take advantage of your good fortune - or misconstrue it's meaning. Be businesslike and attentive. The publisher will be pleased that their opinion matters to you, that you were businesslike and friendly, and will remember your meeting for future contacts.

If the publisher seems uninterested, and will not set aside any special

ProFile

Professional: Barbara Kesel - Managing Editor, Dark Horse Comics
Credits Include: Editor on *New Teen Titans* and *The Watchmen*, DC Comics; freelance writer on *Hawk and Dove*, DC Comics; Editor for *Aliens: Genocide, Aliens: Hive, Star Wars: Dark Empire*, Rick Geary's *Blanche Goes To Hollywood*, and trafficker for *John Byrne's NextMen, Danger Unlimited*, and Mike Mignola's *Hellboy*, all with Dark Horse Comics; writing *Golden City* segments and its sequel *Will To Power* from Dark Horse Comics *Comic's Greatest World*.
Question: Do you think conventions can help aspiring professionals? What advice can you offer?

I feel they play a very important role as long as newcomers don't make the most critical error in comics: "Never expect an editor from any comic book company appearing at a convention to carry home anything that you bring along to give to them." If you're an artist, bring a physical portfolio of your work to show. If you have copies you want to give out, send them separately to the office. Do not hand them to the editor. If you're a writer, the editor will probably not have time to read a story at the convention. Simply meet them, say hello, get them to establish your face with a pleasant personality (also, please bring deodorant, please wear it, and please bathe daily!) and ask them if you can send something to them at the office to review. It is, and always has been, easier for an artist to break into the industry than a writer. Anyone can look at a page of art and see right away if there's personality and character to the work being done, in addition to skills and talent. But you can't look at a page of script and tell if it's a good story or not. You have to spend more time on it. For a writer, often the best thing you can do at a convention is to hook up with an artist and produce at least a low-level story for something like a fanzine, just so you can work your way through the mechanics of writing a script for someone else to interpret visually.

I also think it's important for each person, no matter what their specific interest (a colorer, a letterer, whatever they want to do) to have a concrete idea in mind of what role they want in the comic industry. I prefer to have somebody ask something specific like, "Hi! Can I work at the mailroom at Dark Horse?" Most everyone comes up and says, "Hi! I want a job at Dark Horse!" Well, good! Good for you! So does everybody else! I don't want to hear, "How do I get a job at Dark Horse?", but more like, "I have the following background; I've studied story structure in English. I've written the following things: reviews, short stories, novels, plays, fiction, letters to the editor. I've studied art. What do I need to know to draw professionally?" Let us know who you are, what your skills consist of and what your background and training are. Then ask, "What else do I need? What can I do to make myself a viable candidate for what you do?"

The bigger companies use a lot of interns. They have programs where they draw people in at the bottom, and kind of work them up through the system, training thme as they go. Some of the mid-range companies, like us, have a lot of people employed, but they tend to all be very specialized jobs. I only have one general assistant in editorial here at Dark Horse. Everyone else has some sort of editorial experience. They're either full editors or on the verge of working their way up. But they all have a publishing or magazine background. Almost nobody came to us cold. So, I'm not interested in employing some fan for any kind of staff position, nor as a writer or artist. I'm interested in hiring someone with the background necessary to draw them into the field they want, and the potential to push it as hard as they can and do as well as possible.

I think " Come focused" is the most important thing. I'd rather have someone come up and ask me two well thought out questions and disappear than monopolize my afternoon to the detriment of everyone else. Any professional is likely to get a little impatient with somebody who begins to monopolize their time.

But do feel free to ask questions. It's okay to ask "What does an editor do?" You'll get a different answer every time. But the common description tends to be; read scripts, make assignments of writers and artist, and put the package together. At some companies it can start with contacting freelancers and negotiating contracts. Other companies start with an assignment where you're told, "Here is your story. Here is your creative team. Just traffic it." So you could try asking every person that you run into what their job's like. That will give you an idea of what working for each of the companies would be like. And where you'd be most interested in working - both as staff and as a freelancer. As a freelancer, you might want a relationship where you have a steady paycheck on a monthly book. You also might want to have complete creative control and freedom, and work on your own schedule. Well, Marvel and DC Comics are going to be more receptive to the first type and less to the second.

But of course, no one passes over good work. Good work gets followed. Good work gets noticed.

YEAH... MAYBE HE'S REALLY ANUBIS, BUT THE ARROW GOES INTO HIM WITH A RED, WET NOISE LIKE ANY KIND OF FLESH GETTING *SLICED.*

Art from Mignola's *Hellboy* by Dark Horse Comics

time to review your work, then stop by periodically to see when the crowds subside, so that you can have their captive attention.

2. Professional Critiques

Take time to approach pros appearing at the show for feedback on your work. They aren't interested in hiring you, but they are often willing to provide you with constructive feedback on your samples. Make sure you wait for a moment when they aren't inundated with people - signing, doing artwork, conversing with attendees - before you approach them for a critique. The same advice applies here as with the publishers. If the pro is distracted, they won't be able to give your work the full attention it deserves. Choose *your* times carefully to make the best use of *their* time.

Critiques of your work by established professionals can be very valuable. Don't be anxious. Most pros will be honest. They are comfortably secure in their work, and won't feel threatened by a potential newcomer. If your work has strengths, you'll hear about them. You'll hear about the weaknesses, too. If you present your work to an established pro for critique, be prepared for just that. Although they aren't interested in hiring you, they do remember what it was like getting started. Most pros are eager to help any newcomer who is prepared to work at both the business and their craft. But help takes on a variety of forms, and here it will be (hopefully) a constructive review of your portfolio and/or samples.

Listen carefully to their critique, you can even make notes if it'll help you remember, and absorb any useful information on improving your skills. Keep in mind they are *established pros*. That means that they've used the skills they're trying to impart to *you* to gain employment in this industry. That should be some indicator of the validity of their comments. On the other hand, keep in mind that people can make mistakes. If a suggestion or comment seems too far off base, or confuses you, consider a second opinion. After the convention is over, review everything you've learned from both the creators and publishers. Disregard anything you deem not useful, and extract that information that will best help you pursue work in the industry.

3. Panels and displays

Frequently panels are made up of publishers and creators in the comic industry. The number of panel topics is infinite. Review your program information, and choose panels with subjects you think will be useful, or which feature professionals from whom you hope to gain insight. Try to attend the panel with some questions planned which are related to the topic. During the panel listen carefully, and pay attention to any information that can help you in your quest for employment. Feel free to ask questions, but keep in mind that there is an established topic, and that this is a public forum. Other members of the audience are unlikely to have interest in your unrelated personal inquiries.

Also, take time to attend any pertinent displays set up at the convention. If there is an Art Show, make a point of going. If there is a

ProFiles

Professional: Marc Hempel - Owner of Insight Studios; Writer, Artist, Painter, Designer

Credits Include: *Sandman:The Kindly Ones*, DC Comics/Vertigo; *Breathtaker*, DC Comics/Vertigo; *Gregory I-IV*, DC Comics/Piranha Press; *Hellraiser #20*."The Girl In The Peephole", Epic Comics.

Question: How do you feel about the part conventions play in getting into the comics business?

I think conventions offer a great opportunity for young artists to have their work seen and critiqued by professionals. Working pros can point out their strengths and weaknesses and help steer them in the right direction. It's also important that less experienced artists carefully inspect original comic pages in order to take note of the various working techniques and materials employed by the pro.

In today's sea of bland and imitative artists, it's crucial that newcomers find their own honest, unique style. They need to draw from their own heart and soul and be inspired by their own feelings and experiences as opposed to simply copying the work of other comic book

Art for *Sandman: The Kindly Ones* from DC Comics

artists. They should throw themselves into their artwork as completely as possible (without getting ink stains on their shirts!) To this purpose, conventions are an opportunity to see how similarly artists work in terms of drawing style - and they also offer a chance to view the work of mavericks who are breaking away stylistically. Meeting and talking with any working professional can be very enlightening.

I would stress that when showing samples, artists should make their work presentable - using the correct materials, if possible - and show only

their very best pieces (not the stuff dating back five years to junior high!).
It's also very important that they include actual comic pages in order to
demonstrate their ability with sequential storytelling. Pin-ups are relatively
useless!

Plus, at larger conventions, virtually everyone shows up and you just
can't beat that for contacts. Also the in-person experience can often be much
more persuasive and effective in getting work. It's much easier to be rejected
or ignored through the mail.

The most important thing to remember when going to a convention,
especially for less experienced artists, is:"Leave your ego at the door!" I
sometimes encounter very talented people who have more ego and ambition
than willingness to learn, and they don't take criticism very well. Without an
open mind and the proper attitude their chance of success is greatly
diminished.

large body of professional work, it will give you an opportunity to examine
the work of established pros - allow you to look at techniques, methods and
mediums. If there are many works by non-professionals, consider it a
learning experience. Examine the work for strengths and weaknesses, and
compare these to your own samples. It will give you an idea of what kind
of talent you're competing with for employment.

> *No matter where you go, always bring your work with you.*
> *No matter who's in the room, always show it to somebody. Don't ever*
> *tell yourself they don't want to see it, especially in a convention*
> *situation because that's why they're there. Always be confident.*
>
> *Michael Kaluta, Illustrator (**Starstruck**, Dark Horse Comics)*

4. Socializing

Although this aspect may be somewhat limited for a nonprofessional,
take advantage of any opportunities to mix with publishers and
professionals. Frequently major distributors or retailers, and even
publishers, will host social functions that enable general attendees to
socialize with established pros. If events of this nature are offered, don't
hesitate to attend. Make sure you bring a good supply of business cards,
and a small notepad. But don't bring your portfolio! This is a *social event*.
Make contacts, introduce yourself, hand out business cards, get information,
but let the poor pros enjoy some downtime. If you're just itching to show
your wares to a particular target, then introduce yourself, explain your
interest, and schedule convention time to bring by your samples. But use
the social event for just that - socializing.

This is an excellent opportunity for a newcomer. Very few newcomers realize the value of 'pressing the flesh.' To meet someone on a social level provides you with an opportunity to make an impression outside the convention crowds. You'll become a face with a name, rather than one of the anonymous masses.

Some very important points:

■ If you're short on social skills (have trouble carrying your end of a conversation, that sort of thing) then take time before attending an event to prepare a couple of questions and/or comments that you can use as an icebreaker. Familiarize yourself with the professionals and publishers at the convention so that if an opportunity to talk presents itself, you have some information you can use to open the conversation. Questions about their interests, current projects, how they work, past work history; these are good openers. Just remember, most people love to talk about themselves. A good, interested listener is valuable. Also, you can make a great contact - even friendship - that could help you down the road professionally.

■ If you see a professional you're just dying to talk to, but they're already engrossed in a conversation or otherwise distracted - DO NOT INTERRUPT OR HOVER!! I cannot emphasize enough how annoying this social faux-pas can be. If you just *have* to talk to them, fine. Keep half an eye on them, and when they are finished, or there is an appropriate moment, then wander over and introduce yourself. Otherwise, wait until the next event or con day. A negative impression of your meeting can carry even more weight in consideration of future work possibilities.

■ If you've managed to start up a conversation, but there is a lull, or apparent disinterest on the part of the pro, then conclude your exchange with the appropriate thanks, and release the poor individual to continue their socializing. Many pros have trouble excusing themselves, and don't want to appear rude. Cut them some slack. Their gratitude will be evident when they look forward to talking with you next time around.

■ Keep it brief. Although you may be excited and delighted by the chance to have a friendly conversation with an individual who has until now seemed "out of reach," keep in mind that they are at this social event for the same reasons you are. They want to socialize, talk business with editors and publishers, and meet other people. For many professionals living scattered around the country, a convention is often the only opportunity they have to socialize with their peers. So if you get the chance to talk, keep it brief. Be friendly, but don't tie them up for long periods of time. If they seem receptive, set a time to meet again - maybe over a meal or a drink - and let them get on to their 'schmoozing' while you continue with yours. I guarantee they'll be grateful, and will remember you in a most positive light when next you meet.

■ If an opportunity to talk with a good contact or a potential employer presents itself, take it in a friendly, but businesslike manner. Introduce yourself (your first *and* last name), comment on your interest in that individual, and use some of your icebreaker questions and/or comments.

ProFiles

Professional: Mark Wheatley - Owner of Insight Studios; Writer, Artist, Production and Consulting

Credits Include: *Breathtaker*, DC Comics; writer/artist/production on a two-part *Batman: Legends Of The Dark Knight*, DC Comics; writer/artist/production for ongoing series, *Radical Dreamer* from Blackball and Mark's Giant Economy Size Comics; art direction/production for the *Vertigo Encyclopedia* from DC Comics; writer on *Flash 1994 Annual* for Marvel Comics; creator of a new *2099* series at Marvel; developing *Argus*, a new series for DC Comics

Question: How important a role do you feel conventions play for an aspiring professional, and what advice would you give on attending?

In the comic industry, we have an international community, and conventions are the only time we can get together. I think it's vital to attend cons as early as possible, because that's when you make friends with the people who will eventually be your contemporaries working in the industry. The importance of the social aspect is usually overlooked. You see, even if *you* don't get work, friends might get jobs and you could eventually get work from, or through, them.

Plus, it's fun! It's important to realize that just because 'networking' might sound dishonest, the thing to keep in mind is that it's fun, and real. You're going to make friends.

***Radical Dreamer* art from Blackball Comics**

My advice for when you know you're going to meet a pro at a convention, or any time you get to meet a professional, is to reread their work and read anything you can about them personally. This lets you familiarize yourself with their interests, and makes it easier to talk with them. Try to talk about something that you both can relate to. For example, paleontology is popular with pros in the comic industry. An old sales technique that works really well, is to start talking about something external - like the guy passing that just spilled his coffee - that sort of thing. It's a good place to open the conversation, takes the pressure off and will make it a lot easier to strike up a conversation.

Keep in mind that all the working professionals used to be aspiring pros, too. Try to remember pros aren't the unapproachable two-dimensional superhero comic characters like they work on, but real people with real families and real lives.

Finally, get involved. Help the people who put on the convention. Offer to help anywhere it's needed; the art show, registration - no job is too small. Remember, convention organizers tend to put on shows regularly. If you've been good to them, they'll be much kinder to you once you're an established professional.

When you deem it the appropriate time to depart, offer them your business card, shake hands, and express your pleasure with meeting them and how you look forward to talking again. By following this very simple strategy, you will have left the individual with the impression that you are friendly, businesslike, enthusiastic, and considerate. And you will have primed them for another meeting - hopefully sometime later at the convention. This will provide you with fertile grounds in which to plant the seed of your possible employment.

If you're only interested in being the flavor of the month, then by all means imitate only the current, hot comic book writers. But if you want a long career as a writer, the key is learning to create real stories.

Wendi Lee, Writer (**Elfquest: New Blood**, Warp Graphics)

■ Follow through. This is imperative advice, whether you are socializing, meeting at the convention, or corresponding. Do not expect the individual you contact to follow through for you. The responsibility is yours. You're the one looking for work, and you'll be the one hanging over the phone like a jilted date. Don't sit around waiting anxiously. If you feel you've made a good contact, then follow through while you are still fresh in their mind. If you've talked at an evening social event, then stop by during the next convention day to talk again, briefly. If your contact expresses interest in seeing your work, then visit with them at their earliest convenience during the convention. However you do it, just remember to *follow through*. Even established pros realize the importance of following through.

Keep in mind that publishers and editors are often doing the work of more than one person. They have little in the way of free time, and no matter how wonderful an impression you've made, it is a courtesy to them to help out in your business relationship by following through. This frees them of the responsibility of trying to remember everyone they've talked to and every little thing they said. They will appreciate your consideration, and by following through you display your professionalism and interest.

Using Feedback

Ultimately, whether it comes from an established creator, or whether it's imparted by a potential employer, you will get comments on your work. They may be accompanied by queries about your availability for work - in which case, plan to celebrate - or they may be the precursors to comments like "I see you have a way to go. Keep working on it, and check back with me next year." Or worse. Whatever is said, there are many ways you can react to this feedback. But the best thing you can do is work with it.

If an editor or publisher advises that your work doesn't fit with their line, then concentrate on tailoring your samples more effectively to their requirements.

If they suggest it lacks polish, or shows weaknesses in technical expertise, then get back to work. Practice, practice, practice.

If a creator suggests new or better methods for approaching your work, try them out. If they indicate strengths, cultivate them, if they point out weaknesses, then work to eliminate them.

But whatever you have to do, pay attention to the critique. Essentially, what that professional is telling you is that your work doesn't meet their standards at that time. In the case of the employer, it doesn't mean they won't hire you *ever*. It just means they don't feel you're ready to hire now.

Also, keep in mind that a large part of a critique is personal opinion. What one professional tells you can be the direct opposite of what another will say. It is a good idea to get a variety of critiques, from both potential employers and potential creative peers. With this type of range, it will be easier for you to decide the validity of the critique comments. If the same comment comes up repeatedly with different pros, then you should consider that it's probably correct despite your own feelings. Try adjusting your work accordingly, then have it critiqued again, and see what the response is.

Always keep one thing in mind: you are trying to secure work in a specific industry. Publishing is a business, so publishers tend to be attracted to marketable material and are generally conservative due to financial constraints. If your style is grossly divergent from what is considered acceptable in our wildly eclectic business, then you may have trouble getting work. That doesn't mean your work isn't valid as it stands. It simply means that there is nobody currently available or interested in publishing work so divergent from the norm. Perhaps someday you can get it published, but getting started often means making small compromises. Keep that in the back of your mind. Get yourself established, then if you feel ready, try shopping your more unusual stuff around again. It may be received more agreeably in the future once you're an established name.

For now, however, you just want to get your foot in the door, so listen to the critiques and learn.

Summary

Now you can see how it all ties together in this first step toward approaching potential employers. It is critical to remember the importance of *attending conventions.*

When attending a convention, you will want to organize a strategy that includes *finding out the portfolio review times* and showing your work samples, getting *professional critiques* from attending creators, sitting in at *panel discussions* and checking out any *displays.* You will also want to take advantage of any specially scheduled *socializing* events such as cocktail parties, dinners, dances, or gatherings hosted by professionals that are open to both pros and convention attendees.

Conventions present you with a variety of methods for meeting possible employers, including *introducing yourself* at both the convention and any related convention social events, *showing your portfolio* to publishers, editors and creators and *using feedback* from their critiques of your work to improve your chances of gaining work in the future.

Chapter Four
Approaching Potential Employers Part 2:
The Mail Route

Sending samples by mail and introducing yourself via letter, in combination with other methods of approaching possible employers, can provide a good base for breaking into comics. This gives editors and publishers a chance to peruse your work and mark your progress. If you are diligent about mail contact, it can even lead to professional comic jobs all on its own. But regardless of your approach, it's important to follow the correct procedures and etiquette for mailing samples.

Some Benefits of Taking the Mail Route

In the comic industry, a large percentage of the professionals live scattered across the country, and even overseas. For these people the mail system, together with courier services like Federal Express and United Parcel Service (UPS) and fax machines, provides an invaluable connection with their employers. Not only does the mail route provide a system for sending in completed work from wherever they may live, but initially it also provides them with an avenue for contacting potential employers, and following up on contacts made in person.

As I mentioned in the last chapter, conventions are a crucial component in securing work and gaining exposure as a newcomer. I also emphasized following up on those convention contacts by mail. This is one place where the mail system is indispensable.

The mail route also saves a hard working newcomer much of the time and money it would take to hoof it to a publisher's office for the *slim possibility* of a personal interview. Most American publishers are located in a few major U.S. cities; New York, Chicago, Los Angeles, Portland, etc., but as I mentioned earlier, most professionals are widely scattered. The same holds true for newcomers who ultimately must concern themselves with the costs and gambles of an unsolicited trip to see one of these publishers.

Should I Send Samples?

One of the first steps in making your presence known as an aspiring pro is to send samples of your work, with an introductory letter, to editors and publishers with whom you'd like to work. Many suggestions I made for assembling a portfolio (See Chapter Two) apply to sending samples by mail. We'll review these shortly. However, the question to keep in mind at all times is: "*Has my work reached a sufficiently professional level?*" If you feel that your work stands up to the quality of workmanship currently being handled by a publisher you wish to approach, then send your samples.

The best possible result would be that they see your stuff, love it, and contact you immediately for work. The worst case scenario is that they reject you soundly, and admonish you to consider another career. However it's most likely, if you follow the proper procedure and etiquette for mail-in samples, you will get a polite - and sometimes encouraging - acknowledgment that your samples were received, and will be 'put on file.'

Don't be discouraged. To get a response of this nature should be considered great reassurance. This indicates there is some interest. If you follow through diligently and reliably (by all avenues, including the mail route) with a solid showing of hard work, that interest could ultimately blossom into a real job offer.

If you've been able to attend a convention, and had a chance to meet some publishers and editors with whom you wish to work, now is the time to follow up on that good fortune. A week or two following the convention, you should be sending a note and more samples to those individuals you contacted. Use the mail route to keep your name and your work fresh in their minds. Most publishers and editors have an extensive and busy convention travel circuit. They have neither the time nor the inclination (unless you've shown the abilities of a new Leonardo Da Vinci!) to keep track of everyone or follow through contacting them, the minute they return to their offices. By using the mail, you ensure that you are remembered, and even considered for upcoming projects.

What Mail System Should I Use?

As I've said, there are a number of mail systems available to you. Besides the Postal Service, you also have a variety of courier services at your disposal. Be forewarned; the correct procedure for sending unsolicited samples and introductory letters to a publisher is to use the regular mail service. Although a courier service can often get your material there much quicker, it is considered inappropriate to use this method for submitting new work for consideration. In addition, you are looking at costs astronomically higher than is truly feasible, if you are seriously contacting several publishers regularly.

There are some things you should do to ensure that your system for sending out materials is streamlined and efficient.

1. Familiarize Yourself With the System

Take a trip to your local post office. Talk to a postal worker, and find out about the different types of mail classes available to you. Ask about approximate delivery times for your target cities, so you can better estimate the time to allow before following up on a submission.

Keep in mind, there are lots of little tricks and pieces of information you can use to make your mail submission system effective and efficient. Don't be afraid to ask questions of both the postal workers and any other business people you have contact with.

2. Stock Up on Mailing Supplies

While at the post office, invest in a few items. First, get a *postage rate schedule*. These are free for the asking, and provide a good reference in your home or studio/office. With a postage rate schedule you can figure out the correct postage for small packages you're sending out. It will also help you calculate the correct postage required for self-addressed, stamped envelopes (S.A.S.E) which should be included with all submissions.

It is also worth investing in an *inexpensive postage scale*. You can pick these up at any office supply store or through mail order catalogues. With the scale and the postal rate schedule, you will save yourself countless trips to the post office, and will make your regular submissions procedures much more efficient. This will ultimately leave you time to do what you enjoy most - honing your work skills.

With the thought in mind of conserving time wasted on multiple trips to the post office, you should also seriously consider investing $15 to $20 in *postage stamps* to keep on hand. The best way to calculate how much you should have convenient is to make up a submissions package and determine the postage required using your rate schedule and scale. As an example, let's say your standard package requires about $1.85 in postage, and you are enclosing standard size S.A.S.E. bearing 29-cents in postage. That puts your total at $2.14 per package. Let's say you'll want to send out packages to five different publishers, at a rate of once a month. In this case, it would be wise to keep a minimum of $10.70 in postage on hand, to save you those trips to the post office. Keeping in mind that you're likely to have other business-related postage requirements, it wouldn't hurt to pick up some extra stamps and round off your postage inventory at $15.

If you decide to purchase a stock of stamps, have the post office give you an assortment of denominations that you can mix and match as required. They all spend the same, whether you use a single $1 stamp or three 29-cent, one 10-cent and three 1-cent stamps. Keep your postage in a clean dry storage area (separate envelopes for each denomination is a good organizational practice) to ensure you don't spend an afternoon steaming apart gummed-together stamps. Unfortunately, I learned this the hard way my first year in sunny, *humid* Florida!

Besides postage materials, you should also invest in a package of

ProFile

Professional: Chuck Wojtkiewicz (pronounced Voyt-kevitch), Comic Illustrator
Credits Include: *Mecca*, Dark Horse; *Superman: Man of Steel, Justice League International*, DC Comics.
Question: Do you use a business card or sample sheet when approaching potential publishers? Do you think they make a difference in acquiring work?

I use a business card, and I do think it makes a difference. Especially if you have a snappy business card. People tend to remember you better. And it lets you give them your name and number in a 'no-hassle' manner.

I've never used a sample sheet, I've always given out packages of samples. I find they help a lot too, when you're looking for work. It gives them [editors] something to remember you by. I update my samples regularly, and believe you should always make it your freshest material - and your best!

The cleaner and more memorable a presentation - for your card or samples - the better. I've always sent my samples in an 11" X 14" envelope, with a reduced illustration pasted on the front of the envelope. You can also get different colored envelopes these days. You should have your name and address screaming across the side of the envelope too, so when it gets in that big pile [of submissions] it'll stick out. Because, it is going to go into a heap, and you just want yours to be constantly falling out where it can be seen.

**Justice Leage International
from DC Comics**

plain manila envelopes. These can be acquired many places but shop around, since prices can vary greatly. Avoid the urge to use brightly colored or decorated envelopes (this includes your own art flourishes). It may seem like this would better catch the eye of a potential employer, but what it will really say is that you a) are spending too much time doing silly things instead of honing your skills and b) haven't yet learned correct professional business procedures. There's an old joke principle called KISS; **K**eep **I**t **S**imple, **S**tupid. That's a very good philosophy to follow when handling any type of business, including mail submissions.

When you purchase your envelopes, remember to determine what size will best hold your submissions. If you plan to send 11" X 17" photocopies, make sure your envelope can hold them. Should you want them to stay flat, purchase a larger envelope. If you're not concerned about folding them in half, save some space and money, and buy a smaller envelope. But remember, that doesn't mean you should turn your copies into paper accordions just to save on the cost of larger envelopes! One fold is sufficient.

Also, remember to buy some standard legal size envelopes - those are the long white ones your bills sometimes come in - to use for S.A.S.E.'s.

3. Organize Your Own Mail-Out System

Once you decide to begin sending out samples, you should have an organized method for proceeding. This will ensure two things: that you send regularly to publishers without accidentally doubling up or omitting one, and that you have a record of who got what and when.

> *Always remember - it's not just fun; it's a business.*
>
> *Keep good records. That's probably the most vital piece of information I can communicate. Keep track of all your paperwork; your receipts, your deductible stuff, your contracts, everything. Keep good records, and keep them neat, so you can really find stuff.*
>
> *Twenty years ago, if you worked for Marvel or DC Comics, you did superhero books and that was it! There were no contracts to speak of except an exclusive agreement, or something like that, but that was about it. You weren't dealing with contracts on any kind of regular basis. There weren't any lawyers in comics, on the freelance end of it. Now, of course, there are a number.*
>
> *It's absolutely vital that you keep everything straight. In terms of business, that's the starting place.*
>
> *Walter Simonson, Artist/Writer (**Thor**, Marvel Comics)*

One way of tracking your mail submissions is to keep a log and file system. This means keeping a file folder on each publisher. In each folder, keep any notes you might have on that publisher (your contacts, their responses, etc.) and copies of whatever samples you sent.

Your log should be a notebook or another file folder. In it you should keep details about what you sent, to whom it was sent, and when it was sent. You should also note what the submissions package contained, the amount of postage you used, when or if you received a response, and any additional comments you might have about the entry. This type of log may seem excessively organized, but if you're frequently sending out multiple submissions, this allows you to track who gets what, when and how much it cost you. You will be able to balance your investment in the various companies against the responses you get from them. It will let you add or delete possible employers, and make changes in the actual contact person. It will also allow you to keep track of when to send updated samples and to whom you should direct them.

There are many other ways of tracking your mail submissions. If the log and file system doesn't work for you, then develop one that does. Just keep in mind, if you begin to practice good business skills at this early stage, not only will this help you down the road when you've established yourself professionally, but it will also serve to impress upon the publisher that you are a serious, competent and reliable business person. In combination with good creative skills, this may make the difference for you getting the job over someone who is as artistically skilled, but who may show less professional prowess.

What Should I Be Sending?

In Chapter One I outlined the procedure for getting the submissions guidelines for each company. Additionally, Appendix G at the back of this book provides the submissions guidelines for various publishers. Once you have established that information, and you've organized your mail out system, the next step is to decide what you should be sending. This is determined by a variety of factors, including: whom you are sending to, what type of work you're doing and whether this is a first-time, unsolicited contact.

First-Time versus Follow-Up Contact

First Time Submissions: If this is a 'cold' or unsolicited submission, then the package you send should include samples of your work, as outlined by the company's submissions guidelines as well as an introductory cover letter (see boxed suggestions) and a business card. You should also make sure to include an S.A.S.E. for a response and/or return of your samples, if you want them back.

Your cover letter should be brief and to the point. Editors look at literally *hundreds* of submissions each week. If your cover letter looks like the first chapter of *War and Peace*, it's likely they will toss it aside and only scan your submission, rather than taking the time to look it over carefully.

Your cover letter should include very basic information about yourself and your experience. It should also reflect your sincere interest and commitment, in addition to taking a professional tone. Keep in mind that the editor is taking valuable time from his work day to consider your samples. Be courteous and considerate, and thank them for their time. Do not make demands or issue ultimatums - that will only guarantee that your samples will quickly be filed under 'D' for Disposal! Try to think of this in terms of a job application. You are approaching a potential employer, and you must impress upon them that you are the best candidate for hiring, not only for your work skills, but because you will be a valuable asset to that company as an employee.

Follow-Up Contact: If you are following up on a previous meeting - for example, from a convention or store appearance - your sample package should reflect this. If your first contact was simply voiced interest, then treat this as a first time submission but mention your meeting with the editor in your cover letter (see boxed suggestions). On the other hand, if you had the opportunity to give the editor a business card, show your portfolio, or leave samples with that editor, then your first contact has been made, and now you should simply follow up as a courtesy. Send additional copies of any samples you may have presented in person, assuming that the editor might have misplaced them in his travels. This will ensure that you are not accidentally swept under the rug. If you have new, improved samples, then enclose a couple of pages with the copies, or in place of the samples you initially provided. Again, include another business card and an S.A.S.E., for the editor's convenience.

For follow-up contact, your cover letter can take a slightly more personal tone, but DO NOT assume that you have been burned into that editor's memory, or that you are suddenly his best buddy! He is still a potential employer you hope to work with. Treat him with that respect.

> *Don't be so excited about working in comics, that you allow yourself to be taken advantage of. Check out all offers thoroughly.*
>
> *Terry Beatty, Penciller/Inker (**Ms. Tree** for DC Comics)*

It's always best to assume that you aren't remembered. Providing him with a reference point and reintroducing yourself is a professional courtesy.

Keep in mind, these people are meeting and doing business with thousands of individuals each year. If they only met you once, briefly, at a convention, it is most likely that you will have to jog their memory. They will appreciate the reminder, and you will impress them with your professional expertise. That will help to get you noticed.

Types of Samples You Should Send

Sample Format: You should carefully follow the submissions guidelines for each company. Try to restrict your samples to two or three pieces, and send only your best and most recent work. Each company follows different submissions guidelines, but they have many features in common.

In the case of art samples, without exception, publishers are interested in good, clean copies only - NOT originals! It is also a good idea to include copies that reflect the full size of the artwork, as well as copies reduced to printed comic page size. This serves two purposes; it allows the editor to see how your work would look when reduced for reproduction, and it makes it much easier to file. If your copies are 8 1/2" X 11," they will easily slip into a standard file folder, and therefore will be more accessible to an editor perusing his new talent file. If you send oversized 11" X 17" copies they must be stored in a flat file, or folded in half to fit a standard file.

And remember, don't staple mixed size pages together. Keep the smaller pages together, or your samples will be damaged when pulled apart for filing. Paperclips are always the best method for joining your sample pages.

It is also important to label, carefully and clearly, *every* page of your samples with your name and contact information.

Writers should follow standard script format as provided by the company's submissions guidelines, or as outlined by a writer's manual. Comic script pages share much in common with screenplay format, and this should serve as a guide if you are unsure on how to proceed.

It doesn't hurt to date your sample pages, either. This will give the editor a reference point when they scan the new talent file. They will know at a glance how frequently you update your submissions, and will be able to track your degree of improvement. This is another indicator of your business professionalism.

Sample Contents: Editors want to see what you can really do. This means, if you pencil and ink, you should send copies of BOTH. For example, some pros are stellar pencillers, but once they ink their work, it takes on an amateurish look. By providing copies of both, you allow the editor to assess ALL your skills. You may find yourself hired for a job just as the penciller or inker, because that's where your greatest ability lies. Don't sell yourself short by combining the two. Make sure that all aspects of your work skills are showcased.

Breaking into the comic industry as a writer can be fairly difficult. To increase your chances of being considered, it doesn't hurt to provide a variety of samples; an outline, sample script pages, and if possible, a page where an artist has illustrated the script. Many editors recommend writers find an artist to team up with. This provides both talents with the best way to showcase their skills - plus an editor is more likely to use a good established *team* who can work well together, than spend extra man-hours trying to track down a pencil-inker team for an unproven writer!

Whatever type of work you do, just make sure that you keep your samples to a few, high quality pages and strictly follow each company's submissions guidelines.

Who Should Receive Your Samples

Your samples are essentially your job application. Therefore, you should direct them to the companies with whom you wish to gain employment. If your interests lie exclusively with superhero subject matter, then you should restrict your mail-outs to the mainstream companies like D.C. Comics, Marvel Comics Malibu Comics and Valiant. If your interests are a little more diverse or esoteric, then consider some smaller, independent publishers like Eclipse, Dark Horse Comics, and Caliber Press.

Whatever material you are interested in, just remember to send samples to a variety of editors representing that company, and to continue sending samples regularly and consistently. Many editors pass around or share samples from newcomers with other editors in their company, but as I said earlier, these are a very busy group of professionals, and they don't always have time to circulate the new samples that come in. Additionally, if they are out of the office for any period and become swamped with a work backlog, your samples may end up buried deep under a stack of other work. It may take months before your samples again see the light of day and by then they will be dated. But if you sent them to more than one editor, they will have made the rounds by this point, and this will significantly improve your chances of getting work.

Which Editor Should I Target?

When sending out sample packages, it's important to do your homework. As I suggested in Chapter One, taking the time to keep a

ProFile

Professional: Les Dorscheid - Illustrator and colorist
Credits Include: *Nexus*, First Comics; *Batman:Red Rain*, *Deadman*, D.C. Comics, *Aliens:Hive*, Dark Horse Comics; *Batman:Dark Joker*, D.C. Comics; *Nexus:Alien Justice #3*, Dark Horse Comics; "Discretion" and "See, I Told You" art prints, Moonlit Graphics; *The Battletech Gallery* print portfolio for SQ Productions
Question: Has mail contact helped you make valuable work connections, and what specific mail methods would you recommend?

It isn't a guarantee, but sometimes the mail does help. In comics, you often get work by doing a job for somebody else. A new editor or art director has talked to that somebody else, then you'll get a call from them saying that your editor was real pleased with what you did, that *they* like what you did, and are you available? If they ask to see samples, then the mail system helps a lot. But it's not always as effective when you're sending it out cold, unsolicited. In comics, I've never gotten work through sending in unsolicited submissions. It's worked fine for my science fiction and fantasy illustrations,

A rockorc from Dorscheid's art print *"Discretion"* by Moonlit Graphics

but not comics. It's always been one job from another, where someone saw something else I did. I got my start going on interviews, and I just happened to stumble onto the studio that was starting to produce *Nexus* (originally published by Capital and First Comics, now published by Dark Horse Comics). At that time, I wasn't pursuing the comic book market at all, so that was kind of fortunate.

Now that I'm established, and because I live in Wisconsin, the mail is pretty important to me. If it wasn't for Federal Express and overnight mail, I wouldn't be doing what I'm doing. At least not from Wisconsin!

I helped a friend, a student, send in mail submissions. What he did was send nice, clean, photocopies of his pencils and inks to a number of different editors. He directed them to specific editors, not just the company in general. He tried to target every editor he could think of in each company, because each one does keep their own records. They do pass samples around to other editors (within the company), but you're not guaranteed that will happen. When he sent submissions to D.C. Comics, I had him send off twelve or fifteen different sets, every six weeks or so. Each time his samples got a little bit better, because he kept practicing at his work. It took about a year, but I think that was mostly because he needed to improve. By the time he got to the quality level they wanted, he started to get the phone calls back. Now he's doing a number of professional jobs, not a monthly book yet but a number of jobs for Marvel. He's done three or four pin-ups and a couple of six page stories. As long as he keeps pursuing it, I think within the next two or three months he'll be full-time busy at it. It only took this long, because his work needed to develop to the point where it was good enough. Had he been at that level to start with, it would have come a lot quicker. By being so persistent, and sending samples over and over to the same editors, it let them see his stuff get better each time. And they knew he was serious, so more dependable.

notebook record of publishers and editors is very important. This will provide you with the information you need to decide who should be the target of your sample packages.

Some companies have a single new submissions editor. This will be specified in their guidelines. In these cases, you should make sure that they receive a sample package, in addition to targeting any specific book editors. Send packages to any editors who work on books you are interested in, or whose work has been associated with books you've enjoyed or believe to be successful.

Keep one important point in mind; don't always expect to hear back from everyone you approach, S.A.S.E. or not. Many editors will be too busy, not interested, or might even be short on professional etiquette of their own. But don't give up. Keep sending out those samples.

When Should I Send My Samples?

Once you have selected the companies you wish to approach, and the specific editors you wish to target, then you should begin sending out your samples regularly. Decide, based on how frequently you produce new work, how often you want to send new samples. A good rule is to send new material every six to eight weeks. This shows both your sincere interest and dedication, and will allow the editors to track your improvement. Additionally, by sending sample packages at regular intervals, you make your name a recognizable quantity in the office.

"Here come Joe Pro's samples, just like clockwork!" Then, when a job comes up where they need someone new or quickly, Joe Pro's name is still on their mind, and he's got himself a job.

Keep a few important points in mind though:

1. *Don't make a pest of yourself.* If you're always sending the same stuff, and don't pay attention to any critical feedback from the editor, this will only serve to alienate them - a guarantee you *won't* get work. Try to keep a reasonable time span between submissions. If you send stuff in too frequently, you'll just annoy the editors.

2. *Don't be too familiar in your correspondence.* If you try to be too buddy-buddy, you may lose a shot at a professional job. Also, try to avoid the 'gushing fan' letters. These do nothing to illustrate your professional skills, and only serve to irritate the editor since they run into that all the time at conventions!

3. *Be sure to reintroduce yourself each time you send samples.* Don't assume that you are so memorable that everyone will know who you are the instant they see your name - no matter how often you send in samples. Remember, these people are looking at hundreds of unsolicited submissions every week, besides all the material from established pros looking for more work. Remind them who you are, when you last sent samples, and what they were. This way, they'll have a reference point, and can quickly locate you in the submissions file.

4. *Don't be demanding.* Despite how often you've sent sample packs, or whether you've ever received a response, don't be surly, demanding or issue an ultimatum in your correspondence. If you feel that your work is going unacknowledged, consider sending your samples to a different editor. Your target editor may be too busy to deal with unsolicited material, or may be too unassertive to send you a rejection. Always keep the tone of your correspondence respectful and polite.

Remember, they're doing *you* a favor by looking at your material; you're not doing *them* a favor by sending them your samples.

If you're dissatisfied with their response, consider sending a simple, polite note with your next sample submission. State that you will be available for future work and then make it your last submission to that editor.

5. *Keep target editors informed of your employment status.* Just because Editor A hires you before Editor B, doesn't mean that you won't ever get work with Editor B. Drop them a note with updated material - perhaps once or twice a year - and notify them of any professional jobs you do find, accompanied by a copy of the published material. This will show your 'hireability' *and* reliability as a freelancer. Nothing encourages employers more than knowing someone else thinks you're worth hiring!

Also, just because you get one professional comic job, doesn't guarantee you're set, career-wise. A noteworthy characteristic of being a freelancer is the need to constantly pursue new work, line up leads on new

Professional: Karl Kesel, Writer/Inker
Credits Include: Inker on Steve Rude for *World's Finest* series, and on John Byrne for *Superman*, DC Comics; writer for *Adventures of Superman*, *Superboy* from DC Comics; writer and artist for *Indiana Jones and The Sargasso Pirates* mini-series for Dark Horse Comics.
Question: What business tactics would you recommend to help newcomers avoid being 'pigeon-holed' creatively?

The problem with the industry, and especially editors, is that they like to know *what* you do. They like to 'pigeon-hole' you. It becomes very difficult to convince people that you have goals beyond that.

In my case, I was pigeon-holed as an inker. Even though I was getting positive reception to my writing ideas from various editors, it was not until I started to pointedly turn down inking work that people started to take me seriously. So from my experience I would say that it helps to work in the field, hopefully in an area in which you are accomplished, so as to establish a name for yourself. Once you've done that - unless you're phenomenally luckier than I was - you will actually have to start turning down those really nice assignments to get the types of work in which you're interested. I turned down some very nice assignments - nice, if I wanted to make my career exclusively as an inker. But I always made it very clear that the reason I was turning these down was my interest in writing or writing/inking assignments. I used my inking reputation to help me get some of those

writing assignments. And you have to make sure word gets out that those are the jobs you're looking for.

You may run into people who will say, "He should have stayed with what he was good at." But at that point, you just have to have faith in your own ability.

Cover art for
Adventures of Superman #511
from DC Comics

jobs and promote yourself. You'll have to work hard at staying regularly employed, so make sure you keep your contacts with various editors alive.

Making Use of Critical Feedback

One benefit of sending an S.A.S.E. with your sample submissions, is the likelihood of getting a professional critique of your work. Now, don't cringe! This sounds much worse than it is. Try to take a philosophical, learning outlook to reviewing criticism from your contacts.

If you are fortunate enough to receive more than just a form rejection letter, use the comments to guide you in improving your work skills. As with convention critiques, pay close attention to the comments. When you start to get similar comments from more than one source, then this is a good indication that you have a weak area that bears some improvement. If you get an isolated comment, which seems off-base to you, ignore it. Keep in mind that these are *individuals*, many who are not artists or writers themselves, offering you their personal opinion based on their own experience and industry knowledge. The key here is to keep in mind that it is their *opinion*, not necessarily the law.

Also, remember that individuals have bad work days whatever the industry in which they work. If their comments seem particularly harsh and out of line, consider that they may be having some problems or difficulties in their own career or personal life. Whatever you do, DON'T TAKE CRITICISM PERSONALLY! It is not intended as a personal attack, but in general is offered as suggestions for improvement. They want you to be good, so they can have a new creator to work with. It does not benefit them in any way to mislead you intentionally by providing criticisms that are lies. But they *are* people, and they *can* make mistakes. Use your best judgment in determining the validity of the comments, and use that information to boost your skills, and ultimately your career. Acknowledge the value of their feedback when you next send samples, and point out areas where you've applied their advice to improve your skills. This will show your ability to listen and work cooperatively with an editor. When your work skills meet their approval, you will be quickly considered a valuable asset for your ability to work well with others on a creative team.

The Response Card - An S.A.S.E. Alternative

If you don't require that your submission samples be returned, conserve on postage by including a response card instead of an S.A.S.E.. The S.A.S.E. will require a minimum of 29 cents in postage, whereas a response card will cost only 19 cents. That 10-cent savings can add up pretty quickly as postage for additional submission's packages.

A response card takes a little bit of work to design, but can be quite valuable. Simply, it is a postcard that lists preprinted responses an editor can check off, and a comment box. There are many benefits to this method, but most importantly it provides the editor with an inexpensive, quick and easy way to acknowledge receipt of your material. This is particularly useful if they are simply updating your file.

Publisher and Editor:_____ (*Print this information prior to mailing*)_____

Attention Editor;
      This response card is provided for your convenience. If you could take the time to check the appropriate box or boxes, I would be very grateful. Thank you for your time.

☐ We have received your samples and placed them on file.

☐ We may consider you for future projects.

☐ We are interested in your work, and will be contacting you shortly.

☐ We regret we are not interested in your work at this time.

(**NOTE: Publisher information and your return mailing address should be on the front.
Make sure you provide sufficient postage.)

Example of a *Response Card*

If they wish to contact you for a job, they will follow through independently. In addition, if you note the publisher information on the card, when you address it, you can keep a detailed record of responders, and any comments they may take the time to note. The response card shows your commitment to the business aspects of working as a freelancer, and will not go unnoticed by the editor.

Summary

By using these various steps to contacting a potential employer through the mail, you will be ready to move on as a freelancer.

Remember to consider *the benefits of sending samples by mail*, and *which mail system* will best serve your purposes. Then you must *decide if your work is of sufficient quality* to merit consideration for employment. If you decide it is, the next step is to *familiarize yourself with the mail procedures, stock mail supplies* for making and sending sample packages, and *organize a system* for tracking the samples you send. Once this is done, your next step is to *get a copy of the submissions guidelines* for the companies you wish to approach, and *decide which editor or editors to target.*

Make sure you *use the correct submissions format* depending on whether your samples are being sent *unsolicited* or if you are making a *follow-up contact.* You should make sure you include an *introductory cover letter,* a *business card,* and an *S.A.S.E. or response card.* If you are following up on a personal contact, this should be reflected in your cover letter. *Send samples out consistently,* and with a demonstrable level of improvement each time. Keeping a regular *system of updating your samples* will allow the editors to mark the increase in your skill, as well as proving your professionalism.

Finally, *use feedback to improve your work.* Display your professionalism by applying any critical advice to your benefit, and expressing appreciation for the time taken to provide you with that feedback.

Chapter Five
Approaching Potential Employers Part 3:
The Personal Interview

Many newcomers believe that the personal interview is a critical step in finding work in the comic industry. Many scrape together their limited funds for a trip to one of the big publishers in the hopes that a personal interview will secure them that elusive comic work. But our industry operates slightly differently than most other career fields. Many professionals never meet their editors or publishers, but that doesn't stop them from lining up new projects. Business is primarily conducted via telephone, mail, courier, and fax machines. If you have success getting work through mail samples and convention contacts, then save your funds, and invest them in improved work materials and business equipment.

That's not to say a personal interview won't make a difference. On the contrary, sometimes being in the right place at exactly the right time can mean the difference between obscurity and employment. If you are a committed, businesslike individual, follow the correct procedures for securing an interview, and have the work skills necessary for getting the job done, the personal interview can be a valuable tool.

> *Don't take it personally. Whatever it is, don't take it personally.*
>
> *Mike Carlin*
> *Executive Editor, D.C. Comics*

However, always keep this in mind: There's no such thing as overnight success. Success is a long road of hard, dedicated work, and the personal interview is just one small section of the pavement. Your first steps should be in the form of preparing your portfolio and samples, attending some conventions to familiarize yourself with the industry and how business is conducted, and taking the time to regularly submit samples of your work by mail. If after all that you still decide that an interview could be of help to you, then there are several steps you can take to ensure some success.

How to Get a Personal Interview

I hear the rustle of people moving to the edge of their seats, as I broach this topic. I'm sorry, though; there is no simple little trick or piece of advice that will secure you this elusive prize. To gain a personal interview, you must do a lot of hard work, plenty of preparation, and invest much time and energy.

Your best shot at an interview will manifest itself if you've followed the recommended steps of preparing a professional portfolio, attending conventions to make professional contacts, and sending out samples by mail.

One or all these techniques can open up the opportunity to approach a particular editor or publisher at their offices - sometimes even at their request. However, this route may not appeal to everyone. If you think you have enough talent and business savvy, and you are fortunate enough to be conveniently located near the publisher you are targeting, then you probably could take advantage of the interview process without the preliminary steps I've recommended. Keep in mind though, the preparation of a professional portfolio is very critical to a personal interview. Also, making connections in person at conventions, and through mail submissions, can establish a friendlier, more familiar and relaxed interview setting.

Most publishers have regularly scheduled interview/portfolio-review days and times. If you wish to pursue an interview uninvited, it is in your best interest to call ahead and find out when these activities are scheduled. If possible, you should always make an appointment. This is an indicator of your professionalism. To simply show up at the publisher's office requesting (or worse yet, demanding) a personal interview is the ultimate in rudeness and inconsiderate business practices. It will do nothing but damage your newly developing career, and alienate you with that particular company.

Assuming you've followed all the steps necessary to reach your goal of a personal interview, and provided you have the means to reach the publisher's office in person, there are a number of things you should consider to ensure you make a good impression, including good preparation, personal presentation and proper interview etiquette.

Getting Ready For Your Interview

First off, it's important to prepare properly for your interview. This preparation takes a variety of forms. Things to consider include familiarity with the company and their published works, the segment of the market they tend to target, their use of new talent, the editorial staff and their credits, and how your work will fit into their publishing line.

Knowing the Company

As I suggested in Chapter One, it is in your best professional interest to familiarize yourself with the comic industry and the publishers. If you want to create the product, in this case comics, then you should be familiar with that product, how it's produced and by whom.

There is a broad degree of variety in the comic industry, both in the subject matter and the style of the product. There are more than 120 different actively publishing companies, and 25-30 of those are firmly established and well-known. Within that range of publishers, there is a massive degree of diversity. Although many newcomers frequently associate comics with superheroes, subject matter also includes horror, cutting edge/alternative, movie-licensed characters, westerns, war stories, classic literature, novel adaptations, funny animals, erotica, and an infinite number of combinations and permutations of these and other subjects. You will also find many different types of comics, including the regular series, limited series, one-shots, graphic novels, illustrated story-albums, anthologies, collected works, and experimental formats.

> *If you want to work in comics, the best way to get in is to go and meet the editors and publishers - the people who are handing out the work - in person. Go to conventions, go to shows. If you can, make appointments to go up to the offices of the publishers - if you can swing a trip to that city, or if you live near a particular publisher - then face-to-face is the way to go.*
>
> *Chuck Wojtkiewicz, Comic Illustrator*
> *(Justice League International, DC Comics)*

There are as many *styles* of comics as there are subjects and types. There are color comics - flat-coded, painted and computer-colored - and there are black and white comics. Artwork and writing can be mainstream, design-oriented, stylistic, impressionistic, cartoony or even caricaturistic. And within each publishing house, within each comic line, and within each series or graphic novel, any and all these characteristics can change.

In any given month, there is an average of about 2,500 different comic and comic-related products solicited for sale. This includes comics, books, magazines, cards, toys, games, posters, prints, and T-shirts, to name a few. Seem overwhelming? Well it is, not just for you as an eager newcomer, but even for the established professionals currently working in the industry. Therefore it is important that you do two things in preparation for a personal interview.

1) Familiarize yourself with the products produced by the company interviewing you. This does *not* mean you should learn the names of every book or character the company produces so you can try to impress your interviewer by reciting that information. It means to familiarize yourself with the books they are promoting heavily, any works that have produced accolades or attention for the company, and most important, books on which you would be interested in working.

I cannot emphasize this point enough: If you are set on working on a particular book you must be familiar with the character, their background and history, and what material is currently being published on that character. It is not in your best interest to show up at the interview, state "I really want to work on Batman, and I've got this totally cool idea . . . "

and then have the interviewer look at you astounded, and tell you "We just did that story two months ago! Don't you read the book?" This would be bad. Very bad.

Learn about the characters, books and company that you are pursuing. Knowledge can be a very powerful tool, and good preparation shows your interviewer that you are a professional ready to work.

2) Don't be a geek.

Sorry to be so harsh in my terminology, but there are certain behaviors that are completely unacceptable for an aspiring pro. Sure, it's exciting and wonderful that you finally scored a personal interview. Hey, it could mean they think you've got some real potential. But now, it's time to act like a professional. ***Do not*** recite every tidbit of trivia you know about the company, employees, creators or books. And most important, don't go on about other publishers and their works - that's their competitors, and they really don't care what you think about them. They're only interested in your knowledge about *their* company. Really.

Don't gush and fawn. If you want to seem like a professional, then act like one. Sure, it's okay to be excited and enthusiastic. Many publishers are looking for that fresh outlook and new blood. They don't all want jaded cynics, they sometimes want open idealists. But if you can't stop going on about how faint you are from excitement, or that you ". . . can't believe you're in the same room with the 'famous editor/writer/artist' of a book you've been reading since you were born . . .," then you're going to lose out on a valuable opportunity - you won't even be considered for hiring, because they won't be convinced that you're serious about a professional career.

Just try to keep in mind that it's a *job interview*. Treat it like any other important job interview, and you'll have much greater chance of success.

> *If you can get on staff at an actual comic publishing company, that can be invaluable experience. There is no substitute for actually knowing what a publisher wants, and when they want it. And if you look at most publishing houses, they tend to reward staffers with chances to write, and other types of assignments. This is particularly important if you're a writer, since they depend on the opportunities that are presented. If you're an artist, everything depends on your samples.*
>
> *Chris Ulm, Editor In Chief for Malibu Comics/Writer*
> *(**Rune**, Malibu Comics)*

Their Target Market

It's also important to understand which segment of the market the company targets. If they are focusing on kids, then you will have to be

ProFile

Professional: Mike Carlin, Executive Editor, DC Comics
Credits Include: Editor of the *Superman* books since 1986; co-writer of 15 episodes of the *Superboy* T.V. series; editor on the sequel to the *Death Of Superman* series, *Superman: Doomsday*, and *Power of Shazam.*
Question: Do you think a personal interview is important for an aspiring comic professional, and what advice would you offer to an interview candidate?

Nope, I don't think it's important. Speaking from my own experience, and from just observing, the work should speak for itself. Because we don't have to work in the same room together, or spend hours and hours and hours together, I don't think the personal interview is that important. If you can draw or write well, and on a timely basis, that is more important that if I get along with you on a day-to-day basis. Obviously we have to get along when it comes to the work, but with the fax and Fedex, I don't think the personal interview is critical. I've worked with guys for years who I've never met, and I'm happy with the work and we have a good relationship over the phone. On the other hand, if I'm interviewing for an assistant editor, or somebody I have to live with, the interview is essential.

My main advice, and my biggest pet peeve, is people showing up without an appointment. You'd be surprised how many people just show up, stick their head in, and say "Hi, I'm Joe Blow. Do you have a minute to look at my stuff?" That's not good. It forces me to be the bad guy by not having the time to see them. I do see a lot of people. I see almost everybody who calls for an appointment.

My other advice to creators is don't put down other people's work. *You're* being interviewed. If you thing your work is better than someone else's, or your mother told you that, it may be. But you're talking about people you don't know and also aspects of the work you don't know. For example, even if Don Perlin is not your favorite artist, people use him because he does tell a story clearly, *and* he is reliable, *and* he is a nice guy. People can build careers on that sort of stuff. So don't come in and say, "I'm better than so-and-so," because chances are you're not. And you make a bad impression.

aware that your creative product must be geared for that audience. If they are interested in the general mainstream audience, then it's unlikely they will be interested in your erotica samples. Knowing their product and target market will ensure you have a better chance of being considered for hiring.

Use of New Talent

Some companies make it a policy to limit new unproven talent. Other companies make it a policy to regularly hire new, unproven talent. It's in your best interest to check out the published work of your target company to see where they may stand on hiring newcomers.

If you regularly see new, unknown names, there's a good chance that the company likes to search out talented newcomers to supplement their staff of established, name professionals. These companies are frequently more willing to give you a shot. Other companies, who may operate on a tighter budget, tend to focus on established professionals because of the reduced risk of poor sales. This doesn't mean they won't consider new talent. It simply means your chances of being hired may not be quite as good.

When arranging a personal interview - perhaps at the time you ask about interview/portfolio-review days - you should look into their policy of using new talent. This will help provide you with some insight and guidance about whom you should aggressively approach, and who may require some extra groundwork and preparation.

The Editorial Staff and Their Credits

It is understood that most people appreciate recognition for their work. Consequently, it doesn't hurt to familiarize yourself with the credits and credentials of the person who will be interviewing you. If it is a creator or editor whose work you are already familiar with, great! If their name is less familiar to you, then do a bit of research at your local comic shop, and find out what books they've been involved with, and whether they have any awards or special accolades to their credit. You may discover things about your interviewer that will provide you with some common ground, or give you a bit of extra confidence for your interview.

This can also be a useful technique, if the interviewer is involved with any books on which you are interested in working. Your familiarity with material they are regularly involved with will impress upon them both your professional knowledge of the industry and your interest in their work, and may help you establish yourself as a professional worth considering for future projects.

How Your Work Fits the Company Line

If you tend to work very stylistically - that is non-traditional comic art/writing - then you should be aware of what types of work the company that interviews you produces. If they publish standard, mainstream superheroes, exclusively, then it is unlikely your alternative work will be of interest to them. Likewise, if you don't even have any *interest* in standard superhero material, then there's no real reason to interview with the company.

To summarize, familiarize yourself with the company and their product, be aware of what segment of the reading market they are targeting with their work, learn about their use of new talent and whether there will be a place for you, the newcomer, in their ranks. Learn a bit about the editorial staff and their own accomplishments and credits, and make sure you understand how, and if, your work will fit into the company line.

Personal Presentation

At last, you have finished researching your interviewer and the company. Your portfolio, samples, and business card are organized. You're ready to go, right? Wrong. There's more. Although for some of you, this section may seem redundant - possibly even insulting - for others, this section may make the difference between being seriously considered a professional and never being interviewed again.

Personal presentation. What does it mean? It means personal hygiene, the way you dress, your mannerisms and how you speak. I'm not here to provide you with charm school, but what I do want you to consider are a few important aspects of personal presentation that are considered by *all* interviewers when they sit down with a new job candidate.

Personal Hygiene - Although it may sound simplistic and biased, your personal hygiene will significantly influence the outcome of your interview. Clean, combed hair, brushed teeth, bathing, and deodorant are essentials. Sorry to get personal, but these are frequently mentioned points of contention with many hiring professionals. If your interviewer is badly distracted by your powerful body odor, your interview will be hurried, and leave a markedly unpleasant impression despite your overwhelming talents. Take the time prior to leaving for your interview to ensure that you've been meticulous about your personal appearance and cleanliness.

The Way You Dress - This goes hand in hand with personal hygiene. There's no point in spending undue time cleaning yourself up if you plan to dress in the same dirty clothes you've worn for the past week. Clean clothes are also an essential part of personal hygiene.

The type of clothes you wear isn't quite as important for a freelancer interviewing for work, as it might be for an office worker. But to make a good impression, a neat, clean appearance is essential. Don't wear clothes that are in disrepair, or badly worn out just because they're your favorite, or have always been lucky. You'll just make a bad impression. On the other hand, a freelancer who shows up in a tux and tails will make just as bad an impression. Dress appropriately, neatly and businesslike. Casual is okay, but this doesn't mean sloppy jeans and a faded, dirty T-shirt.

Oh, and don't show up for an interview with Company A, wearing

ProFile

Professional: Kelley Jones, comic book artist
Credits Include: *Batman: Red Rain*, *Dark Joker* (graphic novel), *Batman: Bloodstorm (Red Rain II)*, *Batman: Haunted Gotham* monthly series, all from DC Comics; *Aliens:Hive*, Dark Horse Comics.
Question: Do you think the personal interview is a critical step in acquiring work as a comic professional, and what advice would you offer to an interview candidate?

No, not really. I never met anybody I ever worked for personally, and it really comes down to the strength of your work. If you're good, they'll publish you. The only time a personal interview or meeting the person is important, is after you're already working. At that point, your work speaks for itself, and it's just a question of whether you can get along and get it done. It's really the quality of your work that matters.

I haven't really had any interviews, per se, but I have had to go in and make my pitch for work. But I have two pieces of advice; one is don't come off like a flake - and in that case it helps if you aren't one. Second, don't cop an attitude - keep in mind we're all very replaceable. I always try to keep in mind when I'm working that there's probably a good hundred people better than me. Humility is important. Realize too, that drawing well isn't everything. You have to be able to think well, too. The two go together.

My advice would be to go in there with your stuff, and if they start nitpicking it, don't have an answer for everything. Listen to what they have to say. If it's someone who's experienced, and who's work you respect, then pay close attention. If it's someone who you're not that crazy about, well just keep in mind who's talking. That's the big reason I like working with Doug Moench. He's someone who's told stories for so long he knows exactly what he's doing, and he's always fresh. So if he says something isn't quite right or doesn't work, I say, "How do I make it better?"

Batman art from
***Batman: Red Rain* by DC Comics**

clothing sporting the logo of Company B! If you insist on wearing logo-covered clothing, make sure it's Company A's!

Your Manners - Good manners don't come naturally to everyone, but they should. Respect, consideration and courtesy are the foundation of good business relations. Be polite - not just with the interviewer, but with the secretary, the receptionist, and any other individuals you meet. Practice good manners in your day-to-day life, and it will come naturally in your interview. Some examples of what I mean by good manners:

- Call ahead to arrange your interview, don't just show up and expect to be seen.

- Leave your full name and contact information when you make your appointment.

- Learn and use the names of the secretary/receptionist and your interviewer, but err toward *formality* (Ms. Bastienne, Mr. Reed) rather than *familiarity.*

- Be punctual. Show up a few minutes before your appointment time, and politely notify the secretary/receptionist that you have arrived. This responsible behavior is one indication that you can handle deadlines and assignments.

- Sit quietly and patiently until you are called. Your politeness will cultivate a professional response.

- Make eye contact and shake hands firmly. When you are met by your interviewer, thank them for seeing you, and be open and friendly. In doing so you will help set the tone of the interview and make a positive impression.

- When asked, state clearly and concisely what you believe the purpose of the interview to be, and what your goal is.

- Answer questions politely, honestly, openly and with good humor (that doesn't mean crack jokes!)

- Don't interrupt the interviewer, don't drone on incessantly about unrelated personal matters/thoughts, and do listen to what is said.

- At the end of the interview, regardless of your perception of the outcome, thank your interviewer for their time. Also don't forget to thank the secretary/receptionist as you leave.

In all exchanges, keep in mind how you would feel if your positions were reversed, and imagine the manner in which you would want to be spoken to - let good sense and common courtesy dictate your manners.

The Way You Speak - This is closely linked with your manners, but is important enough to merit mention on it's own. The way you speak can influence the behavior of those around you. Use proper English, avoid slang, expletives and fashionable terminology. Make your statements and questions clear and concise, and you will avoid confusion and misunderstandings. Don't try to be 'cool,' just try to be sincere, polite and enthusiastic. And be yourself; a contrived personality is transparent, irritating, and could negatively affect the outcome of your interview.

The Interview Check List

Here is a summarized check list of important points to remember.

✓ Always, always, always arrange an interview appointment. DO NOT just 'show up' and expect to be well received.

✓ Familiarize yourself with the products produced by the company interviewing you, their target market, and how they handle new talent.

✓ Don't be a geek - behave like a professional and you'll be treated like one.

✓ Make sure you are meticulous in your personal appearance. Good personal hygiene, neat and clean clothing, nice manners and being well-spoken can greatly influence the outcome of the interview.

✓ Be punctual.

✓ Make eye contact and shake hands firmly. Be open and friendly. In doing so you will help set the tone of the interview and make a positive impression.

✓ Answer questions politely, honestly, openly and with good humor

✓ Don't interrupt the interviewer, don't drone on incessantly about unrelated personal matters/thoughts, and do listen to what is said.

✓ Never, ever criticize another creators work.

✓ Don't compare your interviewer, their company, or any of their published work to their competitor(s).

✓ Organize your portfolio in a professional and easy-to-read manner and put together a sample package you can leave with your interviewer, including a business card.

✓ Prepare yourself to accept other material/assignments if they're offered - you have to start somewhere!

✓ Go in with a positive, friendly and enthusiastic outlook, not a negative, arrogant or know-it-all attitude. It's a job interview, you *need* to make a good impression.

❖

Interview Etiquette

Interview etiquette is closely related to good manners, and the one rarely occurs without the other. By interview etiquette, I refer to the way in which you conduct yourself in the interview - which behaviors are acceptable and expected, and which will ruin your chances of gaining employment.

In the previous section on manners, I listed some items that also fall under the heading of interview etiquette. These include calling ahead to arrange the time; leaving your full name and contact information; arriving punctually; waiting patiently until called; being friendly, open and polite;

> *Even if you don't get the job, it's not always your fault.*
> *Rejections aren't personal.*
>
> *Let's give it fifty percent that it is your work. But if you go to an art director, and they've just had an argument with their spouse, or someone shot someone else on their commuter train coming in to work, then you're not going to get the job! If you go the next day, and they've woken up early and made wonderful, passionate love to their spouse, the commute went smoothly, and the art director is in this incredible expansive mood, then you've got the job!! ·*
>
> *When I used to hang out at Marvel, I got any number of covers because I happened to be walking down the halls when an editor had seen me and said, "Hey! I need a cover. Can you do it?" It's a large part of being in the right place at the right time.*
>
> Charles Vess, Artist/Writer
> **(Spiderman: Spirits of the Earth,** Marvel Comics)

listening carefully; stating your goals clearly; answering questions honestly and in a friendly manner; sticking to the interview subject (don't digress into personal areas); and thanking your interviewer for their time, whatever the perceived outcome of the interview.

In addition to these aspects of interview etiquette, here is a list of Do's and Don'ts you should familiarize yourself with before you go in.

- **Don't** compare your interviewer, their company or any of their published work to their competitor(s). Focus on *them* - they're the one interviewing you!
- **Don't** ever criticize another creator's work. You're there to be interviewed, not provide a critique. This is guaranteed to make a very bad impression.
- **Don't** think for one second that your "massive talent" will carry your lack of professional organization because it won't!
- **Don't** prepare a list of requests or demands - this will only guarantee you *won't* be hired.
- **Don't** memorize the company's complete published works and then recite them to your interviewer.
- **Don't** go in with a negative, arrogant or know-it-all attitude. It's a job interview. You *need* to make a good impression.
- **Do** organize your portfolio in a professional and easy-to-read manner.
- **Do** put together a sample package you can leave with your interviewer, including a business card.
- **Do** list the types of characters and/or books on which you'd like to work, and be prepared to describe this to the interviewer.

■ **Do** prepare yourself to accept other material/assignments if they're offered. After all, you have to start somewhere!

■ **Do** go in with a positive, friendly and enthusiastic outlook. It's a job interview; you *need* to make a good impression.

> *Diversity is the key to success. As a freelancer it's helpful not to have to rely on one publisher or a single source of income.*
>
> Dave Dorman, Illustrator (**Aliens:Tribes**, Dark Horse Comics)

Summary

As you can see, the personal interview can be a useful, if not always necessary, tool on the road to becoming a comic professional. Although it can help secure work, other avenues such as portfolio revues, convention contacts and mail submissions can be more efficient. However, when deciding to pursue a personal interview it is important to consider some important guidelines.

You should prepare for your interview by ensuring that you have an *appointment*. Don't just surprise them, or make an unwanted, unannounced visit. You should *familiarize yourself with the company* and their work, what types of product they produce, which markets they target, how and if they use new talents, how your work might fit in with the company publications, and the people who make up the editorial staff, and the background and credits of your interviewer.

Make sure your *personal appearance* is neat and clean, that your manner is *polite and courteous*, and that you speak well and avoid slang or foul language. Don't behave like a flake, and you won't be treated like one. Also, make sure you *understand the structure of an interview*, and the types of behavior that are appropriate: punctuality, politeness, courtesy, open and honest answers, and listening.

If you can master all the skills required to be successful in an interview, then you are one step closer to securing work as a comic professional.

Chapter Six
Approaching Potential Employers Part 4:
Feedback and Critiques

In this chapter I'm going to focus on one of the most important aspect of approaching potential employers: getting, and making use of, feedback and critiques.

First, let's look at what is meant by 'feedback' and 'critique.' Technically, they mean the same thing - obtaining opinions and comments on your work from industry professionals, including other creators, publishers and editors. However, feedback is generally considered a more informal response than a critique. Feedback comes in many situations, but most commonly when you show your work to others on a casual basis. A critique is generally a more structured feedback session, sometimes with comments provided in note form.

Do I Really Need The Criticism?

Many newcomers are afraid to be criticized. That's not an unreasonable fear, it's just non-constructive. Basically, no matter how long you've worked, or how popular you are, it helps you as a professional to have feedback from your peers and superiors.

And absolutely *nobody* is too good to be critiqued.

> *No matter what anybody tells you, you always have to have enough belief in yourself and your abilities to keep striving on. There are very few people who 'make it' overnight.*
>
> *At the same time, you should never be so closeminded that you look down on suggestions or criticisms that could help you improve. You have to be flexible, and able to adapt to the needs of the company, or other creators you work with, or the needs of the fans. If you're set in stone, basically you'll just crumble. You have to be flexible, you have to be able to adapt and grow.*
>
> Dan Danko, Senior Editor at Malibu Comics/Writer
> (*Warstrike*, Malibu Comics)

Now, many creators might say that they are 'good' enough to no longer need that professional feedback. But those are the same creators who will never grow or improve as a talent. Whether you are an artist or a writer, you should constantly be striving to learn and grow and improve. There is no such thing as 'achieving perfection.' Perfection is a fleeting, momentary state of satisfaction; you should find yourself motivated by your successes to reach further and strive harder to attain an even finer degree of accomplishment. This perpetual state of searching and improving will serve to make you a talent worth watching throughout your career.

Sure, nobody likes to be criticized. Sometimes it can be very painful to sit still while someone picks apart your work of love. But self-confidence is the key here. Always remember that you are a growing talent, that you should strive to improve and hone your professional skills. Listen to what is said about your work, and turn it to your advantage. And keep one thing in mind at all times. If the critique is done properly, you shouldn't feel as though your work (or you) has been berated. You should be getting comments about the strengths and weaknesses of your work. And you should be able to determine what's worth remembering and what you should ignore as petty.

So How Do I Get Critiqued?

There are many ways to obtain a critique of your work. Through this book, we've looked at a variety of ways to get your work looked at; attending conventions, sending samples by mail, and making a personal interview appointment. Each of these avenues has its pros and cons, but all are valuable as they represent an opportunity to get constructive criticism on your work.

Conventions

At many conventions publishers schedule *portfolio reviews*, where a more formalized critique of a number of aspiring artists will occur. Sometimes these are done in an organized appointment fashion, and sometimes it's a big line, where it's first to come-first to be served. Regardless of the format, take advantage of these reviews. From the feedback these publishers and editors give, you will be able to further improve and tailor your work to better suit that company's requirements, and thus improve your chances of being hired.

Some conventions also schedule readings. These vary from show to show, but can be composed of established writers reading their own works, or occasionally are set up for new writers to read excerpts of their own work for interested editors and publishers. If you have the opportunity to read at a convention, don't miss out. Not only will this enable you to acquire valuable feedback you can use to improve or hone your writing skills, but reading your work aloud will help you get a feel for the flow of your storytelling ability. This is also a useful technique to use at home.

In addition to portfolio reviews and readings, conventions offer you the opportunity to show your work to other creators. Pay attention to the comments they make - even when they're painful - and file the information away for later reference. Always be gracious when getting a critique, regardless of whether you liked what you heard. Keep in mind, that the creator has taken time from their work (and a convention is work for a

ProFile

Professional: Dave Elliott, Publisher of Blackball Comics
Credits Include: *A-1*, Atomika and Marvel; Publisher for Tundra UK; Publisher of Blackball Comics
Question: When you critique a newcomers work, what are some of the things you focus on and what type of behavior or ettiquette do you expect?

The first thing I look for is storytelling, especially when I see pencils or inks. It's best to see both, because some people are very good pencillers, but they can ruin it once they've inked it.

Also, I tend to be as honest as I possibly can. The worst critique I ever gave to anyone was to someone who must have been in his late 30's or early 40's. He'd been patiently waiting in line to show me his portfolio. I couldn't lie to him - especially someone at that age - about how bad his work was. Sometimes you see people with genuine enthusiasm who are 14- or 15-years old, and their artwork is really bad. But they have time to go to art school - something I always recommend - so that they can get access to lifedrawing, not just tracing off comics.

Art from *"Edge"* in *A-1* by Atomika and Marvel

Always remember that when you get criticism, you're getting it from that particular person's point of view and tastes. Keep that in mind. When you're showing your portfolio you should know the person giving you the critique. If it's a publisher, like myself, you should know what company they're from and the sort of material they publish. You should also consider whether your material would fit with theirs, otherwise, they will be critiquing you on what *they* want. So, for example, if you want to draw *Texas Chainsaw*

Massacre comics and you're showing your work to Mark Gruenwald [Marvel Comics], it's a bit pointless. I think a lot of people do that. They just want to show their portfolios to *anyone* and get a response. Unfortunately, that can work against you. You can get some very negative critiques just by talking to the wrong people.

When getting a critique, you should listen. You're asking that person for their opinion, so you should listen carefully. If you've got a difference of opinion, it's probably because your feelings are hurt. I try to be reasonable. If I've been particularly harsh on someone, I'll ask them afterwards, "Do you think what I've just said is fair?" A lot of them will grudgingly agree. On the other hand, a few people will turn around and shout at you, "Well, what do you know?!" But if you're asking for a critique, you need to learn to accept the feedback.

You can't just ask your mum and dad for a critique. They'll always say, "You're absolutely brilliant!" They'll drag you around, showing you off to all the relatives and your family, saying, "Isn't he good?" But they aren't the ones giving you work, and they (most likely) don't know comics.

You've got to be prepared to be hurt, and for negativity. But you've also got to know to take it positively.

professional!) to give you some feedback on how you're doing. Their opinions may not always seem on target to you, but they took the time to do you the favor of looking at your work, so don't forget to voice your appreciation with thanks.

Similarly, use the convention event as an opportunity to take your work around to the publisher's booths. If they are willing to look at your work on the spot, take advantage of the opportunity. Sometimes, outside the time pressure of a portfolio review, they can provide you with a more detailed and expansive critique.

Mail Samples

As we have discussed in the past, sending samples of your work by mail to prospective employers can also be helpful in refining your abilities. Most publishers, on receipt of samples with a self-addressed, stamped envelope (SASE), will take the time to give you a fair critique. Sometimes it can even lead to work! Pay attention to what feedback you are given, and make the appropriate adjustments to your work. Essentially, that publisher/editor is providing you with the keys necessary to eventually obtain work with their company. Put that information to good use, and you may find yourself gainfully employed.

Responses to submissions by mail take a variety of forms. They can be a quick note, a full and detailed letter, and as often is the case for busy publishers - a form response.

Sample Of A Form Response *(Courtesey of Caliber Press)*

Dear Creator/Talent

     Please excuse this generic form that covers your submission but it is the only way we can handle the volume of submissions received. Please look over the checklist and see which are applies to you. In any case, we do appreciate you taking the time to send us your submission and thank you for thinking of us. If your work is not accepted by us at this time, we hope that you continue to work at your craft and wish you the best of luck in this often difficult "to break in" medium.

_____Yes, we are interested in your work, please turn over and fill out the areas on the reverse side of this sheet.

_____No, sorry we are not interested in this submission at this time for the following reason(s):

_____Not suitable for us as far as the type of material we want to produce.

_____Generally just lacking in a quality level to consider for publication.

WRITERS:

_____The story is something that is working on a level of audience that we are not actively seeking, _____or within a genre we have no interest in.

_____The characters in the story are lacking motivational factors to bring out their actions in the story.

_____ The dialogue needs additional work.   _____ Plot needs additional work.

_____ Too much implausibility in story.   _____ Story lacks structure.

ARTISTS:

_____ The samples sent don't show us enough to give an example of your work

_____ no/too few continuity pages   _____ lacking enough samples

_____ The samples generally indicate an artistic level not ready for publication

_____ Areas where we feel you need improvement:

_____anatomy   _____faces   _____architecture   _____perspective

     _____layouts   _____ storytelling   _____camera angles

_____ Please send us some more samples, we'd like to see more soon.

_____ Practice some more and give us another try later.

75

A form response is a pre-printed card or letter with a variety of replies. The editor/publisher checks off the appropriate items in response to your submission. But don't be deterred! A form response doesn't mean your work didn't merit a 'real' critique. Never take the response personally. ALWAYS, ALWAYS remember - this is a *business*. It's just business, not a personal attack. The most likely reason for a form response is that the target publisher/editor is swamped with submissions and deluged with work. Be happy when you get any response. There will be many occasions where it will take multiple submissions before you hear a peep out of them!

Finally, don't let a form response - even if it's less than positive - deter you from future submissions to this company. Unless they state outright that they ". . . are not accepting submissions at this time," then you should send updated samples periodically, and utilize any feedback they (or anyone else) provides to tailor your samples to their individual needs.

Keep a disciplined work regimen. It's better to be consistent and maintain a daily routine for work, instead of waiting to the last minute to crunch on a deadline. And this applies to any task. It may seem slower, but in the long run you're actually working more efficiently. Also, don't promise to do work that has a deadline that you feel would be impossible to meet. Keep an even keel, and everyone will have better expectations of each other.

A friend once gave me a valuable piece of advice. I had just stayed up for three days straight to meet a deadline, and I was regaling him with my tales of suffering when he said to me, "So, are you going to do this when you're sixty?"

I said, "Well. . . no!"

His reply was, "Then why are you doing it now?"

Sean Taggert, Trading Card Editor for DC Comics
*(**Batman: Saga Of The Dark Night** card series)*

Personal Interviews

If you are fortunate enough to be able to score a personal interview with a prospective employer, take full advantage of this golden opportunity. Even if it becomes clear in the course of the interview that you won't be hired at that time, pay full attention to everything your interviewer has to say about your work.

If you have a small recorder, ask permission to tape their feedback, so you can review it later. You can also make notes so you don't forget what is said about your work, or invite them to make notations on your copies (but never originals!).

Most importantly, be gracious. You have taken up a portion of the interviewer's work day. The interviewer is providing you with the chance to demonstrate, through your work, if your skills are refined enough for the company to use. Don't be cocky, don't be rude. Behave exactly how *you* would want a prospective employee to behave if it were *you* doing the hiring. Be polite, honest, and attentive.

Finally, if your interview ends without the possibility of gaining employ at that time, check with your interviewer to see how long you must wait before you can come back for another appointment. Indicate that you intend to apply the feedback they have provided, and suggest a return appointment a month or so down the road. If they are amenable, this can provide you with the opportunity to apply what you've learned, and better your chances at working with this company.

The Anatomy Of A Critique

Wherever you end up getting your critique, and regardless of who does the critique, it will have the same basic characteristics. People will look over your samples, and tell you what they think. However, it is at this point that there can be significant variations in what makes up the critique.

Depending on who is doing the critique (a fellow creator, an established professional, a potential employer, or your mom), the time constraints under which it is done (a crowded convention hall, a quiet office, or your friend's house), and the skill level of the critique-giver (PhD in Fine Arts, a professional with 20+ years experience, your kid sister who has created her own comic book series for her friends, or your bored friend who's *trying* to watch the *Beavis and Butthead* show) the critique is going to have a great deal of variation. So here are some points to remember:

■ A good critique talks about both your strengths and weaknesses
■ A good critique looks at improvement in your work over time (ie., older samples versus newer work)
■ A good critique never dwells on how completely 'amazing!' you are, or how completely 'awful!' you are. That's getting personal, not objective. There should always be a balance, since your work will have both good and bad points
■ A good critique looks at a reasonable amount of your work - not just one page, and not the three forty-page volumes you dragged along with you!
■ A good critique analyzes not just the mechanics of your work, but the overall effect - The Big Picture. For artists, it's not just the actual pencils/inks/colors, but how you put it together as a page of storytelling-with-images. For writers, it's not just whether you can create a really cool character concept, but if you know how to tell a real story with that character (i.e., beginning-middle-end, conflict, resolution, excitement, action, humor, plausibility, realistic dialogueing, etc.)
■ A good critique involves questions and verbal interaction with you. The person doing your critique should try to find out information about your

background, experience, and interests. This information will help them provide you with useful and constructive advice

■ A good critique considers your feelings, without babying you. You should never be treated unfairly, or rudely. If they don't like your work, there are many ways of saying so that are fair and tough, but considerate. On the other hand, you shouldn't take personal offense if they seem overly blunt. Just keep in mind, it's your work they're criticizing, not you as a person.

Draw a lot. Get in print. Don't give up your day job. Make sure you have an understanding partner.

Matt Feazell, Minicomic artist
*(**Death of Antisocialman**, Not Available Comics)*

Critique Etiquette

Now that you've finally talked someone into looking at your work, you must remember your own behavior is important. Most professionals who look at your work are providing you a valuable service free of charge. For that reason alone, you should be grateful. Show your appreciation by being polite and attentive to what they say. And always thank them for their time, regardless of whether you agree with what they've said.

As important as it is for a person critiquing your work to abide by certain guidelines, it's equally important for you to follow a certain etiquette or behavior. There are plenty of things to remember to do and not to do, but if you follow the standard behavior when being interviewed for a new job, you won't go wrong. In the meantime, here are some points you should make a note of:

■ Close friends and family have a hard time being completely objective and honest. After all, they *love* you. They think you're great. Try to temper that unabashed adoration with more objective critiques.

■ Always listen carefully to what the person critiquing your work has to say.

■ Don't interrupt to make explanations or excuses for parts of your work they might criticize.

■ Don't be demanding, rude, flippant or cocky. It's fine to be self-confident, but there's a thin line between confidence and arrogance.

■ DON'T, DON'T, DON'T, compare your work to anyone else - whether as a put-down on them *or* yourself. The person looking at your work doesn't care if you think you draw as well, better, or worse than anyone else. They'll tell *you* if they think it's worth mentioning.

■ NEVER put-down or criticize the work of the person/company critiquing you, whether you believe your constructive input is valuable or not. Write them a letter some other time. Just now, they didn't come to *you* for feedback, you came to *them*.

ProFile

Professional: Michael Kaluta, Illustrator
Credits Include: *The Shadow* series for DC Comics; *Starstruck: The Expanding Universe* and *The Shadow* (writing and art) from Dark Horse; *1994 J.R.R. Tolkien Calendar* from Ballantyne.
Question: When you critique a newcomers work, what are some of the things you focus on and what type of behavior or etiquette do you expect?

First, before I even look at their stuff, I put my hands on their portfolio and I ask, "Do you know my work?" If they come to me for a critique, I would assume that they know it and it's *my* opinion that they wanted. If they say "No, I just want an artist's opinion," I tell them "Before I even look at your work, I have to tell you, I don't draw superheros. I do very personal work, and I'm going to critique this as art. But I'm also going to tell you what I would expect an editor to say. Now, do you want to work for Marvel or DC or Malibu?" If they say yes, then I say "I will tell you what I would imagine they would say." I'll be just like them when I do that part of the critique. But I also have another hat; I am an 'artist' artist. If I see art there, I'll commend them, but I'll say whether I think they will make a dime off it.

Then we open up the portfolio. With luck, the material is good enough for their age. Sometimes I'll ask how old they are, in amazement, because the work is very strong. Sometimes I ask, and then I don't know what to say, because it's *so* miserable.

I look for proportion first. I want to see if they understand it, because a lot of young people are attracted by the gloss, the surface, the exaggeration - the icons of comic book art. This as opposed to being able to draw people doing things. I look to see if they've done mundane scenes, and if it's in a comic book format. If it's just a bunch of portfolio pieces - single image things - I ask them if they're planning on getting work in comics. If they say yes, I tell them that they can't show this material. You can have a few of these pieces, but you've got to show them three or four pages of story - continuity. It's got to be continuity if you want to do comics. That's all they're going to look at.

Then I tell them, "Now, understand that an editor knows *exactly* what they're looking for." If an art editor opens up your book for a look and takes only five minutes, don't be insulted. They know exactly what they're looking at. This is their job. They know this in and out. So, they'll know whether or not its what they want, and they'll tell you. Believe what they say, and try to make it better. But don't be disheartened, because you're only learning what that *one* company is specifically looking for. It doesn't necessarily mean you have to change your style. It may mean that you're not ever supposed to work for that company!

If there is storytelling work, I'll look at it and ask questions based on the content of the work.

Even if the portfolio is miserable, I try to find some strength. If it's really bad, I have to ask some probing questions to find out what their expectations are. Sometimes they're living in a fantasy world, and they expect to get a job by showing their portfolio to someone.

Sometimes they just don't understand how it works. I know this fellow who's very accomplished, but he draws in a European style. He was upset, because he wasn't getting jobs at DC or Marvel. But there was no way DC and Marvel were going to use his stuff. He had 64-page stories with none of their characters in them. What did he expect? It was good work, and with that work he could get jobs with them, but he couldn't sell what he had in his portfolio. At this point, he would have to self-publish, or try to get someone to do it for almost no money. That's what happens.

It's rare that you get a completely polished artist. There's always something to be worked on. Years ago Frank Frazetta put it bluntly when he said, "Why even bother to look at it or talk to them, they live in a complete fantasy. They think their work is the best in the world, they think they're already professionals, and nothing you can say will get through to them." I haven't found that to be exactly the case, but I certainly have run into that.

If you want a job, there are things that you've got to do. You have to realize that the editorial opinion is *the* opinion. Your opinion doesn't matter. You're just a pair of hands that they're going to make work for them. It's a business. It may be your fantasy life, but it's really a business. If your work is good enough, you'll have a job. Just like that! If your work is headed in a direction that's good enough, they will nurture you.

I also ask if they've shown their work to Marvel or DC. If they say no, I ask them if they want a job, or just a critique. If they're looking for work, they've got to take it to people who will give them work. I can't give them work. I'm an artist, all I can do is tell them I like it. My opinion doesn't matter. An editorial opinion matters. . Editors are the ones who can say "Seventy bucks a page," and you're in! All of a sudden you've got a job, and you're a professional.

■ At conventions, don't corner a professional to "take a quick look" at your work, when they're bogged down with convention business or talking with fans. Especially if you want a critique - that should never be "just a quick look." Wait your turn and be polite

■ Don't just show up at a publisher's/editor's office unannounced and expect them to take time out of their busy, planned, work day to look at your samples. Prove you're a professional and make an appointment.

■ When making mail submissions, ALWAYS include an S.A.S.E. if you expect a response. Publishers receive literally hundreds of unsolicited submissions every week. This represents hundreds of dollars in postage - a prohibitive cost for any business. Many are unable to respond with more than a form letter, but it's a guarantee that without an enclosed S.A.S.E., you won't be hearing from them at all.

■ Don't argue with the person critiquing your work. Sure, they may not understand what you've been trying to achieve with your work. Sure, they may seem somewhat harsh in their comments. But always keep in mind; you went to them to ask their opinion. Now keep quiet and listen to what they say. You can always ignore their comments and advice later, just don't argue with them while they're talking to you.

Applying Critiques and Feedback

Applying what you've been told is the most important aspect of having your work critiqued. It's all well and good to drag your samples from convention to publisher to the post office, but if all you do is show the same stuff over and over again, without listening to the advice you're given or applying the feedback you get, then you will never improve as a creator and your chances of becoming gainfully employed in the comic industry are very slim.

Granted, it can be painful to have your work criticized. But listen carefully to the comments you get. If you hear a repeating theme in the feedback (eg. "Well, your drawing skills are strong, but you use too many front-on shots, then vary your 'camera angles' more), there's probably a good chance that it is a weakness you need to work on. Possibly one that will prevent you from getting work in the business.

On the other hand, if a single person delivers a critical, and seemingly unwarranted, blow to your ego, consider carefully what they said, who said it, and the circumstances in which it was said. (eg. You meet another newcomer at a convention, and when they look at your work they criticize your anatomy as being "too artsy," in a very sarcastic manner.) People are only human. Sometimes they hide their own insecurities by lashing out at others. If you are shocked by a particularly vicious attack on your work, step back and take another look at the situation. If you still can't understand the motivation behind the 'attack', then ignore it, move on, and get a second opinion.

If, after a series of critiques, some consistent weaknesses in your

ProFile

Professional: Gary Reed, Publisher of Caliber Press
Credits Include: Co-creator/co-writer, *Baker Street* (Harvey Award-nominated); writer, *Mechanoids*. As publisher, Gary Reed is responsible for: *Realm of the Dead, Roadkill:A Chronicle of the Deadworld* and it's sequels *December* and *Heat*; *Sinergy*; *Deadworld*; *Realm*; *Negative Burn*; *Joe Sinn*.
Question: When you critique a newcomer's work, what are some of the things you focus on and what type of behavior or ettiquette do you expect?

As far as artwork goes, assuming a basic level of competency such as anatomy and drawing skills, you're basically looking for how they compose the story. How are their various storytelling aspects? Are they changing the camera angles? Are they moving the characters around in a logical, coherent fashion as opposed to 'jagged cuts', where they're jumping from behind to the front of the character? There's a technique called 'the 180-degree turn.' Every step you move the character should be going in that flow of 180-degrees. So basically, just how the storytelling and how the character situations move. You don't want to have the flow of the story interrupted by these jarring shots, which may look good - make really great pin-ups - but they don't help the story along. Also, one thing you don't want to see all the time are these straight-on, waist-high frontal shots, which you see from a lot of new people.

Writing is a lot harder. For one, it takes a lot longer to tell if somebody's good. And a lot of times, I think that in art you can sometimes get away with telling one story, or type of story, really well.

THE FOLLOW UP TO THE SMASH HIT ROADKILL

Cover art for *Heat* from Caliber Press

That can also be true in writing, where they can handle one type of situation really well. Then you have to look at how they handle the transition, how they handle the dialogue. I can't believe how incredibly bad a lot of comic dialogue is! You just have to look at all the same components you have to look at in a story, first, without the artwork. You have to look at how the story is structured and how it's put together.

One thing that irks me more than anything else is when somebody comes up and asks for a critique, and even though you try to make it clear that you're just one person and that it's your personal viewpoint of their art or story, they start arguing with me. If I say 'Well, I don't like the way this is drawn,' I don't like it when they start arguing with me or trying to justify the way that it's drawn. Basically, it just comes down to 'I don't like it.' If I don't think it works, it doesn't matter what reason there is behind doing it that way. Whether the agree or disagree, this is my opinion, and I don't care if they totally disregard it. I just don't want to spend 15 or 20 minutes arguing over a small point. This can influence whether they're hired or not, but Caliber Press is a bit different, in that we do creator-owned projects, and take the package complete, warts and all. But I can see how if would affect a lot of other publishers who are looking for a specific style of art or type of artist. If they're going to argue over a small point like this, then what's going to happen if they're hired and the editor has to go in ask for a change? If the artist is going to balk and fight them every step of the way, it's not worth the editors time.

work are pointed out, then take that information home and consider it. Carefully look through your work, and compare what you've been told to change how your work looks. You will begin to see the places where you should change and improve your work. Using this feedback, check out some books at the library or your local college that can provide you with instruction and guidance on how to execute the recommended changes.

Never understimate your ability to screw-up. Deadlines, contract obligations, capacity for timely production, business decisions, etc. - we all overestimate. We never really know how much we're going to go awry, so give yourself some room to move.

*Scott Hampton, Illustrator (**Batman:Nightcries**, D.C. Comics)*

And Practice. Practice, Practice, Practice. Almost nobody starts out proficient at anything they try for the very first time. If you play a musical instrument, did you start out able to play a concerto the very first time? Pretty unlikely. If you're any good, it most likely took you long years of practice to get there. The same thing goes for your craft, be it writing or art. You can only hone your skills by practicing.

It also helps to search out advice and instruction from experts, other professionals in the field, teachers and publishers. Strive to continually improve your skills through every possible avenue, and it will serve to make you a better professional.

Summary

As you can see, constructive criticism from a formal *critique* can help you as a talent, and as an aspiring comic professional. To shy away from this valuable industry 'service' is to stunt your growth creatively, and to possibly miss out on the clues a publisher can give you for gaining employ with their company.

It's also important to remember that there are many places to have your work critiqued, including *conventions*, through *mail samples* and in *personal interviews*. Take advantage of any and all these avenues. Aim to have as many professionals look at your work as you can. Each will bring their own expertise and experience to the critique, and can provide you with valuable insight in improving your creative skills.

Always keep in mind that a good critique has many characteristics, but that regardless of the type of critique you receive, *good etiquette* as the recipient is crucial.

Whatever it takes, strive to grow as a creator. Use feedback from critiques, practice, get good advice and instruction - these will all serve to improve your skills. By making the effort to apply feedback, you will demonstrate to a potential employer your ability to work as a team member and a reliable employee.

Chapter Seven
The Legal Business of the Biz

If you have achieved a sufficient level of creative expertise that you are now being offered work, this represents many legal and business ramifications. Let's look at how they can, and will, affect you as a professional.

There are many critical aspects to conducting yourself as a business professional. Your first question might be, *"Why do I have to know this stuff, or how to do it?"* Simple. Not only does your knowledge of these elements protect you as a new professional, but they prove to the company hiring you that you are an accomplished, organized and reliable businessperson.

You might also ask, *"Can't I just hire somebody to handle all this stuff for me?"* Probably, if you have sufficient funds. But do you really want to turn over your livelihood and working future to a stranger or trusted family member, and be a) unaware of what's really going on, or b) shocked when you discover that this trusted relative/employee has bilked you or screwed up a crucial deal? Neither of these situations may necessarily arise, but always keep one thing in mind: it's very hard to discuss a potential project with an editor if you have to say, "I'll have my agent/lawyer call you to sort out the details." As a newcomer this is both

---

It's important to talk to an attorney periodically, to have them read your contracts. It doesn't necessarily have to be an attorney with a great deal of experience in the comic industry because - although that would be preferable - any decent attorney ought to be able to figure it out. In many ways, this is not a very complicated industry, but it is a risky industry because of the transient quality of the publishers.

Rod Underhill, Attorney/Computer Fine Artist/Writer
(Airlock, Eclectus)

---

pretentious and foolhardy, as it prevents you from familiarizing yourself with how the industry works, and what types of expectations are reasonable to maintain. Once you are firmly established as a popular pro, then you can feel free to employ a whole entourage to take care of your every need. And at that point a rep may help you save money by taking care of the 'drudge' work while you concentrate on your creative work. But in the meantime, let's address this issue as a creator just getting started.

Business and Legal Practices

There are a variety of components that make up the business and legal practices of our industry. They share many characteristics with other careers in the visual and print mediums (such as magazine illustrators and photographers, book writers, freelance journalists, etc.). *Negotiations, contracts, standard forms, copyright, ownership of original works, reproductions, licensing, merchandising and taxes* are just a few of the items that fall under this heading. There are extensive volumes of material available on these subjects. For the purposes of this book I'll just give a brief overview of some of the more important areas, with an emphasis on how they apply to the comic industry. It is advised that you make use of the reading list I provide at the back of the book to learn more about each of these subjects.

Negotiations

Negotiating a work agreement involves the creator and publisher representatives striving to accommodate each other's needs, while determining the elements of the contract. The terms of a contract are reached by negotiation. The purpose is not to defeat the other party, but for each party to feel that their needs have been satisfied. An editor must decide whether the work to be provided by the creator will suit the needs of the project, and will fall within financial budget. The editor must also ensure that the creator can meet the project deadlines. The creator, like any business person, must cover his overhead and make enough profit to live on. Therefore, the more information each party has about the other the more effective the negotiation.

If a creator knows ahead of time how much a company generally pays for work, then the creator will be better able to figure out what asking price will be reasonable. The editor's offer is constrained by company guidelines and project restrictions, so any information they have about the creator's business requirements will help the negotiations go smoothly. If either the creator or the editor is unable, or unwilling, to meet the needs of the other, the negotiation will fail and the editor or creator may seek a contract elsewhere.

To ensure negotiations are conducted fairly, it is important for you as a creator to approach the situation armed with knowledge. Familiarize yourself with the standard contractual agreement used by the company. Also, secure a copy of Fair Practice Guidelines (see reading list at the end of this article), to ensure you are informed about how negotiations should be conducted.

In our industry negotiations vary depending on the degree a professional is established. If you are a name commanding some attention and long established in the industry, negotiations go quite differently than those with a newcomer. As a new professional, you should listen carefully

ProFile

Professional: Mark A. Nelson, Illustrator
Credits Include: Aliens: Book One, Dark Horse Comics; *Nightbreed #11 & #12* and *Feud*, Marvel Comics; interior illustrations, *Dragon Magazine; Blood and Shadows*, DC Comics; *Pencils and Inks* feature Hero Illustrated Magazine
Question: How much value do you place on written contracts and the importance of creator-owned rights versus work-for-hire agreements? What business advice would you offer to newcomers?

I think that newcomers should really get a contract. Get it all spelled out so that later on in the game if someone says, "Well, no. We didn't say that," then you've got it on paper. So instead of going verbally or with a handshake and just trusting people, it's better to have it in writing. Then you both know where you stand. I think that a lot of times (in our industry), on

**Nelson's art design
for *Feud***

regular, monthly books it tends to be a handshake. I think there is a lot of turnover. For example, I haven't received any contracts from Marvel for *Nightbreed.* That was a handshake, but that worked out. But on creator-owned projects, that's different. For example, on *Feud* we went through a lengthy contract.

Sometimes it's fun to do work-for-hire, because you are working on projects that you want to work on. *Aliens: Book One* was work-for-hire. There was no way I could do Aliens without it being work-for-hire. On the other hand, *Feud* (of which Nelson is a co-creator) has been an absolute blast, because I got to create everything with Mike Baron. So that was a lot of fun. The same holds true for *Blood and Shadows*, which I'm working on with Joe Lansdale. We got to bounce ideas off each other and came up with a project that's been a slice of heaven.

It's also important for newcomers to be aware of filing Quarterly Estimate tax payments. That's what we (Nelson and his wife Anita, who is also an illustrator) are doing. We also have an accountant and we have a lawyer. Sometimes a lawyer is a good person to have go over your contracts with you, so you know what you're getting into. There can be a lot of legalese. It puts you in a better bartering position, so you can barter a little bit on creator-owned stuff, and hopefully work out a good deal between the two parties.

I think it's a good thing to have an accountant because he/she will help you figure out all your financial matters. Our accountant helps us keep track of our business expenses. This covers everything from materials, mileage, phone bills, postage, to mortgage or rent.

to what is offered, assess the value and desirability of the work contract, and make a decision. Don't dawdle in deciding, and be firm in your decisions. Sometimes I am saddened to learn of a newcomer who has hurriedly accepted a publishing agreement without familiarizing himself with the company's reputation. The burning desire to 'be published' blinds him to the facts. There are many disreputable publishers who prey on naive newcomers. Your best defense is to be as informed about your work negotiations as possible. Do some research, make some phone calls. Ask a lot of questions. Only these things will keep you from getting burned down the road.

Contracts

What is a *contract?* Physically there are many, many different contract forms. They can be preprinted forms and specially typeset agreements. They can also be found in the fine print of purchase orders and payment invoice chits provided by the publisher. They can even be stamped on a payment check. Pay attention to what you're signing. It might just be your contract!

The contract is by far the most important business aspect of becoming a professional. I cannot emphasize this enough! No matter how

> *Check out those contracts!*
>
> *Make sure you understand the contract. I recommend that anyone who works, work with a contract just so you'll have something to fall back on if a publisher won't pay you. If you live up to your part of the bargain, you can always fall back on the contract when there are problems. But, a lot of companies will try to screw you over with the contract, especially if you're not used to looking over contracts. An example of this is a moderate sized game company that uses a contract like a paperback novel contract! Once they get your artwork, they can do anything they want with it; they can cut it up, they can crop it, they can use it as many times as they want without paying you. I go through that kind of contract and I scratch that out. I stipulate what I want, and change anything I'm unhappy with. Then I send it back and tell them I'm not going to do any work until the changes are initialled and they agree that it will work. Unfortunately, a lot of new people starting out aren't going to have that kind of clout. I've never used a lawyer to look over my contracts, and so far I haven't gotten 'bit.' But you never can tell if something will happen.*
>
> Tim Bradstreet, Freelance Illustrator
> (**Dragon Chiang**, Eclipse Comics)

badly you want to work and establish yourself, nobody wants to work free. A contract is protection for both you and your employer. I can't begin to count the astonishing number of aspiring, or newly established, professionals who have poured out a horror story about how they were brutally exploited by a publisher. It happens a lot in this industry. Because of the casual nature of the convention circuit and related social angle, many "agreements" are formed over a drink at the bar - often without so much as a simple handshake.

Here's an example: Joe Editor leans over his beer, slaps Joe Creator on the shoulder and says "Hey! We've got this really hot project we'd like *you* to pencil. We'll pay you $200.00 per page, and the deadline is pretty open." Joe Creator's eyes light up, and little cash register noises go off in his head. He says, "Man, that's great! I won't let you down!!" Six months later, Joe Editor and Joe Creator are doing the 'Courtroom Two-Step.' Joe Editor cries about missed deadlines and his subsequent lost revenues, and Joe Creator cries about the lack of payment and his inability to meet Joe Editor's unreasonable - and previously unmentioned - deadlines. This might sound like a silly scenario but, except for the names, it has happened time and again in our business. Don't put yourself in this situation.

Types of Contracts

Work for Hire

According to copyright law, in a work made for hire, 'the employer or other person for whom the work was prepared is considered the author/artist for purposes of this title, and, unless the parties have expressly agreed otherwise in a written instrument signed by them (the employer or other person for whom the work was prepared) owns all the rights comprised in the copyright.'

> *Read Your Contracts! Find out where you stand as the artist/creator, what your rights are, royalties, and what options you have.*
>
> Mark A. Nelson, Illustrator (**Blood and Shadows**, DC Comics)

Note that a work only becomes a work for hire when there is a signed (by both parties) written instrument expressly agreeing that the work is to be considered a work for hire. In addition, it is sometimes possible to reserve certain rights, such as the right to reproduce the work in other media. This should be considered when the negotiating is done.

In the comic industry, the *work for hire contract* - also called a work made for hire contract - (WFH) is a double-edged sword. On one hand, you are generally being offered the opportunity to work on an established character owned by a major company. This means that an established fan following most likely already exists for work produced around this character, and the potential for income-generation is great. Also, depending on your WFH contract, your royalties may help deter the cost of losing any rights to reproduction of your work. On the other hand, you did lose any rights to reproduce your work. To use an art example: If you produce a truly 'kick-ass' pin-up or splash page, say hello to plenty of exposure and advertising without payment. On first glance, this might seeman ego-gratifying experience, but on retrospection, you may find yourself feeling bitter about the benefits to the company that don't trickle down to you. Remember, it's a double-edged sword. Just be sure you know which side you're on and how much it matters to you before you sign all your rights away. (See Appendix B for an example of a WFH contract.)

Creator-Owned Rights

Another type of contract available in our business is the *creator-owned rights contract (COR)*. For many creators this is the contract of choice. Depending on what agreement you negotiate with the publisher, this contract represents the most control for the creator. It provides that the creator is the sole author and owner of the material they create, and lets them decide where, when, why and how their work is reproduced.

The COR contract does not always equal immediate financial success. Sometimes the initial monies produced by a creator-owned property are

ProFile

Professional: Mark Verheiden, Writer
Credits Include: *Aliens, Predator, The American* and *Timecop*, Dark Horse Comics; *The Phantom*, DC Comics; Unproduced screenplays: *The American, The Doomsday Conspiracy*; Produced screenplays: *Timecop* (Universal Pictures), *The Mask* (New Line), *Darkman II* (Universal Pictures)
Question: How much value do you place on written contracts and the importance of creator-owned rights versus work-for-hire agreements?

I put a lot of value on written contracts, though maybe not for the reason you'd expect.

Most people think they need a contract because a written document will protect them from being ripped-off. That's not really true. The sad fact is that most companies have far more resources - financially and legally - than the average freelancer. If you're wronged, you really have few options. Lawsuits are absolutely the last resort - lawyers are extremely expensive, the amount of money at issue usually isn't that much, and results are certainly not guaranteed. Basically, if someone makes an active decision to rip you off, you're taking a trip to the world of pain.

On the other hand, a contract *is* important, because it codifies various points with the people who *aren't* planning a Hawaiian trip on your royalties. Things come up, and it's easier to deal with these "things" before the temptation of money colors the discussion.

Case in point; when I created *The American*, I had no idea there'd ever be movie interest in the project. Well, I got a movie deal - in fact, I've had several movie deals on the project. The fact that my agreement with Dark Horse provided shared veto power over ancillary projects - and the fact that publisher Mike Richardson was and is an honorable guy - made it possible for me to insist the property only sell if I had the job writing the screenplay. And that's how I broke into the movie business.

I have no fundamental moral problem with work-for-hire, as long as the deal is understood up front by all sides. Given my experience, I think it's rather foolish to create new characters under a work-for-hire agreement - but again, it's a matter for each individual writer or artist. In the old days work-for-hire became an excuse to rob writers and artists of the ancillary benefits of their creations; happily, we now live in more enlightened times, where there are options to a "sign it or get out!" ultimatum.

I've created or co-created three titles - *The American, Stalkers* and *Timecop*. I've worked on several work-for-hire projects, including *Aliens, Predator* and *The Phantom*. There are advantages and disadvantages to each. With work-for-hire, you may simply feel like you have something to contribute to an established character or title. Maybe you're trying to establish yourself in the marketplace. Sometimes established titles just plain *pay* better than a creator-owned book.

But there is something extremely satisfying about working on your own concept and exercising control over the end result. And occasionally creator-owned projects can work out beyond your wildest dreams. I share the copyright on the comic version of *Timecop*, I wrote the screenplay for the movie, and now I get to watch a $30 million version of my baby hit the screen. *That's* satisfying!!

Art from *Timecop* by Dark Horse Comics

small. But over time, and if the work is properly promoted, it can represent a substantial financial gain. Sometimes, at a later date, a creator may choose to sell all rights to their creation. That is fine, but remember they would never have had that right if the initial contract was a WFH agreement.

COR agreements can also give the creator a say in how their work is reproduced. With a WFH agreement, once the work is in the publisher's hands, the creator relinquishes all quality control. Whereas a COR agreement allows the creator some control in how the work is reproduced, and the markets at which it's directed. It can also allow the creator the right to reproduce the work as often as they wish.

Basically, the COR agreement gives the creator more latitude and control than the WFH agreement. However, from a publisher's standpoint, the WFH is more desirable, and so you will find that most of the major publishers use the WFH agreement, with the COR agreement residing primarily with the smaller, creator-supportive independents. (See Appendix B for an example of a COR contract.)

There are a great variety of contract types, and each offers different rights and compensations. To find out more detail about contracts, check out some of the books noted on the reading list at the end of this book (See Appendix E).

Contract Pointers

Here are a few things you should know about contracts:

1) Always, always, _always_ have a written contract. Although the belief that a contract must be in writing to be enforced is false, it is foolish to believe that enforcing a casual verbal agreement is an easy process. There are a multitude of reasons for having a written contract. Mainly it protects both you and your employer's interests. But most importantly it outlines, in black and white, the specifics of the agreement. This allows you to check on established deadlines, payment, royalties, complimentary copies of published work, the copyright holder, and any other features of the agreement, at any time during your work on the project. Simply put, it eliminates your questions, and serves as a written guide to what must be done, by whom and by what date, in exchange for what compensation.

> _Get everything in writing. Read your contract. Do your work on time and the best you can._
>
> _Mitch O'Connell, Artist_
> **_(Good Taste Gone Bad,_** _Good Taste Products)_

2) Read you contract. Make sure that all the details that have been discussed are included in the written contract - right down to the number of free copies of the published work you should receive. If you don't outline it at the beginning, you may regret it in the end.

3) Make sure both parties sign the contract. Too simple? Apparently not, as there are many creators who sit on their contracts (out of laziness, busyness or forgetfulness) until after the project has been completed, then cry the blues when there is nothing to force the employer to honor their end of the bargain.

4) Ensure that you get an original copy of the contract. Two originals should be executed. The creator and the employer should each get a copy of the original. If legal problems arise, do you really want to try to explain to your lawyer why you only have a photocopy?

5) Make sure you understand all the language and items listed in your contract _before_ you sign it. Yes folks, legalese is still alive and well, and confusing the best of us laymen. Don't be overwhelmed by it all. If the

ProFile

Professional: Mitch O'Connell, Artist

Credits Include: *The World of Ginger Fox* graphic novel for Comico; *Good Taste Gone Bad: The Art Of Mitch O'Connell* from Good Taste Products; illustration for *Spy Magazine, Playboy Magazine, National Lampoon*; advertising work for *Seven-11, Burger King, MacDonalds Restaurant , Coca-Cola*, and *Kelloggs*.

Question: Do you believe that hiring an agent or lawyer is/has been beneficial for your career? Would you recommend this practice to newcomers?

I've found it beneficial, as a commercial artist, to have reps. I have one in New York and one in Chicago, and I'd like to get one in L.A. They're helpful, because they know a lot more about the advertising ins-and-outs than I do. I'm not always confident enough to quote a price for different advertising jobs. They're much better at it than I am. It also doesn't hurt to have a couple more bodies showing off your art. They handle the advertising stuff, and I usually handle all the editorial and miscellaneous work. I'm happy to have them, but of course they take thirty percent off the top of any jobs they get. But I'm still doing pretty good.

On the other hand, I don't think you need a rep to draw comics.

Art from *Good Taste Gone Bad: The Art of Mitch O'Connell*

language of your contract is too heavy for you to wade through, first talk to the publisher about it. If they are unable or unwilling to simplify the language - or can't explain it to your satisfaction - then consider spending a small sum to have a business lawyer look it over for you. Don't balk at the idea of the cost! Not all lawyers are costly, cutthroat, or inept. Most areas have a lawyer referral service, lawyers for the financially burdened, or a law school brimming with eager students. Use any of these avenues to have your contract deciphered. Don't sign it until you understand it, and are satisfied with the conditions.

Standard Business Forms

Formal contracts are not the only way to confirm an agreement in writing. There are a variety of standardized business forms you can use in the place of specifically drafted contractual agreements. Some of these include the *letter of intent, an outright bill of sale, permission to reproduce work in a publication, and billing invoice.*

Letters of intent signed by both parties can also serve as a form of contract. A letter of intent is simply a letter outlining the intent of both the creator and the publisher with regard to the creation of work, assignment of rights, and compensation for said work. Be cautious in your use of the letter of intent, however, particularly with publishers who avoid a formal written contract. Their avoidance may represent a private agenda that will not benefit you as the creator. These can also be dangerous, legally. Sometimes they are enforced as contracts, sometimes they are not. Sometimes they are considered "quasi-contracts" on which one can make a claim based on reliance even though there is not technically a contract. It is worth the extra two or three days it may take to hammer out the agreement rather than depend upon a letter of intent.

The *bill of sale* does not always apply to the publishing portion of the comic industry, but is still an important aspect of which the creator should be aware. Your original artwork is generally considered your property, even in the cases of WFH. The only restriction in WFH cases, is the fact that you are usually not free to reproduce the image. However, you are free to sell the original artwork if you so choose. In these cases, the bill of sale comes into play.

The bill of sale stipulates to the buyer just what rights they purchase when buying an original work. If your original publishing agreement is COR, then you have the freedom to sell reproduction rights to your buyer, in addition to the original work. Outline these features in your bill of sale description to ensure there is no misunderstanding about just what is being purchased. (For more information, and a sample of a bill of sale, please refer to the reading list at the end of this book - See Appendix E.)

The *form granting permission to reproduce a work in a publication* is a simplified contract form. Keep in mind, unless all aspects of the agreement are stipulated in writing and signed by both parties, there can be problems - because of a lack of communication or understanding - at some point in the future. However, the permission form is an excellent starting point for newcomers, and most publishers use a modified version of this form (Examples are available in the refrence books listed in Appendix E.)

The *billing invoice* is a common method of formalizing the written WFH agreement for the major publishers in our industry. For example, both DC Comics and Marvel Comics provide creators with a payment chit or invoice. When the work is turned in, the invoice is filled out and signed. Small print on the invoice forms the contract agreement that, generally, is signed only by the creator, not the publisher representative. Read these 'mini-contracts' with care. You may be surprised at just what rights you are freely signing away.

Another version of the billing invoice is a simple bill for work done. These types of billing invoices are generally produced and provided by the creator. However, don't denigrate their value. By executing and submitting such a bill, and on its acceptance by the publisher, a form of contractual agreement takes place. Granted it is a simplified contract that describes work produced for specific compensation, and that does not outline rights or royalties. But it is an agreement (generally enforceable) all the same.

Although these preprinted or standard forms can be convenient and efficient, use them with care as there are some risks that are inherent. Problems with preprinted forms include inaccurate descriptions, accidental (or intentional) omission of parts of the agreement, and inadvertent creation of obligations and rights that were never intended by either party. Approach the use of standardized forms with the awareness that the form, as it stands, may not be a comprehensive expression of your actual agreement.

Find a good lawyer to look over your contracts - especially one who is skilled in copyright law. Don't just sign it!

Marc Hempel, Writer/Artist/Painter/Designer
(**Gregory,** DC Comics/Pirahana Press)

Copyright

Copyright is a complex issue that we have already touched upon under the contract heading describing creator-owned rights. The ability for a writer or artist to make a living is greatly dependent upon their ability to control the authorship of their work. In one sense, this characteristic is what sets the comic publishing market apart from other visual and print mediums. In our industry, many works on which we are employed as creators, have already been 'authored' by another creator. We are simply brought on board to continue to develop the property, ie. , continue the series. Under these circumstances, it is not unreasonable for the publisher to expect a creator to 'work for hire,' as they are technically the 'author' of the materials on which you as a creator will work.

There are many critical details about copyright law in this country, and it is in your best interest as a creator, and a professional, to research how this information applies to you, and protecting your career.

Copyright Notices

Copyright notices are a subject of great confusion. Unless you are working under a WFH contract, you should always put a copyright notice on all copies or publications of your original work, or see that the publisher does. The notice should start with the copyright symbol or the word "Copyright" followed by the year of first publication and the name of the artist. For example - Copyright © 1994 Joe Blow. However, in WFH contracts, the copyright will belong to the company hiring you, which no doubt will put the copyright notice on all copies.

Until recent years, this notice was a legal requirement to record your copyright in the federal Copyright Office. It is no longer legally required, but it is still *strongly recommended.* Many people misunderstand the law of copyrights - they believe that if there is no copyright notice, the work is "public domain" and may be copied freely. That is not the law, and it is a good way to get sued! However, if you put copyright notices on all copies of your original work, then you reduce the risk of unauthorized copying.

Trademarks

Unlike the copyright notice, you cannot use the federal trademark symbol - ® - until you have been granted a federal trademark registration. This is a long, and sometimes expensive, process. However, you can use the letters "TM" under any character or logo that you create but have not registered. "TM" notifies people that you are claiming a "common law" trademark in your characters or logo. You could conceivably claim a trademark for any character that has come to symbolize the origin of your goods or services (like Superman for DC Comics). If you do not plan to re-use the character, copyright protection is all that needs to apply.

Ownership of Original Works

As mentioned earlier, in the comic publishing industry creators are generally entitled to keep the original work reproduced by a company for publication.

For example, if you are hired to pencil an issue of *Green Lantern* for DC Comics, the standard artist agreement is a work for hire contract. Since DC Comics owns the rights to the Green Lantern characters, you as a creator are simply being employed to produce new artwork for their

ProFile

Professional: Paul Chadwick, Artist/Writer
Credits Include: Creator, artist and writer of *Concrete* from Dark Horse Comics; *Dazzler* (penciller) for DC Comics; various anthology stories and pinups for DC Comics; *Stalkers* and *Open Space* (painted covers) for Marvel Comics; *Concrete: Killer Smile* four-issue series from Dark Horse/Legend
Question: Do you believe that hiring an agent or lawyer is beneficial for a professional's career? Would you recommend this practice to newcomers?

I've always relied on my agent, Mike Friedrich, to stay current with the field for me. Things just change to fast to keep up. I also like the fact that since he plays the tough guy in negotiations and dunning for payment, I remain the "nice artist."

Although I think an agent is an excellent idea, if you live near your clients (in New York for instance) you might be able to effectively represent yourself and hang on to what you'd pay an agent.

Paul Chadwick's *Concrete*

existing property. You will most likely be paid a flat pagerate for each page of pencils you produce, and a small royalty (which you will share with the inker and writer), based on the volume of sales. You will not be entitled to reproduce the work in any form, without the permission of the publisher. However, you most likely will retain ownership of the original artwork, which you are permitted to sell as an original work (although *not* for reproduction.)

Read any contract agreement carefully, however, as there are many publishers who wish to purchase not only all rights, but the original artwork as well. This is usually stipulated in the written agreement. If ownership is not mentioned, be sure to include - or insist they include - a line describing who retains ownership of the physical work. Nothing can be more heartbreaking than finding out you signed away your favorite piece of work!

Reproductions

The comic publishing industry in which you now search for work is basically a big reproduction business. Your contract agreements assign *reproduction rights* to your publisher(s). This is a complex and multi-faceted subject that cannot be easily covered in this overview book and merits some additional research and reading. Be sure to look into this subject in the reading list at the end of this book (See Appendix E.) However, there is one aspect I would like to address, since it is a relatively new angle affecting reproductions of original works.

According to an article in the May 1993 issue of *The Artist's Magazine*, recent changes in copyright laws (due to a surprise ruling from the Copyright Office) have affected the ownership of reproductions of original artwork. What this means is that until just recently, on reproductions of a creator's work (ie. lithographic prints, photographic prints, color photocopies, etc.) the creator retained the copyright. However, since a derivative work can be copyrighted in their own right, a recent ruling by the Copyright Office significantly affects copyright of a creator's work. The Copyright Office determined that a derivative work is any "work based upon one or more pre-existing works, such as a translation . . . art reproduction . . . or any other form in which the work may be recast, transformed or adapted. A work consisting of editorial revisions . . . or other modifications, which as a whole, represent an original work of authorship."

Simply (and frighteningly) stated, this means that any employee of a copier shop or printer who fiddles with the color or line or magnification controls when reproducing your work, has provided sufficient editorial revisions to consider themselves the author of a derivative work, and the copyright holder of that - and any subsequent - reproductions. Aaagh! To make this even clearer, according to the *Artist's Magazine* article, this means that every time you have copies or prints of your work made, you need to have the company and/or its representatives sign a release of copyright back to you. Or, you need to include a text line stating copyright details for both the original image and it's reproductions.

You may be saying to yourself, "So what's this got to do with getting into comic the business?" Well, if you are a professional business person, you will keep careful documentation of your work. Photographs and photocopies don't just help keep your records straight, but they also protect you against shipping accidents that can result in loss or destruction of your work. After all, it's much easier to reproduce a page of pencil art if you have a photocopy of the original from which to work! So keep in mind, while you conscientiously reproduce your work for documentation purposes, you must get a signed release to protect your reproduction rights.

> *Get the money up front. That's not always possible, but I'm always willing to offer advantages and discounts for the money up front, and people will often take you up on it. That's the best arrangement, get the money up front.*
>
> Mark Wheatley, Writer/Artist
> (**Radical Dreamer**, Blackball and Mark's Giant Economy Size Comics)

Licensing

The subject of *licensing* can be divided into two categories in the comic industry. There's the creator work on licensed material, and the licensing of materials produced by the creator. Huh? Let me explain.

Work on licensed materials means that you are hired - on a WFH basis! - to produce material based on established characters. The publisher who hires you has purchased a license from another company to create original materials based on those characters. The license entitles them to hire under WFH agreements only. All materials produced become either the joint possession of the publisher and the license holder or, as often happens, the sole possession of the license holder. An example of this would be the case of Lucasfilm and Dark Horse Comics.

Dark Horse currently holds the license to produce original *Indiana Jones* and *Star Wars* materials. This agreement limits them to comic book materials, but they are free to negotiate other licenses with Lucasfilm. Lucasfilm, the copyright holder of the *Indy* and *Star Wars* characters, becomes the owner of new materials produced by the creators who work for Dark Horse. Lucasfilm is free to resell those materials to other licensees, such as computer game companies, without compensating the original creator of the material. On the one hand, many newcomers would be delighted to have an opportunity to work with these firmly established - and very popular - characters. On the other hand, the financial gain is limited, and the control the creator exerts over reproduction of their work is nonexistent. Consider these facts carefully before signing a WFH agreement for licensed material.

Licensing of materials produced by a creator is another matter altogether. This means, if you create a particular character, then you can control the licensing of that character and image. You can sell licenses to various publishers and merchandisers, and you control what is produced, and make a substantial profit from those reproductions. An example is comic professional Matt Wagner.

Matt created the character of *Grendel*, which was published by Comico for many years. When Comico changed hands (and after a fierce

ProFile

Professional: Rod Underhill, Attorney/Protem Small Claims Court Judge/Computer Fine Artist/Writer
Credits Include: *Airlock #1-3*; *The Forbidden Airlock #1*; *Wonderwall #1*; variety of fine art prints by Eclectus, story for *Caligula* (art by Topper Helmers), graphic novel; *Nutopian Digital Pin-ups*, a series of fine art pin-ups done in conjunction with Homage artist, Brian Haberlin, for CompuServe.
Comic Clients Represented: Hero Comics, Barb Rausch, Topper Helmers, Howard Simpson - all pro bono

Question: Do you believe that hiring an agent or lawyer is beneficial for a professional's career?

There is some controversy about that. When I was reading through the Comic Book Superstars, there was a very famous artist who was quoted on that subject as saying, "This is comics! Don't be ridiculous!!" Personally, I don't know. I've never represented anybody in that [agent] particular capacity, so I don't have a great deal of experience with it, but I suppose agents can be pretty valuable.

If you can deal with the expense of having a lawyer, I think it's a good idea - especially for reading over your contracts. You should *always* have a lawyer read your contract before you sign it. Another question is; "Do you need a lawyer to be your agent at the same time, or would you be better off having an agent represent you?" It's strange that there are lawyers in the industry that represent comic professionals in the guise of being an agent, too. I don't know how comfortable I am with attorneys being agents for people. There's nothing wrong with it, but it does seem a bit on the odd side.

David Scrogge [who is now VP of Publishing with Dark Horse Comics] was a real textbook example of what an artist's rep should be. I was really comfortable with how he ran his business.

Question: How much value do you place on written contracts?

You should always have a written contract. A written contract defines, basically, what's going to happen and what you can do about it if it *doesn't* happen they way it should. So, you've got to have a written contract. Comic professionals should endeavor to have the publisher draft the contract, because any ambiguities in the contract would therefore, by law, be construed against the people that wrote the contract.

I think it should be a formal contract, rather than a letter of intent, and should be signed by both parties. A letter of intent can be, in effect, binding depending on how it's worded and who sent it, but it doesn't really substitute for a good, written contract.

There are a couple of things you should get in a contract. One, is permission to sue the publisher in your home state, if they fail to pay you. But even if you get permission to sue in your home state, that doesn't mean you can *collect* in your home state. You still have to register the judgement in the state in which the publisher operates. Collecting is a major problem for freelancers dealing with out-of-state publishers that refuse to pay. It's a real nightmare. With that in mind, the second thing is that you should probably get as much money as you can up front. Naturally the publisher's not going to want to pay you up front, because you may not produce the work in time, or you may have a poor or unproven business reputation. So, you've got to reach some kind of common ground.

A good guideline is; the newer the publisher, the more risky they can be. Although, there are several notable large publishers that have gone under. What I advise creators to do is to share as much information as they can. If a publisher doesn't pay you and you don't tell other professionals in the industry about that, it can go on for quite a while, and a lot of people can be hurt. The first people who find they aren't getting paid should spread the word. There should be some sort of forum to disseminate this kind of information. The computer forums are a good way of doing that, I think. You can reach a lot of people, world-wide, instantaneously. I've posted notices on the Pro-Only part of the CompuServe Forum indicating problems with various publishers that people should be aware of.

If a publisher refuses, or stalls on, a written contract then there is a dilemma. If you're trying to break into the industry, they've kind of got you over a barrel, naturally. If you're willing to do the work for free, but you're *hoping* you'll get paid, then I'd say go ahead and do the job depending on how much work you're putting into it and how much damage would occur to you if you didn't get paid. However, if this is the money you need to eat, then it's not such a great idea. If you're a newcomer and you're working full-time in some sort of a job with your comic work an after-hours sort of thing, and you're willing to risk not getting paid then it might be worth it to you. It's really a personal choice. Even if you have a contract, that doesn't mean you're going to get paid. The company might go out of business or might go bankrupt. Just having a contract doesn't ensure that you're going to get paid. However, a rough rule of thumb: Have the contract before you do the work.

Question: What importance do you place on creator-owned rights versus work-for-hire agreements?

It depends what you want in your career. If you want to try to build up a, more or less, steady income then you're going to have to work for other companies on characters that you don't own. If you're trying to "win the big prize" and make a great deal of money, then you're going to want to own the character. For me personally, as a comic book writer and artist, I only do characters that I own myself, because I already have a steady source of income. I'd rather control my own characters. That's pretty much what I want to do, although there are some characters owned by DC Comics that I'd like to work with, just for fun.

Dave Sim places a lot of emphasis on owning your own characters, and I think what he's done is fantastic! He's got a really nice thing going. But there are problems with owning your own characters. The first one is having to finance the publishing yourself. If you create a character, that you own, and you want to have someone else publish it, there are some issues to consider. If I was advising the publisher, I would say, "Don't publish characters unless you own at least a piece of them." I interviewed Steve Shanes many years ago shortly after Pacific Comics failed. He was mourning what a tragedy it was that he didn't have at least a *piece* of *The Rocketeer*. At that time it had been optioned by Disney, and was eventually made into a film. Steve was saying, "Jeez, if I'd just owned twenty percent of it, who knows how much money that would be!" So, there is a hybrid relationship that publishers canwork out with the creators. The publisher can say "I'm putting all this money out to do this. It may be a big winner, and I'd like to own some of it, so I'd like twenty percent." I think

Art from Underhill's *Caligula*

that's fair. The risk compared to the gain makes it worthwhile. The [Teenage Mutant Ninja] Turtles is a good example of this. They were turned down by publishers numerous times, and were finally self-published. If somebody had taken the risk, and taken that five or ten percent, they'd now have the equivalent of five or ten percent of, seemingly, almost all the money in the world!

legal struggle) Matt was able to take his character to other publishers, recently licensing its use with DC and Dark Horse Comics. Another example of licensing is Dave Steven's character, *The Rocketee*r. For many years, Dave also licensed out the use of his character; however, within the past couple of years, Dave sold his rights to Disney/Touchstone Pictures.

There is a distinctive difference between the two forms of licensing. Make sure that you are clear on which one is specified if licensing is included in one of your contract agreements.

Merchandising

Reproduction of your work on materials other than the original book publication falls under the heading of merchandising. This can include prints, T-shirts, toys, sculptures, buttons, caps, pogs (cardboard milk-cap collectibles), trading cards, and anything else a merchandiser comes up with on which to place your work image. This subject relates primarily to artwork rather than writing, although sometimes quotes of text have been reproduced. Technically, merchandising of your work is covered under licensing and work for hire.

Following a WFH agreement, the publisher is free to use your image/work on any merchandise they choose. Unless the contract stipulates compensation from a merchandise reproduction, be prepared to see your work adorning everything under the sun, but don't expect to get paid - even in items - for your popular image!

Under a licensing agreement, you would sell reproduction rights of your work to a merchandiser, following successful negotiations as to the nature of the merchandise and the payment you would receive. You may need to store this information away for the future, as the newcomer with a hot licensable property is practically unheard of.

Taxes

Wait, wait, don't close this book! I guarantee I will not bore you with dry tax details. The simple matter of taxes and the freelancer is not nearly as boring or difficult as everyone believes it is.

First, let's look briefly at what type of taxes affect you.

Like everyone else in the world, you must pay *Federal Income Tax*. Your Internal Revenue Service (IRS) forms provide you with all the information you need to complete your tax return. Don't let the language of the forms scare you. It is really a very simple, straightforward process. Carefully read each step. There are many areas of the tax forms that will not apply to you. When you have completed your return, simply keep a copy on file that you can refer to the following year, and use it as a guide for which areas you must complete.

The other side of being a freelance writer or artist, is that you are now self-employed. This means that you must complete the portion of the IRS Tax Return Forms for those who are self-employed. Again, once you complete your first return, keep a copy on file to refer to, as a guide, the following year. **But, most importantly, you must pay *self-employment taxes and social security.***

Now, I emphasize this portion of the tax section, because it is the area where I have heard the most problem stories from new freelancers. Your self-employment tax and social security are going to equal about 20% of your paycheck. If you were an employee, the money would automatically be withheld by your employer. However, as a freelancer, you must withhold those funds yourself.

Now don't, for one second, think you can make it up at the end of the year. Wrong!! Many experienced professionals spend March and April scrambling to take on more and more projects, and sell even more originals, trying to scrape together the money to pay their taxes.

The IRS has set up a *Quarterly Estimates* payment system. This system requires you to make four estimated tax payments (based on the previous year's income) over the year. The benefit here is that it alleviates your tax payment burden come April. It also eliminates the penalties the IRS charges you if you fail to make you quarterly estimates!

So, set aside 20% of each check, right off the bat. Establish a savings account, where you can save that money until your Quarterly Payment is due. Don't procrastinate and don't be waylaid by unexpected extravagances and indulgences. The 20% now is nothing compared to the substantial end-of-year bill and subsequent IRS penalties. You'll spend years playing catchup, and it's only *you* who'll live to regret it - possibly from inside a prison for tax evasion! Start out your career with good business habits and you'll find that it makes doing business much easier and a lot less stressful!

Summary

Like any business or profession, the comic industry is a complex intermesh of employers and employees. There are many rules and guidelines that stipulate how business can, and should, be done. Established ethical and professional guidelines do exist, and are available from a variety of source. It is in the best interest of the aspiring professional to familiarize themselves with the various aspects of doing business within this unique profession.

In this section we have looked at some of the more important aspects of the business and legal practices of the comic publishing industry. We have looked at conducting *negotiations* with a potential employer to determine the terms of an agreement that are mutually acceptable. We have also discussed the importance of a *contract*, and the two most important forms that affect us in this business - the *work for hire agreement* and the *creator-owned rights agreement*. I have also illustrated the usefulness and restrictions inherent in *standardized forms* such as *letters of intent, bills of sale, publication reproduction permissions*, and *billing invoices*. We've reviewed *copyright* rules, how this applies of *ownership of original works*, and how it affects *reproduction rights*. I've also given you some examples of *licensing* and *merchandising*, and how this can affect you as the creator. Finally, we took a brief, but important look at *taxes*, and your responsibilities as a self-employed professional.

Remember that as a professional you are responsible for the business and legal aspects of your work as well as its creation. If you fail as a *business* professional, you will have only yourself to blame for your downfall as a *creative* professional. Use your mind and your common sense as a guide, set your passions and feelings aside when conducting business. If you can take an objective and businesslike stance, you are well on your way to proving your professionalism and closing important work deals.

Chapter Eight
You Got The Job: Keeping Your Humility,
Pursuing More Work, and Fans

In this chapter we will take a look at some of the things you must consider once you've finally secured that seemingly elusive job.

It is important as both a comic professional and a business person to remember that there is more to getting work than just being offered a job. Even in the simplest of businesses, an employee or worker - whether salaried staff or subcontractor - is expected to maintain certain business practices and behaviors to keep that job. In that respect, the comic industry is no different from any other business. There are a variety of tasks and skills that are almost mandatory to continued success as a freelancer. Some of these skills include social and business interactions with peers and employers, the methods to follow for securing more work, and the behaviors expected of you when dealing with customers and fans.

> *Don't over-estimate your chances. Remember not to badger the editor from who you got your first piece of work, purely because they may have just done it to you to give you a chance. Don't feel that because you've submitted an 8-page story, that you'll be immediately leaping to a graphic novel or mini-series! I think too many people submit huge proposals. It's rare to get a proposal for a 5 or 6 -page story. Everyone's got a graphic novel, everyone's got a mini-series.*
>
> **Dave Elliott, Publisher of Blackball Comics**

Keeping Your Humility

All newcomers must consider the concept of 'keeping your humility'. There are a great variety of attitudes about this subject. Three common stances are the "I'll *never* forget where *I* came from," school of thought, the "I hope I have a chance to reach that pinnacle someday - *then* I'll deal with it," perspective, and the "At last they all see just how truly great/talented *I* am," point of view.

Here are some important points to remember when considering this issue:

- Whatever your work skills, there will always be somebody out there who admires your work - even if it's just your friends or family - so admirers don't always equate with you being a great talent

- If you attend conventions as a professional, there will always be fans. Some of them may claim to love your work without ever having seen it. Some will be legitimate hard-core fans who've stumbled on your work and admire the burgeoning talent they see

■ Most professionals will be unfamiliar with your work until you're a bit more established, but that doesn't negate the quality or value of what you produce. Low recognition is just due to your lack of exposure and the volume of product produced by the industry

■ Whatever your personality type - introverted vs extroverted - there are many ways of dealing with success that are polite and considerate. And humble.

■ Humility is a consideration for every individual that works in any public forum. Nobody likes an arrogant, self-involved butthead!

The most important thing to keep in mind about your success is that you were an industry 'nobody' until you got your first job, and if you don't work hard at being a pleasant business person, you will go right back to being a 'nobody' just as quickly if publishers refuse to hire you. The true "legends" of the comic industry are few and far between, however there are plenty of transient "stars." Some are still around because they work hard and are good to their fans. Some of them are still around because they minimize contact with the fans (eliminating the 'alienate your readership' factor) and rely heavily on old friends in the industry to get work. And some are simply no longer around.

Here are a few guidelines to help you in keeping your humility:

■ *Don't forget the people who helped you get your break.* If you're fortunate enough to have family or friends who helped you get where you are, don't forget them once you get there. Sometimes help takes the form of parents or spouses willing to support you while you struggle to get established. Sometimes the help takes the form of financial assistance. Sometimes guidance and advice from established pros will help you get your foot in the door. Once you're through the door though, don't forget how you got there!

■ *No matter how popular you get, just remember that you wouldn't be there if not for the publisher and the fans.* The fans are technically your employers, too. If they don't buy the books, the publisher can't print them. Think of the publisher and the fans as a business partnership. Make sure you treat your bosses respectfully and with consideration.

■ *There's always room for improvement.* Nobody is so good that they can't get better. Sometimes getting better means changing with the times. Sometimes it means keeping up with technology. Sometimes it just means growing and learning as an artist or writer. Just remember, who you are when you start out will not remain the same. The industry will affect you, and hopefully you will affect the industry. Given that you should always be changing and improving, it shouldn't be too hard to stay humble. Nothing is more humbling than learning that you don't know everything!

■ *Just because you're great doesn't mean you'll get the job - and just because you got the job doesn't mean you're great.* There are many talented creators out there, all of them vying for the jobs available in the

ProFile

Professional: Joe Rubinstein, 'Cary Grant-like' Inker and Fine Art Painter
Credits Include: *Wolverine* mini-series and *Captain America,* Marvel; *Superman* and *Batman*, DC Comics; *Penthouse Comics*; various and numerous projects for Malibu Comics, Dark Horse Comics and Image.
Question: What tactics would you recommend to newcomers for acquiring more work once they've completed their first comic job?

Willingness to learn, willingness to accommodate, and honesty.

Joe Kubert once said to me " The hardest job to get is not your first, but your second." That's because, in general, people have spent six months getting those samples just perfect, just right, and then they've gotten their first job. And then they discover it's got a very real deadline that has to be met. Maybe they don't do as good a job [as on their samples], or they take shortcuts they ordinarily wouldn't have because they just want to please the editor and meet the deadline. Well deadlines, of course, are very important but I think, ultimately, every job should be taken quite seriously and as a showpiece. But I've spoken to people who seem to have this sort of 'I'll get better and after all, it's only my first job' attitude.

On top of that, I think it's important to establish with the various editors that you are willing to listen, willing to learn, willing to make changes as are necessary, or don't demonstrate that you think you know better than other creators on a project by making unauthorized alterations - based on your own tastes - to another creator's work. I think ultimately you have to be honest and willing. I think there's an inclination that freelancers have, more often than not, to lie. If you've got a deadline, and it's Tuesday for example, but there's no way in hell you're going to make the Tuesday deadline, don't mail it on Thursday. Instead, call up on Monday and say, "Look, I've got a problem." Keep them aware, keep the communication going. Because if there's one thing that drives editors crazy, it's somebody who can't be gotten a hold of. Frequently the editors can be accommodating if the excuse is a legitimate one; you broke your arm, you got a cold, your mother got sick. Willingness to learn, willingness to accommodate, and honesty.

**Rubinstein's inks on *Batman*
for DC Comics**

industry. Sometimes the work will go to a creator who doesn't seem to be as talented, qualified or experienced. Just remember, jobs aren't doled out based on talent alone. There are a multitude of other influential factors, including your work relationship with the publisher (established or new), your proven track record (can deliver proven quality on time or proven failure to meet deadlines), ability to work out business details (acceptance of deadlines or financial compensation), and timing (if you were in the right place at the right time). Keep in mind all these factors, and you'll increase the odds of securing that job. Forget them, and you may find yourself nursing a wounded ego!

> *Cooperation and communication are very important.*
> *That doesn't mean you capitulate on every creative point - it doesn't mean you have to capitulate on any - but commercial comics tend to be team sports, requiring a certain amount of give and take. All the elements of the creative team need latitude to do their best work.*
> *So always listen. Try to understand the other points of view. And when you think the other guy is wrong, make sure you have a cogent argument to support your case. "You're full of it!" isn't really an argument, even though it's often true. But if you're right and you know it, stick to your guns - because the end result is going to have your name on it and reflect on your career.*
>
> Mark Verheiden, Writer (**Aliens**, Dark Horse Comics)

■ *No matter how good you are, there's always somebody better.* Guaranteed. If not a current peer, the another up-and-comer will be there dogging your heels. If you don't practice humility, it may be forced upon you!

■ *Listen to what the fans and publishers have to say about your work.* Take heed, but with a grain of salt. Just because they like your work doesn't always mean they understand what you're trying to express. On the other hand, keep your artistic integrity; but just remember, integrity doesn't pay the bills. Sometimes we have to compromise to please the boss. Just be sure you can live with that idea before you jump into this industry. The comics' field is a business, and there's no room for creative prima donnas!

■ *Just because your peers ask your opinion doesn't qualify you to be patronizing.* Hopefully you will have peers with whom you will interact in the business (other artists or writers). There will be occasions where your opinion of their work will be solicited. As suggested in chapters Three and Six (Feedback and Critiques), a critique should be constructive, not destructive. Always imagine yourself on the receiving end of your

Not-So-Nice Guys Finish Last
or How To Break The Rules And Fall Behind: A True Story

To illustrate some of the mistakes you should avoid once you get the job, here is a true, personal anecdote about a newcomer who made a lot of the classic mistakes.

A young fellow David and I were friends with was struggling to "break in" to the business (for the purposes of this story we'll call him "Charles"). For years David provided him with technical instruction and advice. We advised "Charles" on his portfolio, samples, provided him with contact names and information, made personal recommendations to publishers, gave him encouragement and moral support, and goaded him into attending conventions. He had trouble getting any substantial work until at last we convinced him to attend a large convention. Within a couple of hours of introducing him around to major publishers, to whom he showed his samples, he had secured a job so prestigious that long time established professionals were effectively green with envy. We were delighted, as all "Charles" hard work was now beginning to pay off. Or at least, so we thought. Then "Charles" began to break some very important rules that ultimately affected his career.

Once "Charles" began work on the job, he started to have artistic differences with his editor. Rather than bite his tongue and struggle along, recognzing that he was getting a tremendous opportunity for a newcomer, he broke the first golden rule; *Keep your humility.* "Charles" began to argue with his editor safe in the belief that he must be an invaluable and irreplaceable talent, because of how quickly and enthusiastically he had secured this prestigious job. In short order his working relationship with his editor and the other creators on the project began to deteriorate. As his satisfaction with the work and the work relationships began to wane he broke the second golden rule; *Don't be late on your deadlines - especially if you're a newcomer!* "Charles" editor became so frustrated and disatisfied with his inability to meet the crucial deadlines, that "Charles" was fired before the completion of the project.

Once "Charles" had lost this big job, and his lucrative source of income was gone, he was back to struggling along with small potatoe jobs. Then he befriended another creator with whom he shared a good personal and work relationship. Riding that other creator's popularity, "Charles" was able to secure another great job with different publisher. About this time, "Charles" broke another golden rule; *Don't forget the people who helped you get your "break."* Without any apparent reason, "Charles" simply stopped staying in touch, stopped phoning, and ceased visiting with us - even when in town to visit with his family. Quite simply, he became rude and inconsiderate. We had gone out of our way to help him get his start, and then were snubbed once he believed himself to be firmly established, and no longer "in need" of our assistance. Very sad.

"Charles" attempted to use his new job to reestablish himself. But developed the same deadline problems he had with his first big project. As a result, he now struggle to secure himself big jobs. He picks up the occasional small project, but few publishers are interested in taking a gamble on his ability to make deadlines and be professional.

"Charles" is a nice guy. He's pleasant to talk to, and doesn't come across as arrogant or rude. It's probably that fact in combination with his creative talents that have continued to gain him piece work, and keep him in the business. But as long as "Charles" is unable to meet his deadlines, or operate from a more humble, fair-minded, flexible position he will find it hard to get the "big" jobs in the industry. And as long as he ignores the hand of friendship, there will be nobody there to help along his rocky career path.

comments, and temper them with humility. Regardless of how skilled you believe yourself to be compared to your peers, don't patronize. Be supportive and positive - it's more effective!

- *Don't trash other creators' work to your editor.* Whether or not you believe all other creators working for your editor are talentless trash, don't bother sharing that little insight with your boss. It's an insult to their judgement, it illustrates how arrogant you are, and ultimately it will jeopardize your working relationship with that publisher. Thanks to word of mouth, it may also cause your reputation egregious harm in the industry and possibly endanger your chances of securing work with other publishers.

Keep these bits of advice in mind while you look for work throughout your career, and you'll find that publishers will begin to search you out, because in addition to your professionalism you will be considered a nice guy to deal with.

To paraphrase Shakespeare, "Nothing so becomes a man as humility."

> *Be true to your word. If you say you're going to hand in an assignment on Tuesday, bend over backwards to make sure it gets in on Tuesday. When you're starting out, your reliability is probably as (and sometimes more) important than your talent.*
>
> *Karl Kesel, Writer/Inker (**Superboy**, DC Comics)*

Pursing More Work

So now you've worked on your first project. You're elated to have secured work you've always dreamed about doing. Now you can sit back and relax as a comic professional.

BZZZT! Wrong!! Your hard work is just beginning.

Unless you've managed to secure a long-term contract with a publisher to produce a regular unlimited series, there's little likelihood that your first big break is going to guarantee you a continuous flow of work. Long established freelancers and newcomers alike must constantly work at lining up new projects to produce a steady source of income. This is not easy work, and requires diligence and a tough skin. There are lots of times you will be turned away, just like any unproven newcomer, whatever the amount of experience you've acquired. As I mentioned previously, timing plays a significant role in finding work - being the right person in the right place at the right time. There are several tactics you can use to pursue more work, and for the most part they resemble those used to get work in the first place. Here's a run down of some of the more helpful methods for lining up more work.

Conventions

Never underestimate the power of a convention. Once you've been published, this provides you with a forum from which to display your newly published samples. Both fans and publishers alike will be interested in seeing your work. Everyone likes to know a potential hot property before they were 'anyone.' Take the opportunities a convention offers to reintroduce yourself to editors and publishers you've previously met, and to make as many new contacts as possible.

Also, invest time in getting to know your freelance peers. They may have a project they're involved with that needs someone just like you. Or perhaps they know an editor who's desperately seeking the talents you have to offer. Make use of the social relationships to get the word out that you're available and looking for work - it really can make a difference.

A convention will provide you with many possible work contacts. Take advantage of these events whenever your time and finances allow.

Be persistent. If you're pursuing a client that you want to work for, send them samples, follow up with phonecalls. Also, find out why they didn't use you on your first inquiry. An art director's advice on what you need to improve can be very valuable.

*Les Dorscheid, Illustrator and Colorist (**Nexus**)*

Mail and Telephone Contact

Just because you've now been published doesn't mean you should stop sending out mail samples to publishers. The same holds true for telephone contact. If you've established a good, friendly rapport with an editor, don't hesitate to give them a call occasionally to let them know you're available and looking for work. Sometimes, if your timing is good, you'll

ProFile

Professional: Jerry Ordway, Writer/Artist
Credits Include: _All Star Squadron_ (artist), _Infinity Incorporated_ (co-creator/penciller), _Crisis On Infinite Earth_ (finisher), _Superman_ (writer/artist), _Power of Shazam_ (writer/artist), _Zero Hour_, DC Comics; _The Fantastic Four_, Marvel Comics; _Wildstar_ (co-creator/artist), Image.
Question: What tactics would you recommend to newcomers for acquiring more work once they've completed their first comic job?

I've known a lot of people who got their foot in the door, but then had a very hard time getting their second job. So my best advice is don't believe you've made it just because you got that first job. It may see print, or it might never get printed. There are no guarantees. So take that first job, do your best work, and make sure your next job is as good. If you don't get that next job, you may have to go back to doing samples. The best thing you can do, is to show whoever you're working for that you're really interested in getting in. Make sure you make your deadlines and that the work is your best. Sometimes that means taking on a job that might have a really tight deadline, but still put as much as possible into it.

Initially, you're going to work really hard when you first get in the business - and you still work hard later - but before you set any patterns for yourself, I think you're better off avoiding shortcuts and going the long way. Whatever extra work you need to put into a panel to make it good, you really should do at the start of your career, to establish it as a work habit. I think that's all part of the Work Ethic. You really can't let up, because there's too many other people there looking to get in [to the industry]. If you got one job, your foot's in the door - but just barely. There's plenty of other people that would be happy to push you out of the way!

Art from _Shazam!_ by DC Comics

land yourself an unexpected but very welcome job.

Also, once you have acquired new, published tearsheets, renew your mail contacts with this updated material. Editors frequently feel more secure hiring a proven quantity than an unproven newcomer. Enclose a brief cover letter describing your published work, and relating how you enjoyed the project and are ready for new jobs. Make sure you include a reference to past sample submissions. Don't assume every editor will remember your last sample pack. It's highly unlikely, so be considerate and provide a friendly, yet businesslike, reminder in your note.

Mail and telephone contact should be a path a new freelancer regularly uses in securing more work. Prove your professionalism and reliability with this method, and you may find yourself more job offers than you can possibly accept.

Personal Interviews

As I've mentioned in the past, this avenue of securing work is not always the most efficient or desirable. However, if you live in a location that easily enables you to drop by the publisher's offices, take advantage of the opportunity on occasion. Make an appointment, and stop by with your newly published material. Also remember to bring any other new samples you may have produced.

Remember, the editor doesn't want to see you every couple of weeks. Save the appointments for times when you have something really big, or extra-special to show as samples. Maximize the time made available to you, or you'll begin to find that the editor is never available when you call.

Related Work Fields

Now that you've finally had a chance to work in the comic industry, you may decide it's not quite what you thought it was cracked up to be. If that's the case, you may want to consider related fields. Your local library or bookstore will carry current editions of *Writer's Market* and *Artist's Market*. These books carry comprehensive listings of markets interested in freelancers. There are listings for both mainstream and small press, including comic listings. For example, you may find that although you thought you'd enjoy drawing a superhero comic, once you competed issue two of Super-Colossal-Hero-Guy, you found you were quite sick of muscular men in tights and the thought of drawing editorial caricatures seems much more exciting. In that case, it's off to *Artist's Market* with you. There you'll find listings for a multitude of publications that are dying to have your artistic skills provide them with heaps of editorial caricatures. These related work fields operate in a very similar manner to the comic industry, so you can probably use similar techniques for securing work.

Always remember this: If you're doing work you don't enjoy, you can't possibly be doing your best. Find the niche that makes you happiest, and pursue it for all you're worth!

Professional: Mart Nodell, Comic Artist
Credits Include: Creator of the *Green Lantern* for DC Comics
Question: What's one of your favorite fan stories?

We have, through the years at shows, made many friends. People from all areas of life; from a 5-year old girl who wanted to know what we thought the Green Lantern #19 - Fiftieth Anniversary issue would be worth to doctors, judges and lawyers. Comics run the gamut of peoples interests.

A most interesting situation came about during our stay at the Chicago Con two years ago. A fan, of about 65 years of age, walked over to us waving two parts of an early Green Lantern book. He explained that his school teacher, in the early '40's, had caught him reading it inside his geography book, and ripped the comic in half. He was proud to have saved it through the years, and we autographed both halves for him. As an aside: In those days, comics were *not* considered good reading material, whereas today literacy organizations regard comics as a good supplement in reading studies.

Through the years we have made many friends in the comic field, both among fans and pros alike. We thank them all for the pleasure of meeting and talking with them.

Fans

Fans are wonderful. They are also some of the most complicated, exciting, gratifying and frightening people you will ever have to deal with as a comic professional. They're people. All sorts of people from all walks of life. And they love comics (or comic-related material.) Sometimes they also love you. Sometimes they don't. They are there whether your good or bad, talented or talentless. Trust me, they'll find you. Once you've been published there's no way of avoiding them.

Fan presence is everywhere in this industry, whether you're an extroverted convention attendee or an introverted hermit. Fans come to conventions, they show up at store signings and they send you mail. They're Joe Average on the street who finds out you're a professional artist/writer. Everyone has some creative streak in them, and the idea that an individual makes a living with their creativity is very exciting and seductive. Everyone knows somebody who's creative, and they'll want to tell you all about them. Be polite. Listen. Then excuse yourself when you must get going. Always keep in mind that you're no better than any fan you meet just because you are a published talent. There are plenty of doctors and lawyers and musicians and rocket scientists and bookkeepers who are fans. Chances are pretty good you'd admire their work too, if you knew anything about it.

Here are some pointers on what to expect from fans and how to deal with them.

Good Stuff About Some Fans

· No matter how bad your day, week, month or life is going, they can make you feel like you're on top of the world.
· They love what you do, and they're generally not afraid to tell you.
· They say nice things about you and your work.
· They bring you gifts to show their appreciation of you.
· They buy your work, which makes publishers want to hire you for more projects.
· They're interested enough in your work to buy original art and commission new work - a great supplement to freelancer pay.
· You get to meet a lot of really nice, interesting people, some of whom you'll become good friends with.

Bad Stuff About Some Fans

· They really can't stand your work and aren't afraid to tell you why.
· They can say some really thoughtless and mean things.
· Even if you cut your price on originals or offer deals on commissions, they'll balk at your prices, or act outraged by what you're asking.
· Sometimes they're not the most socially skilled individuals, and they won't leave you alone.

Dealing With Fans

This is a complicated issue because of the diversity of the fandom. There are, however, some basic 'rules' you can follow. Interestingly, they're also basic common sense, courtesy behaviors. Feel free to apply them to other people in your life.

Always remember this: No matter how much you admire a particular publisher or retail operation, always, always, always remember that *the fans* are technically your employers. Although they don't make out the pay cheque, they buy the product. If the fans don't like you, they don't buy the product and sales will drop. Editors don't hire creators whose work makes sales of the book drop.

Here's how you should treat fans: Be Nice.

Think of it as a customer satisfaction job. You keep the customers happy, they keep coming back for more. Sure, the guy with the bad body odor who spits when he talks is grossing you out. But he buys your book, so Be Nice. For every fan who puts you off, there are twice as many nice fans in the wings. So, Be Nice. The bad ones only seem more noticeable because of their negative qualities. Trust me, there's way more nice fans out there than rotten ones. So, Be Nice. Besides, they can't be all bad. They bought your book, didn't they?

In case you didn't take my point, let me clarify:

Be Nice, Be Nice, Be Nice.

ProFile

Professional: Terry Beatty, Artist/Writer
Credits Include: *Ms. Tree*, *Wild Dog*, and *Guy Gardner* (Inker) all, most recently, from DC Comics; *Elfquest: New Blood* stories (writer) from Warp Graphics; *Johnny Dynamite: Underworld* (artist) from Dark Horse; *Scary Monsters Magazine* (cover artist) from Dennis Druktenis Publishing.
Question: How do you feel professionals should deal with fans? What's one of your favorite fan stories?

Well, I can tell you how fans and professionals *shouldn't* deal with each other!

I attended the Chicago Con once, several years ago, on one of the hottest July days that ever existed. I had driven in from Iowa in my old car, which had no air-conditioning. I'd taken a wrong turn on the highway, and it took forever to get there. I finally got in, got set up in the artist's room with my artwork displayed, and felt exhausted the moment I sat down. The first person who came up to me was a thirteen- or fourteen-year-old kid. He walked up and immediately started complaining about my work. And I blew up at him.

Now, normally I'm a very low-key guy, I'm pretty much able to take everything in stride, but I then made an announcement to the entire room: "The artists at this convention are not here to be beaten up on or complained at. If you have complaints about our work, that's what the letter columns in the comic books are for." I'm sure I scared this kid half to death, and I've never seen him again. I wish I knew who he was so I could apologize to him.

I think that when those of us who are in this business [the comic industry] are meeting our public, when there is somebody who is rude, it doesn't necessarily justify us being rude in return. On that occasion, I crossed the boundary. You don't want people going around telling the story about what an incredible jerk you are because of the way you treated them at a convention.

I figure that these people are my customers. They're the ones who are paying my bills, indirectly. Directly the comic book companies are paying me, but those companies wouldn't be paying me if those fans and readers weren't buying the books. It's their money trickling down to me. So I'm very flattered when somebody wants to take the time to come up to me at a convention and talk, or get my autograph, or ask me to do a sketch. I'm always flattered by that. And I'm always interested to hear what people have to say about my work. On the other hand, I do think that fans would be better served by saying what they *like* about a professional's work rather than coming up and saying anything *negative*.

As for the fans at conventions who may not know the artists in Artist's Alley, a good rule of thumb, if they are interested in finding out about the artists, would be to say "Oh, I'm not familiar with your work, could you show me, or tell me, what comics you've worked on?" As opposed to the typical thing that is usually said which is "Are you anybody?" I try to take that in stride, but when you get a few too many of those, it can start to wear you down. It's a little depressing to be treated in that manner.

Comics fans and comics professionals, for the most part, come out of a similar background. We were the kids who stayed in our rooms a lot. And read comics! We weren't the captain of the football team, we weren't the leader of the cheerleading squad. There's probably some exceptions out there, but we were generally the fat kid with the glasses. And sometimes our social skills aren't what they ought to be. I think that, in general, it's something we all need to work on a little bit.

If you get a reputation as a stand-offish jerk, then who's going to want to work with you? Practicing these manners right from the start will definitely help you be a better professional. And it'll effect both the fans and the people you work for.

Beatty's *Johnny Dynamite* art for Dark Horse Comics

On the flip side of this coin are the fans who seem to go out of their way to make it impossible to Be Nice. Rude fans, people who say mean things about your work or your current project, people who make unreasonable demands and then act like they hate you when you refuse, fans who obviously don't care a lick about your work - just it's collectability (eg., they haven't even *opened* the book, let alone read it), etc., etc. If a fan makes it impossible to be nice, be as tactful as possible. If that doesn't work, just ignore them altogether. Mostly they'll get bored by your lack of response and leave. Minimize the conflict; it's the best P.R. you can do for your career. Plus, the nice fans will remember what a considerate person you were. And most likely, if there are any nice fans around, they will be quick to jump to your defense and commiserate when a problem fan is around. Remember, they're Nice.

If all else fails, remove yourself from the vicinity completely. Why make an ugly scene? The Nice fans will only remember you losing your cool, not the idiot provoking you.

Most important, remember that the good and bad aspects of fans are the same characteristics you'll find anywhere in the world, no matter what your job might be. There are nice guys out there, and there are jerks. Consider being a diplomat as one of your most valuable freelancer skills. It can only help your career.

Have an imagination. Try not to mimic what's trendy or hot. Try to do something different.

*Guy Davis, Illustrator (**Baker Street**, Caliber Press)*

A Special Note On Fans

At the risk of sounding melodramatic, there are a few types of fans you must be aware of in order to protect yourself. Being a 'public' figure brings some risks. There are obsessive fans who will attach themselves to you because of your perceived 'celebrity.' There are fans who will resent your popularity and will try to do nasty (and sometimes dangerous) things to you. There are fans who will come on to you sexually, purely because of your public status. A word of warning about these fans: They can endanger your career, and even your life. Play it cool, be polite and keep your eyes open. Your foremost responsibility is to protect yourself. Don't ever underestimate your fans.

Summary

Now we've looked at a few important considerations to keep in mind once you've secured your first comic industry work. I've outlined reasons why *keeping your humility* is crucial, both from a social and career standpoint. I also emphasized the importance of *pursuing more work*, using the basic methods I previously described for securing work. These included *conventions, mail and telephone contact, personal interviews,* and *related work fields.* I have also explained some of the things a newcomer can expect from *fans*, and the best way of dealing with some fan situations.

As a professional newcomer, it is in your best interest to remember that there is more to getting work than just being offered a job. Make a habit of practicing these business behaviors, and you'll have a much better chance of moving on to your next professional comic job.

Chapter Nine
You Got The Job: How To Be A Good Businessman

One of the most important aspects of being a comic professional is being a good businessman. (Please note, I will refer to both men and women as business men for simplification sake - I am not trying to be antagonistic or politically incorrect!) Raw talent is not sufficient to maintain a professional career. You must master basic business skills.

Sometimes a newcomer will acquire work in the industry through sheer force of talent, or just plain dumb luck. Keep in mind, however, that you need more than either of those qualities to retain your professional status. You need to be a good businessman.

What Does It Mean To Be A Good Businessman?

There are many aspects to being a good businessman. This includes efficient and reliable *communication*, good *organization*, effective *financial management* and demonstrating *responsible business behavior.*

Ask anyone in the comic business what it means to 'be a good businessman' and you're liable to get a wide range of responses. The answer frequently depends on exactly whom you're asking. To a freelancer, it can mean your employer is prompt in paying and that they maintain good, open communications with you. To an editor or publisher, it can mean the freelancer delivers quality work on time, answers the phone and is cooperative and communicative. To production staff, it means quality artwork on good materials and good communications with the freelancer. Marketing people are concerned with the quality of the product, timeliness of delivery, and good contact with the freelancer. The accounting department needs accurate information, on-time invoicing and good communications with the freelancer.

Do you see the pattern here? Communication. *That* is the most important key to being a good businessman.

Communication

Just what is meant by good communication? The dictionary defines communication as ". . . the imparting or interchange of thoughts, opinions or information by speech, writing, etc. . ." Simply put, it means ask questions and be there to answer questions.

What this means is, when you have a question of your publisher - regardless of the department involved - you call and get an answer. Don't procrastinate. Particularly if it will affect the finished product.

It also means Answer Your Phone!! Don't screen calls so you can avoid an irate editor who wants to know the whereabouts of his three-week late book. Don't take the phone off the hook and claim you had calls all day, just to avoid that same editor. If you don't already have call waiting, get it. Or keep your social calls to a minimum during business hours.

As a freelancer, in an industry that doesn't require you to live where your publisher is located, the onus is on you to be available to talk to your employer(s). *That is the first rule of being a good businessman. Be available.*

Good communication also has a lot to do with telephone etiquette and general courtesy. Granted, many freelancers have found themselves drifting into this hermit-like profession because of the relative isolation - and as a result the minimal demands on social interaction. Many freelancers lack the basic communication skills necessary to be a successful businessman. But that doesn't mean success will always be elusive. There are a plethora of books, courses and therapy groups that can help you master the basic social skills needed for good communication - both listening and talking.

If assertiveness is your problem, work on that. If nervousness interferes with your ability to converse easily, practice overcoming your inhibitions. As silly as it may sound, despite the relative isolation of the freelance profession, these communication skills are mandatory. You will find yourself in a position where they are needed at conventions, during interviews, in your letter-writing skills, and in basic telephone conversations. Nothing will more greatly jeopardize your chances at a job than your inability to communicate your needs and wants, as well as your abilities.

Conventions
You will have to meet and greet potential employers, fans, other professionals, peers, and sometimes even come face-to-face with editors you've only ever interacted with by mail or over the telephone. Communication skills are the basic building blocks of self-promotion. You can't hope to 'sell' your skills as a freelancer if you are unable to communicate your abilities. This skill will help you 'get your foot in the door,' show your work, line up tryouts, make business contacts and even new friendships.

Interviews
As you can well imagine, communications skills are imperative for a successful interview. Much like the application at conventions, you will need to be competent at self-promotion for an interview to be remotely successful. If you choose this method for pursuing work, it is crucial that you make a good impression. A difficult thing to do if you're standing there staring at your shuffling feet and mumbling - or even worse, shooting off at the mouth inappropriately!

Learn the accepted format for an interview. Learn about basic conversational skills, your interviewer and the company. Rehearse what you want to say, and answers to basic questions you think might be asked. Try to be prepared; it's the best defense against being left speechless.

ProFile

Professional: Wendi Lee, Writer/Editor

Credits Include: Press Liaison for Renegade Press; co-writer on *Elf Quest #7* and *#10*; writer of six *Jefferson Birch* western novels for Walker & Co.; *Elfquest: New Blood Summer Special* (story) for Warp Graphics; *The Good Daughter*, a lady P.I. crime novel from St. Martin's Press.

Question: Once a newcomer gets work, what business behaviors do you believe are critical to being a successful professional?

The most important thing is; meet your deadlines! And if you can, *exceed* your deadlines.

Also, give the editor credit for having chosen you as a creator. If they have any criticisms, you really should listen to them. You might not always agree with them, and maybe you can sit down and talk about it, but don't disregard what they say out of hand. One of the things I believe about critiquing, is that if an editor is telling you something that is clearly their opinion, then that's something you can probably discuss with them if you disagree. If they're giving you specific reasons why something needs to be changed, as in company policy, then that should be something you should seriously consider changing. Those two are the most important things.

I also think that having a good relationship with your editor is important. Show a genuine interest, to a certain extent, in them as a person. However, it's important to distinguish between genuine enthusiasm and phoniness. You genuine interest will come through, just as it will if you are less than sincere. You want to convey your willingness to work, not desperateness. You should realize that your editor is not that 'big, bad person' standing over you with a whip and telling you to 'meet this deadline'. You really have to treat them like you would anyone in any other business. If you were a sales rep, you'd have to make your quota of sales. You can't not make your quota and expect to stay on the job. Also, getting to know your editor a little bit gives you a better perspective on what they have to deal with at their

"A LONG TIME AGO, LONGER AGO THAN YOU CAN IMAGINE, IN A PLACE FARTHER AWAY THAN YOU CAN KNOW, THERE LIVED A GREAT MAGIC USER--"

Art from *Elf Quest: New Blood* by Warp Graphics

end of things, like deadlines and critical feedback. It's important to understand that when an editor says they want the job by a certain deadline, there's a reason for it. Talking to the editor, and finding out exactly what their job is and how your job relates to that in the production of the work, will help. Show an interest in them.

And always do the best work you can.

Letter Writing

This particular communication skill is required at many levels within the freelance industry. You will need these skills when you first start out, in your inquiry letter. You must communicate concisely what it is you are interested in (acquire submissions guidelines, work, etc.) and how you intend to go about getting it. You will need these skills when you send in your samples (describing your abilities, your interests, and your work situation). You will use these skills once you get the job, both in contract negotiations and execution, and in correspondence with your editor.

> *Always think conservatively about how well a book will do.*
> *And never be married to a project.*
>
> *Kelley Jones, comic book artist (**Batman: Red Rain**, DC Comics)*

If you are unsure how to proceed with a business letter for any of these situations, invest in a book on letter writing or utilize the reference books available at your local library. Ask a friend, parent, or teacher who you are confident has this skill or knowledge to look over your letters or make suggestions on how to proceed. Just remember, keep it clear, keep it simple; that's the best formula for good letter-writing communication.

Telephone

As I emphasized earlier, be available to answer questions and don't hesitate to seek clarification when you have a question of your own.

Telephone communication skills are not significantly different than interview or convention communication skills. You need to listen carefully to what is said, and answer appropriately. Try not to digress, or behave in an inappropriately personal manner. Be polite. And remember: The editor you're talking to is probably swamped with work. They don't always have time for a little chat. Just because you sit at your drawing table or keyboard, wishing for a little digression from the work at hand, doesn't mean your employer has that same interest - or free time! Be considerate of your conversant's time.

Again, keep it simple, keep it clear. And keep it brief!

Organization

I can see all you 'absent-minded professor' types out there cringing at this word like it was some type of heinous weapon. But believe me, good organization can be one of the most effective tools in successful business.

Stacks of books have been published on how to better organize your time, your work, your personal life, your paperwork, your bookkeeping - heck, even your sock drawer! Sit back and think about that. It means a) there are a lot of people out there just as disorganized as you, and b) there must be some good reason for being *more* organized.

There is: It will make you a more effective, even powerful, businessman.

As a freelancer, there are many areas in your professional life that can greatly benefit from better organization. Some of the most effective areas to organize include your studio or office, your work time, and your travel schedule.

Studio or Office Organization

There are many aspects of studio and office organization that will contribute to your success as a businessman. The most obvious of these is the actual physical organization of your workspace.

Make sure that your work supplies and materials are conveniently and readily stored. Keep more frequently used materials closer to hand. Supplies used less frequently can be stored less accessibly. The less time you spend wandering around looking for the right paper, the pencil you want, or clean-up materials, the more time you'll spend actually getting the work done. Keep your work space well organized, and you eliminate a hurdle keeping you from being a good businessman.

If you ship your finished work to your publisher, remember to keep an adequate supply of shipping materials on hand: envelopes, boxes, cardboard, tape, shipping invoices, stamps, etc. If you are running on a tight deadline, you cannot afford to be delayed by a lack of the appropriate shipping supplies. Keep a diligent check on your materials, and avoid last-minute emergencies because of undesirable shortages.

Freelancers frequently collect their pay in a most erratic manner. Sometimes this is due to the payment schedules kept by their employers; sometimes it's due to the irregular nature of the delivery of their work. Regardless of whether you work for a company that provides billing invoices, you should make a habit of keeping your *own* invoices for record purposes. Although this may sound redundant, it eliminates a lot of problems associated with lost invoices, and allows you to better track your income. This can be invaluable for both your bookkeeping and income tax purposes. Keep a good supply of invoices on hand so you aren't caught short when sending out a job.

Also, remember to keep tabs on your other business supplies - the ones that enable you to conduct business: letterhead, business cards, sample

> *If you're trying to get your first job, always show your very best work. That might sound simplistic, but I can't count how many times I've been shown art or a story with the caveat that "it's not my best work, but it'll give you an idea of my potential." Don't bang something out the night before a convention to show editors; you're better off missing that convention and putting together a proper set of samples.*
>
> *I've often heard newcomers criticize a comic - and validate themselves - by saying "that's awful! I can do better than that!" The point to remember is that a **lot** of people can do better than that - the comic book industry doesn't need more mediocre writers or artists. I don't care if you're self-publishing or trying to write Spider Man, you're "competing" creatively with the very best in your particular arena, not the worst. So be honest with yourself.*
>
> *Mark Verheiden, Writer (**The American**, Dark Horse Comics)*

sheets, etc. There will be many occasions where you might be put on the spot to hurriedly provide a potential employer with information. Don't get caught short and end up looking like a novice. Demonstrate your professionalism by being prepared. This advice also applies to your materials. Keep tabs on your paper stock or ink and paint supplies. Don't find yourself in the middle of a critical job and running out of the necessary materials. Your preparedness can profoundly influence your professional career.

Organizing Your Files

One of the most important aspects of being a good, organized businessman is maintaining effective records of your business dealings. For this reason this is a topic worth addressing on its own.

Good recordkeeping serves an important variety of purposes, including protecting both you and your employer's work interests. One of the first tasks you should set for yourself once you decide to pursue a freelance career is to set up a basic filing system.

Don't panic! I'm not proposing you build a new Library of Congress. Just take the time to organize your paperwork in a reasonable manner. There's no need to spend massive amounts of money on this endeavor, as inexpensive (or free!) cardboard boxes will serve adequately as filing cabinets. Invest a bit of money in a bulk package of file folders. Then, sit down and organize your paperwork in a manner that will workbest for you. (A basic organizational plan is illustrated below in Box 9-A.)

By keeping up on your recordkeeping you will be able to better track your work, your income and business dealings with the various publishers. It will also help you keep tabs of your budget, supplies, and various business

ProFile

Professional: Mitch O'Connell, Artist

Credits Include: *The World of Ginger Fox* graphic novel for Comico; *Good Taste Gone Bad: The Art Of Mitch O'Connell* from Good Taste Products; illustration for *Spy Magazine, Playboy Magazine, National Lampoon*; advertising work for *Seven-11, Burger King, MacDonalds Restaurant , Coca-Cola*, and *Kelloggs*.

Question: Do you use a business card or sample sheet when approaching potential publishers? Do you think they make a difference in acquiring work?

Using a business card definitely makes a difference. You need to have a leave-behind after you've shown someone your portfolio, or when corresponding through the mail.

I don't have a regular type of business card that fits in your wallet. I figure that no one's going to keep it, or it's going to get lost, so my business cards are 5" X 7". I usually print them up at the local photocopy center, very inexpensively, and pick one of those real eye-catching Astro-Bright colors in the hopes that they [potential employers] will tack them on the wall or tape them to their desk, so they'll be constantly looking at it.

I change my card art at least once a year, to keep interest going. If you're going to keep showing the same thing, not too much is going to happen with your career. I'm constantly promoting myself and sending out new work. I have two reps [art representatives] who are always showing new stuff. There are so many artists competing for the same jobs, that you have to just bombard the people, who might give you work, with good samples.

I also advertise in the Chicago   and the American Showcase. When you buy those ads you also get as many reprints as you want - usually a thousand. I use those as a tearsheet to promote myself, too.

Art from *The World of Ginger Fox* published by Comico

and financial responsibilities. And believe me, when an editor returns your call about a late payment and is told you can send copies of all the pertinent documents to help in sorting out the problem, they will be both grateful and impressed with your business skills. And ultimately you will benefit since you will be able to better manage your career.

Organizing Your Files

There are a few simple guidelines you can use to better organize your business records. You should have two sets of files - company files and expense files.

Company Files

Your company files should be comrpised of a folder for each company with which you regularly do work, correspond, or receive material from. Companies can include publishers, distributors, retailers, and individual clients. If you regularly send out samples to a particular company, make a seperate file to track those records and their responses. It also helps to keep a small card file to record correspondance dates for sending out samples and receiving responses. There are about twenty well-established publihers, but if you have minimal contact with any f them, create a Miscellaneous file and use that for your record keeping.

Expense Files

As part of your bookeeping practices, you should keep a file for each company or business with whom you do business. These include overhead expenses (rent, telephone, electricity, water/sewer), supplies (office supply firms, art supply companies, furniture sales), services (shipping, mail, printing, lawyer, accountant), and any others that you discover apply when you organize your business expenses.

Box 9-A: Organizing Your Files

Scheduling Your Time

Organizing your work schedule efficiently is also a critical aspect of being a good businessman. To be a successful freelancer, you need to learn how to estimate your work time. If an editor offers you a regular series, assess the workload, and ensure that you can meet the regular deadlines before you head out for that champagne celebration. Because if you are a newcomer who accepts a job and then fails to deliver on time, you will quickly find yourself hard-pressed to drum up work. Editors talk with each other and with other freelancers. If an individual is having problems with a specific freelancer - especially a hot-shot newcomer - it won't be long before word of it spreads through the industry like wildfire. To put it more simply, you'll find yourself blackballed.

Some freelancers - both new and many of those who are firmly established - have an inordinate amount of trouble estimating the time a job will take them. Sometimes this is due to inexperience. Sometimes it's due to plain old laziness. But often it's just due to poor organization.

Your first step to improving your scheduling skills should be to get a calendar. Select one with a large, open, monthly grid where you can make notes about work deadline dates, income due dates, travel plans and any other pertinent business information. Get into the habit of keeping a written calendar record of every job you accept, and the date that it must be shipped to the editor.

When you send out work, and invoice for payment, make a note on your calendar for the date that money should arrive. Keep in mind that many companies have set dates for issuing payment checks, and allow for postal travel time. Keep tabs on those funds due, and followup in a professional manner when they are late.

> *Get in the habit of setting aside 20-30% of every cheque in a special bank account earmarked for paying estimated taxes. There's no worse situation for anybody to be in than to have quarterly tax time come around and be in the hole. Or worse, have to totally deplete your savings to pay taxes at the end of the year. The penalties for under-estimating on your taxes are pretty stiff, so why pay any more than you absolutely have to?*
>
> *Jerry Ordway, Writer/Artist (**Power of Shazam**, DC Comics)*

Also keep track of convention dates - both the major shows and any which you wish to attend. Regardless of whether you attend the larger convention, making note of those dates will allow you to stay in touch with your editor more effectively, and eliminate those 'limbo' days where they are at a convention, 'incommunicado.'

Allow for convention travel time, as well as time to settle back into a work routine once you get home. Try to remember to allow for these trips , so that it will not interfere with your ability to deliver work. Few things can get you canned faster than if you attend a convention and your editor, or an associate of your editor, spots you there when you are late on delivering work!! If you keep track of your travel time, you will find it much easier to manage your work schedule and still fit in time to promote your current projects, and line up new work at conventions.

Travel Organization

Another important area of organization is travelling to conventions. As simple as this may sound, for a freelancer this can be a particularly hectic and critical time.

The convention circuit is meant to help the freelancer promote his projects, line up new work, and make business and social contacts. It

ProFile

Professional: Sean Taggart, Trading Card Editor for DC Comics
Credits Include: Special Projects Manager for Topps; cover art for the *Jerky Boys CD* ; *Batman: Saga Of The Dark Night* card series for DC Comics; *DC Comics Universe Masterseries* trading cards for Skybox
Question: Once a newcomer gets work, what business behavior do you believe are critical to being a successful professional?

I would say that 'professional' is the operative word. I think everyone should have the ambition to be professional, whether they're a behind-the-scenes kind of person or a superstar. It's the best way to conduct business. Essentially, what you should do to be professional, is work out as many details as you can in your initial contact with your editor or art director. Determine what the assignment is, what the dates are for delivery of the work. The bottom line of being a professional is living up to promises. Don't make promises you can't keep. This is a mistake we often see with seasoned professionals who have suddenly become hot. They are being contacted to do a 'million' projects, and being that they're still in the freelancer "feast-or-famine" mode, they end up overextending themselves and everyone loses in that situation.

It's also important to realize that creators and publishers are "all in this together." This is a team effort kind of business. Don't just drop in on an editor without calling him first, though some editors don't care if you just drop by to say "Hey, how are you doing?" When you ask an editor to send you something, don't 'freak out' if it doesn't work out right away. Editors, very often, are buried in work themselves. It's a two-way street for editors and the freelancers, both. They should both realize that everyone's fallible and everyone is busy.

Good communication with your editor is critical. Sometimes an editor will ask a freelancer to do something they don't agree with, but because the editor has an idea of the 'big picture' in mind it's good to deliver on the request. I've had situations where artists have done things I did not ask for, but they thought they were helping me out, but in fact it was the worst thing they could have done. But, no, that was absolutely wrong. Sometimes working on your own initiative isn't a good choice. You also need to figure out *how* to communicate with your editor. Everyone's different, and some people are more articulate than others. When I deal with freelancers, I don't have a general rule, but I know with certain people I have to act differently than with others. I have to approach some people with caution, be demure and soft-spoken. With other people I can be completely up-front, abrupt almost. And they prefer it. So, see how the editor responds to how you approach them, as well. All you need to do is find the right combination of manners and intelligence.

generally entails taking at least a few days (more depending on how far way and how big a show it is) away from your work schedule. There are many things that must be done to properly prepare for a convention.

- *Securing display space.* For artists, even more than writers, securing display space is important for promoting your work, and making sales of prints and originals in an effort to defray some of your travel expenses. You may also wish to secure art show display space. This space is generally at a premium, and usually costs some amount (which varies depending on the show), so making advance arrangements is about the only way to ensure space will be available for you. If you are working as a professional, most conventions will supply you with a table if you provide them with enough lead time to make the arrangements. Organizing your travel schedule early in the year will allow you to make the appropriate contacts necessary to secure display space.

- *Making travel arrangements.* Because of the competitive nature of travel fees (eg., airfare, car rentals, hotel rates) it is imperative that you make your plans far enough in advance to take advantage of the early booking discounts. Also, don't forget to mention the convention rate (which is usually a significant discount) when making hotel reservations. Also, take advantage of any savings coupons (eg. car rental/hotel packages). The money you save on travel expenses can be used to wine and dine a potential employer - or better yet, pay some bills at home! Planning ahead for travel dates will help you save money and the aggravation of an attempted last minute reservation in an over-booked city!

- *Make a travel checklist.* As over-organized as this may seem, making a travel checklist is probably one of the most valuable tools I have developed since I started working as a professional freelancer.

Early on in my career, I would scramble to gather clothing, toiletries, my portfolio and professional supplies at the last minute - sometimes only hours before leaving town. Without fail, I always left some crucial item at home and found myself sorely missing it, or forking out big dollars in a

Travel Checklists

If you've ever travelled anywhere for business or pleasure, you know how hectic getting ready can be, and how easy it is to forget something important. To avoid showing up without the appropriate clothing, toiletries or professional materials, it's a good idea to create a checklist. Especially if you choose a career in the comic industry, with it's many conventions! Here is an example of an actual list that you can use as a guide to create your own personal travel checklist.

Clothing and Personal Items

· clean shirt for each day of trip
(count days away, including travel days)
· appropriate clothing for the climate of the destination city
(check the weather reports)
· at least one dressier outfit for business functions
· appropriate footwear to go with the clothing you bring
· soap, shampoo, deodorant, toothbrush & paste
(all critical items if you hope to present yourself as a pleasant professional!)
· razor (for those who shave - or should)

Professional Supplies

· paper, pencils, eraser, pens, ink, paint, brushes, markers, illo. board - for creating new work
· metallic and/or bleedproof pens for autographing
· portfolio displaying your work
· business cards and sample sheets
· utility knife, push pins, tape, rubber bands, bulldog clips - for displaying and packaging work
· some type of attache or art bag for carrying your materials
· materials to sell - originals, commissions, published copies, prints

An added word of advice: If you plan to travel regularly as a comic professional, particularly if you will be bringing your work to conventions, invest in a compact carry-on duffle bag and a moderately sized portfolio. You are limited by the airlines to two pieces of carry-on luggage. Master the skill of packing your bag with lightweight, non-bulky clothing and materials.

Avoid checking luggage - especially your originals! In this manner you can avoid the distress of lost luggage, luggage pick-up delays or worse, any kind of damage to your personal belongings - including artwork!

Box 9-B: Travel Checklists

strange city to replace the item I needed. Finally, in frustration, I sat down and made a comprehensive list of everything I would need for convention travel. I typed up the list, and keep it in a drawer with my travel supplies.

It's looking a little dog-eared now, and I'm almost ready to make a new copy, but it's been a long time since I arrived at a convention unprepared. (See Box 9-B for an example of some items you could include on your checklist, and the way to go about custom-designing one for yourself.)

If you take the time to plan your convention trips a bit more thoroughly, you will find yourself a lot more relaxed once you arrive at the show. You will communicate professionalism, and potential employers can't help but see that.

Financial Management

Before we get off and running on all the different areas of financial management you should pay attention to, I want to highlight the cardinal rule:

<u>KEEP ALL YOUR RECEIPTS!!!!</u>

Although this might seem like a burdensome task, you will find over time that you begin to do this automatically - it will become a habit. Also, you will find that many of those seemingly inconsequential receipts add up to big deductions at tax time. Now that you're a self-employed freelancer, nobody takes care of your taxes for you. Plus, you will be paying additional self-employment taxes. Now, those receipts are like little slips of gold. Never, never throw them away! With that said, let's move on.

One of the most critical area for demonstrating your professionalism is good financial management.

Don't run screaming from the room with visions of your tenth grade math teacher clouding your mind!! This is much simpler and a lot less painful. But it will require self-discipline.

There are a variety of ways to manage your finances efficiently, from throwing away your receipts and pretending everything is fine to hiring a bookkeeper. However, for a newcomer just getting started in the business, there is a much easier, and less expensive, middle road.

Here's some important steps to better manage your finances:
1) *Invoice for every piece of work you do, and keep a copy of that invoice for your records.*

Regardless of whether a publisher provides your with invoices, make out your own - even if it's just a handwritten slip of paper (although a more professional printed or typewritten form is better) - so that you have your own record of your income that you can track. Many publishers require the freelancer to send in all copies of the company's invoice form, and unless they send back a copy - providing it hasn't been lost - you have no record of the business transaction. A lack of a paper trail makes it a lot harder to collect your pay.
2) *Document the dates you ship the work and when monies are due on a calendar.*

Keep track of income you are expecting. This way nobody will ever get too far behind in paying you, and your own bill collectors won't have to wait to get paid!

3) *Set up a simple bookkeeping system.*

There are a variety of bookkeeping systems, ranging from throwing all your receipts in a shoebox and presenting them to an accountant the week before your income tax is due, to keeping elaborate budget credit/debit records. As a new freelancer, I suggest you keep your life simple. Set up an easy recordkeeping form to track all your pertinent receipts as they apply to your income tax. Keep a file folder, box, tray or some type of receptacle handy in your office, home or studio. Each day when you come in, dump in your receipts. At the end of the month (or every couple of months) set aside time to organize those receipts and record them in your bookkeeping. (See Box 9-C for a sample bookkeeping record.)

At the end of the year when tax time rolls around, you are going to be very happy to have completed the bulk of the work. Additionally, this provides you with a means to track your monthly and annual expenditures on various items like shipping and supplies. This will enable you to better budget your income, and help you in pricing out your work at a reasonable page rate.

4) *Open a separate savings account to use exclusively for tax monies.*

At the end of each year, Uncle Sam will collect approximately 25% of your gross income in federal, state and self-employment taxes. The actual total varies between states, and depends on how meticulous you are about tracking receipts and deductions. It also depends on how much money you're making. Suffice it to say though, if you keep a designated tax fund account, set aside 25% of every check that comes in - BEFORE ONE PENNY IS SPENT!! - you will find yourself comfortably protected at the end of the year when you have to file your income tax return.

Also, once you have established a profit-making year, you will be required to pay *quarterly estimate tax payments* every three months, based on your estimated income for that year. Failure to make these payments will result in big, fat penalty payments to the IRS (automatically calculated and billed by the IRS.) It's in your very best interest to discipline yourself into setting that money aside. A little piece of advice - don't expect that your publishers will pay you a few weeks early, or give you a nice little advance. They are well experienced in the last-minute scramble by freelancers to produce tax payment money, and don't look on the practice too kindly. Few things will jeopardize your professional standing faster.

5) *Maintain a checking account to make business payments.*

Many young freelancers like to keep their money 'cash on hand'. This may seem like a good idea at the time, but here are a few excellent reasons for maintaining some form of checking account:

- *It is impossible to open a business account without some type of checking account already established.* If you want an account with your local art supply or office supply business, or Federal Express, it won't happen unless you can prove established business ties. This means a credit history, which means an active bank account. Open one; use it.

- *It will help you establish a credit record.* It's almost impossible to get credit anywhere without some kind of credit history. An active bank account serves that purpose. You may feel you don't need credit right now but what if you decide to buy a fax machine or a photocopier for your studio/office, and want to do financing? Without that credit history you will find it very difficult.

- *It will greatly simplify your ability to keep track of business payments.* To keep an accurate record of business expenditures, it is useful to have the check stub or copy as a receipt. Since sometimes you may forget to collect the receipt, may not be given a receipt, or may receive an unintelligible receipt, the checking record will greatly improve your recordkeeping abilities.

The best thing I ever did was get an accountant. You can pretty much do a lot of your own legal work, and you can do a lot of self-representation, but I think most creative people have a phobia about numbers. I definitely do. I realized that although it was kind of expensive, but taking care of it [bookkeeping] yourself is so aggravating and stressful, that I'd rather just have somebody take care of that for me. For me it was great, because at tax time I didn't get hammered, although I had been in previous years.

Sean Taggart, Trading Card Editor for DC Comics
*(**DC Comics Universe Masterworks** cards)*

---

6) *Use your bookkeeping records to create a comprehensive budget.*

Once you've laid out an easy to follow bookkeeping record, you can use the information it provides to guide you in budgeting your income. Track the amounts you spend on professional services, supplies and expenses and you will be able to determine how your money is being spent, and how to better manage it. This will also help prevent that last-minute panic at the end of a pay period as you wonder where and when your next dollar is coming from.

Once you've determined where and how your money is being spent, you may find there is room in your income plan to set aside additional savings that you can designate for special circumstances, like travel expenses or financial emergencies (eg., medical expenses, lost work and income, unexpected home or car repairs, etc.)

7) *Make a budget for convention travel and stick with it.*

Since convention travel is a fairly critical part of being a comic freelancer, it's safe to say that you will most likely be attending at least one or two conventions each year. These little trips can be unduly expensive and if you don't take the time to plan a travel budget, you may find yourself tapping into next month's rent money!

A Simplified Bookeeping System

If you follow the catagories allowed for deductions on your income tax form, it is very easy to set up a simple bookeeping system. Here is a easy plan. Feel free to tailor it to your own business needs.

1) Purchase a 14 column, Columnar Book or Pad and use one page for each month. (Alternatively, you can use a 7 column pad or book, and open it to use two pages for each month.) Make your entries on the numbered lines, using the line number to represent the day of the month.

2) Label the first two columns **Income** and **Payer**. These are the places you should record the amount of monies received, and who the monies are from.

3) The remaining columns should be labeled to coincide with the deductible catagories allowed on your tax return. A good sample is as follows:

Dental/Medical - Keep a record of dental and medical expenses, including prescription medicine costs. Don't list health insurance under this heading.

Car/Truck Expenses - If you use your vehicle for work (delivering work, driving to FedEx, business trips) keep a mileage log, and you will not only be able to deduct a portion of your gas and maintenance costs, but you will be able to do devaluation (cost of wear and tear) on your vehicle.

Insurance - List medical, car, home and business insurance payments here.

Freight - This includes courier and parcel services, as well as postage costs.

Business Expenses - These are the costs of coing business, and include office supplies and equipment

Supplies - These are the costs of actual physical supplies required to create your work. For artists, this can include paper, board, canvas, pens, pencils, ink, paint, and reference books. For writers, this can include paper, computer disks, pens, pencils and reference books.

Travel - Here is the place to list expenses incurred during travel, including air/bus/train fares, car rentals, hotel costs, taxis, subway, parking, etc.

Meals and Entertainment - This is where business related meal and entertainment costs should be listed. If you art travelling, the IRS permitts a fully-documented receipt total or a daily allowed budget.

Box 9-C: A Simplified Bookeeping System

If you entertain a business client, in the process of actually doing business, that expense is listed here.

Dues and Publications - List your expenses of business related membership fees and regular business publications to which you subscribe, and on which you depend to conduct business. The IRS continues to vaciliate on the allowability of this expense, but it is valuable to keep a record, just to better manage your budget.

Utilities and Telephone - The IRS allows a portion of your utility and telephone expenses for business use when you have a home office. You will need to know the aproximate square footage of your dedicated business space, to determine it's percentage of your home. That is the percentage of your expenses you should record. This includes, electricity, gas, water, sewer, garbage pick-up, and general maintenance. The total cost of your telephone calls (long distance only) that are made for business should be listed in full.

Other Expenses - list lawyer, accountant, charity donations, or any other expenses that don't fit the other catagories. List the amount, and note what it represents next to it.

Box 9-C: Continued

Plan ahead for travel, accommodations, and meal costs, and then add at least 15% more. This is a good travel budget, with a bit of leeway for unexpected situations that may arise. By planning your travel budget ahead of time, you will be able to set aside the money in smaller increments, which should help minimize the burden on your regular income and bills.

To Conclude

If you start out your freelance career making a point of following these simple financial management steps, you will find it provides you with many benefits throughout your professional career. You will always have a sharp picture of your financial status. It will provide you with the information you need to set prices when lining up new jobs. It will ensure that you don't find yourself hip deep in tax evasion problems (and we all know that messing with Uncle Sam can mean serious repercussions - like jail time!) Most importantly though, you will constantly demonstrate your professionalism to prospective employers and that, in addition to your hard work, will guarantee you a long, and possibly illustrious, career.

Business Responsibility

The fourth facet of being a good businessman is demonstrating business responsibility. This simply means staying on top of your responsibilities as a career professional. As much as we'd all love to immerse ourselves in our work - be it creating art or writing stories - there is always the business aspects of our jobs to attend to. If you are independently wealthy, fine; hire someone to do your dirty work and just do the fun stuff. Perhaps once you've become an established and highly lauded pro, you can hire people to do those jobs. But you will most likely have to handle these tasks yourself, and efficient and responsible handling of these jobs will ensure continued freelance employment.

Meeting Deadlines

Unless you have a battalion of assistants to help you produce your work, you will have to be very conscientious in making sure you meet your deadlines.   When a publisher hires you to produce work, he is operating under a range of very strict deadlines - marketing, solicitation, production, printing, shipping, and so on. To have a successful and popular product means making all these deadlines on time. Therefore it is ABSOLUTELY CRITICAL that you deliver the completed work in the time frame you agreed to. In our industry, failure by creators to meet deadlines is probably the most common complaint of every publisher. And it's not just restricted to newcomers! This problem is uniform across all levels of expertise, experience and popularity. Some publishers overcome the problem by refusing to process a book until the material is completely finished and delivered. Often pay for the freelancer is withheld until completion, too. Other publishers make a point of avoiding working with unreliable creators.

Always under-promise and over-deliver.
This applies to everybody. If you're a freelancer, this means don't tell them your artwork or story will be done, and then fail to deliver it.
George White, President of Top Dog Marketing
(Creator's Edition Cards, Skybox)

Sometimes fans question why one creator, who's work seems merely adequate, continues to be granted prestigious project after another, when other much more 'stellar talents' have very little work produced. In many cases this is due to the inability of those 'stellar talents' to deliver their work in a timely manner. Some freelancers are fine until the deadline pressure is on - which is why their work appears so sporadically - but freeze up and are unable to produce when under deadline pressure. They should be considering another field of work. Publishing is rife with deadlines, and a successful freelancer needs to learn how to budget their time to be a good and respected businessman.

If you can improve your ability to reliably deliver consistently good work, there is a good chance that you will find yourself one of the well-respected creators in constant demand.

ProFile

Professional: Charles Vess, Artist/Writer
Credits Include: *Spiderman: Spirits of the Earth* (writer and painter), Marvel; *A Midsummer Night's Dream*, the illustrated book, Donning; *Sandman #19, Swamp Thing (#121,122,129-139)* cover art and *Books Of Magic #3*, DC Comics; *Stardust: An Illustrated Prose Novel of Fairyland*, written by Neil Gaiman; *Prince Valiant* (writing and scripting) four-issue mini-series, Marvel Comics; *Books Of Magic* (cover artist), DC Comics; "Ballad" series in *Dark Horse Presents*, Dark Horse Comics.
Question: Do you use a business card or sample sheet when approaching potential publishers? Do you think they make a difference in acquiring work?

I tend to give tearsheets of things I've had published instead of a sample sheet. Yes, I use a business card. I think it's very important to have the business card. It makes a better impression. My whole theory about getting a job, is that the person giving you the work is betting *their* job that you are going to do what you *say* you're going to do *your* job. And anything you can do to say you're professional, is better. For example, brushing your teeth, taking a bath - those kinds of things! A business card is one of those things! It shows you're serious. You've spent some money, you've thought about it beforehand. You haven't decided two minutes before you've gone to the convention that "Gee, I want to be a comic artist, or a book cover artist." It means being prepared and professional. And it helps if it's an interesting looking card.

I've used the same card for about fourteen years, and there are still people looking at it and saying "That's really nice!" Only if you were going to change

**Vess' art from *Sandman*
by DC Comics**

your whole style or approach to your work, would I suggest changing the card design. Unless, of course, you've got a black and white card, and after five or six years of working in the business you're making pots of money, and you decide to do a full color card. Also, I've seen these large format business cards, but I think they're really a bad idea as a business card, because they don't fit in a Rolodex. They'll just get put into a file, and the editor or art director is much less likely to see it.

If you're going to send in samples, use the 81/2" X 11" format so they will easily fit in a file. And don't send in a hundred sheets of paper covered with drawings - five or six good ones is more than enough!

Proper Handling of Paperwork

The federal government seems to have nothing on the comic industry when it comes to pushing paperwork. There are many areas of our business that require forms to be filled out - contract agreements, invoicing, correspondence, preliminary sketches, rough drafts, shipping bills, artwork releases, return of artwork forms, checks, etc. It is imperative that you make a practice of completing the appropriate paperwork in a timely manner. Failure to do so not only affects your appearance of professionalism, but can result in late payment for work, lost artwork, and even worse, violation of work agreements.

As I mentioned in Chapter Seven, the legal aspects of the business can make or break a professional career. If you take the time to responsibly review (that means READ CAREFULLY) your contracts, ensure that all appropriate signatures are thereon, and keep copies of all your contracts, you will be well protected in your business. Failure to do these simple things can result in gross violations on the part of less reputable publishers, to which you will have no response or recourse.

Keep careful track of your paperwork trail, and you will always have a clear record of your business dealings. Your publisher will be happy, you will be happy, and you can get down to the business of creating entertainment.

Keeping Your Hat In The Ring

Just because you've finally secured that ever-elusive comic job doesn't mean you're now set for life. The comic industry is a transitory business. Projects, publishers and freelancers come and go before you can blink twice. What seems like a sure thing can be snatched away from you without warning, and unless you have the 'iron-clad contract from hell,' you'll find yourself out of work and lacking income.

With this fact in mind you should make a point of keeping your hat in the ring. Stay apprised of the sales of your project, be aware of the status of your publisher or the line they're using to market the work. Keep feelers

Business Card Etiquette: When Should You Hand it Out?

Many consultants say there is rarely a bad time to hand out your business card. Here are some suggested guidelines:

■ It's inappropriate to automatically hand your business card to people you've just met. They haven't had time to decide if it's even something they want, and it makes you appear pushy and overbearing. Spend at least five minutes with someone before requesting or giving a card.

■ Be discreet when handing out business cards at a social function.

■ There's no excuse for not having a business card. However, if you're caught in a situation where you've been asked for your card and you don't have any, ask for that individuals card and send yours by mail.

■ Never give out badly soiled or bent cards to anyone. It's almost better to write your name on a napkin! It is best, though, to wait and send your card through the mail, perhaps personalizing it by handwriting a note on the card.

■ Carry a card holder so your business cards can be easily found in your briefcase or portfolio.

■ Feel free to augment your business card with sample sheets, proposals or tearsheets featuring your work. You should try to avoid relying solely on your business card a s a point of contact, because they can be lost, misplaced, and don't tell the whole story about you and your abilities.

out in the market to ensure that you have a selection of backup jobs in the wings. You may also want to take on the odd single piece or small one-shot job (scheduling permitting, or course,) just to make sure that your name remains highly visible in the market.

Follow the same steps you took when looking for work, to make your availability known:

- Send out updated sample sheets regularly.

- Occasionally call around to 'shoot the breeze' with new business acquaintances (other freelancers, editors, publishers, convention organizers, retailers). This will give you an opportunity to renew your friendly ties, pick up any news, and keep your name on their mind

- Make sure you take full advantage of conventions. This is an excellent place to continue forging social and business relationships, and a fertile source of obtaining new work. Psychologically, you will be a more in demand freelancer if you're already working. Editors will wonder what they're missing, and you'll find yourself with plenty of work offers and suggestions.

- Court other projects and editors within the company you work for. If you enjoy your work relationship with a particular publisher, there's nothing wrong with doing the majority of your work with that company. Ask your editor, or others in the company, about upcoming projects for

ProFile

Professional: Chris Ulm, Editor In Chief for Malibu Comics/Writer
Credits Include: *Dead Clown*, Malibu Comics; *Robotech*, Eternity Comics; *Rune* (co-writer with Barry Windsor Smith), Malibu Comics; editor on a variety of Malibu Comics
Question: Do you look for a business card and/or sample sheet from newcomers who approach you for work? Does the type of approach they use make a difference?

It absolutely makes a difference what kind of approach they use! The more professional their package of materials, the more seriously I tend to take people. A business card isn't always necessary, but a well written cover letter *is*, accompanying whatever samples are germane. In our guidelines we stipulate that it's always important to make sure that the samples are the best you can possibly do, whether you're an artist or a writer, and that they're relatively brief. You don't want to overload the editor or the submissions person with lots and lots of extraneous information that they can't possibly use. A business card is always helpful for whatever business cards can do, but ultimately it is whatever you can offer that publisher that makes the biggest difference.

Rune **art from Malibu**

At conventions, it really depends on individual situations. Conventions have gone from small gatherings of professionals and fans to enormous consumer shows. There were 30,000 people at the 1993 San Diego Con! When they're that big we often simply don't have the time to spend going over somebody's work. *I* don't have the time, personally, and this makes it very difficult. Also, now that people from Malibu are recognized, there are lots of times where we'll be eating lunch or having a break from the convention, and people will come up and want us to take a look at their work. That's inappropriate because it shows that you're not particularly professional. Also, believe me, anyone who's interrupted in the middle of lunch is not going to look on your work kindly!

We always accept packages at conventions, but I honestly think it's probably better to mail things. If you're going to give a package to an editor at a convention, assume that he might misplace it, or it might not make it back in the transition to the office during the chaos that usually follows conventions. So, the best thing to do is to meet with the editor personally, shake their hand, and give them your samples. They usually will not have time to look over, or read, the sample at the convention so follow that up with a letter and, possibly, that same [sample] package again.

The easier you can make it for an editor, the better. An editor is going to want to say no to a newcomer - that's just the way it is in *any* business. So, the best way to break in is to make it very difficult for someone to say no. Supply them with really great work, on time, and have it well-packaged - show that you're a professional. And follow-up.
That's the most important thing, to continue to follow-up in an appropriate way. In terms of a time frame, I've always found that a good rule is; immediately follow-up on a convention with a letter and, possibly, the same [sample] package, and then follow *that* up maybe a month or two later.

which they might consider you.

- Don't hesitate to approach other related markets. The comic industry has ties and associations with many other markets that would be interested in your freelance skills: games, books, magazines, toy designs, movies, television, trading cards, T-shirts, postcards, novelty items, etc. Don't restrict yourself to the comic industry if you have other interests. Many of these related industries are lucrative sources of income. In addition, they provide you with a second audience that can be drawn over to follow your comic work. Take advantage of any markets that will help promote you as a talent.

Stay Apprised Of The Industry
The final aspect of business responsibility I want to address is staying on top of the status of the industry. It is important to be informed if you hope to be a successful businessman. You need to follow what trends and fads are drawing the readership. You need to be aware of how your work will fit into the market, and which of its characteristics will draw readers.

There are a number of news publications that report regularly on happenings in the industry. In Chapter Eight I provided a list of some of the better know trade publications when discussing convention listings. These included *The Comics Buyer's Guide* (weekly newspaper format), *Hero Illustrated* and *Wizard* (monthly color magazines), *Comic Scene* (monthly newsstand color magazine), *Comic Shop News* (monthly color news flyer) and *The Comics Journal* (monthly black-and-white interview magazine). The distributor catalogues also provide a valuable source of information about what's available in the market. Read one or more of these publications regularly and you will find it much easier to stay on top of where you fit into the comic industry.

Remember to update your business files using information you acquire in your reading and convention socializing. This will pay off both in terms of acquiring new work, and in carrying on an informed and intelligent conversation with new business contacts.

Summary

In this chapter we've covered the four main areas that contribute to being a good businessman - *communication, organization, financial management* and *business responsibility.* I described how good *communication skills* include *making yourself available, asking questions* and *staying in touch* through a variety of means. We looked at *organization,* including how to *schedule your time, organizing your files,* and *planning your travel.* We also covered *financial management,* which incorporated *setting up bookkeeping, handling taxes, invoicing, designing a working budget,* and most importantly, *keeping your receipts.* Lastly, we discussed *business responsibility,* which includes *meeting your deadlines, proper handling of paperwork, keeping your work options open,* and *staying apprised of the industry.*

Being a comic professional means more than just creating the work that is published. Learning these basic skills will make you a good businessman, and that will most assuredly help lead to more work in the comics field.

Chapter Ten
Special Cases and Related Fields or
Creators Aren't the Only Working Stiffs!

As we approach the end of this book I would like to address other jobs in the comic industry that are equally important, sometimes even more demanding, and often just as creative as being a freelancer.

I am of course referring to the myriad employees of our business that are responsible for ensuring that your creation is published and ultimately reaches the hands of your eager fans.

You might wonder why these people are worth mentioning in a manual aimed at freelancers who wish to 'break' into comics. For starters, many of you may find that on closer examination, the life of a freelancer, with all its risks, is not to your liking. You may yearn for a secure, reliable, salaried job that still allows you creative expression and work in comics. You may ultimately decide that you don't "have what it takes" creatively to achieve the degree of success required to support yourself financially. Or, most importantly, you might find that your true talents lie in one of these related areas of the comic industry. If this is the case, then these jobs will be of great interest to you.

> *Comic creators need not neccessarily be business persons, but it certainly would help to have a knowledge of publishers procedures.*
>
> *Mart Nodell, Comic Artist (Creator of **Green Lantern**, DC Comics)*

Who Keeps the Business Running?

There are vast armies of comic industry people responsible for the smooth and continuous operation of our business. Much like the movie industry, these people vastly outnumber the more prominent 'celebrities' or recognized freelancers, and without them we would be unable to deliver our beloved creation to the hands of the readers.

Within the publishing end of the business, depending on the size of the publishing house, there are a variety of specialized areas of employment. These range from the lower-ranked office 'gopher'-type jobs to the more prestigious and demanding positions at the administrative levels. Some examples of these positions include: accounting, administration, advertising, computer coloring, computer typesetting, editorial, international rights, legal affairs, licensing, marketing, office help, production, rights and permissions, royalties, and special projects.

Often many of these jobs will be amalgamated into one area. For example, computer coloring, computer typesetting and production may all be duties for which the production department is responsible. Likewise, rights and permissions, licensing, international rights and legal affairs may all be under the auspices of the company's legal reps.

Outside the publishing and creative end are other equally important positions. Distributors and retailers are just as critical to the sales of your book, and represent a whole separate set of skills and responsibilities. Convention organizers are also significant, and can also be a creative industry career choice.

However, whatever the job, or how the company delegates responsibilities, positions do exist for work within the industry that can be exciting, challenging and creative.

Think of comic books as you would any other business. Don't approach the business as if it were some sort of an anomaly, separate from the way the rest of the world operates. Don't make the mistake of believing that what the rest of the business world does, won't apply to comics. If you're going to learn to write a good press release, or good advertising copy, or if you're going to be a quality control person, you can learn as much - or more - working in other industries as you can in comic books. So if you want to get your training, you have to open up your mind a little bit more to the sorts of things that comics really are, in addition to the stories. It's a printed product that needs advertising and promotional support. If you already have your business training, and then you go to the comic book company and apply for a business job, then you're miles ahead of the game. Plus the company is getting you with skills they need already intact.

Dave Olbrich, Publisher of Malibu Comics

A Closer Look at Publishing Industry Jobs

I'd like to give you a better idea of just what these comic industry jobs embody, and the kind of work you would be expected to do if you chose one of these positions. Keep in mind that each company may expect more or less of a particular employee position, and can often assign tasks that might, in another company, fall under a different job title.

To help you better understand how it will affect the creative product, let's look at these jobs in the approximate order they would handle a comic book project, from start to finish.

The Publisher

Depending on the size of the company, the publisher may also be an editor.

ProFile

Professional: George White, President of Top Dog Marketing
Credits Include: Marketing and P.R. for Skybox Comic Cards, Blackball Comics, Wildstorm Productions, and *Skybox Master Series: Creator's Edition Cards* (featuring work by Dave Dorman, Brom, Julie Bell, Brian Stelfreeze, Dave McKean)
Question: Aside from creators, what other jobs do you feel are critical to the smooth operation of the comic industry?

On the business end of things, solicitation is extremely important. By that I mean how it's description is phrased, getting it out on time - all that paperwork stuff that most creators don't like to, and in my opinion shouldn't have to, worry about. That's why most creators work for companies like Marvel [Comics] and DC [Comics] - because the people at those companies are *good* at doing that stuff. If the solicitation is not correct, or out on time, then you're not going to sell as many copies of your product.

The main reason for this, I think, is that the industry has gotten so big. If you don't 'jump through the hoop' of the big distributors - the hoop being that when you solicit you have to provide 'A', 'B' and 'C' - then they are not going to sell your product. Now, they put those 'hoops' up to act as a kind of gatekeeper, and it's a reasonable gatekeeper. It's designed to make sure that whatever they get is going to be a legitimate piece of work.

The promotion and publicity side is also very important. In most companies, it is separate from the people who work on the solicitations. It's significant, because we're constantly trying to increase our fan base. We want to expand the readership and bring in new people. Once people have entered the market, we want to keep them in and broaden their interests. To do that, you've got to develop all kinds of interesting and neat programs. We all advertise, and we all advertise in the same kinds of places. That's noteworthy, because if you saturate your advertising market, nobody pays attention anymore. It's critical to get the people who are in comics to buy whatever your particular product is, but on the other hand it's also important to go out and bring in new people through unique and differentiated advertising and promotional programs.

George White of Top Dog Marketing

146

The publisher is responsible for tracking and planning for all aspects of the company. The publisher must be knowledgeable about (and hopefully experienced in) the industry as a whole, and how their company fits into the big picture. The publisher must follow industry trends and oversee internal company organization and dynamics. He must assign duties and responsibilities to their management and editorial teams. They make decisions about and plan for the company's product and future.

The publisher must wear many business hats, from host to salesperson to administrator. Although generally a highly paid, appointed employee position, in many smaller publishing companies the publisher is also the owner of the company. Therefore, this position is not always open for pursuit from individuals outside the company.

Editors

Editors are also expected to assume a variety of responsibilities. They are assigned, or may choose, the variety of projects they oversee to completion. The editor is expected to be the quality-control person and the primary communication path in the comic-publishing chain.

Editors often solicit, find or seek out talent for projects under their responsibility. They act as the communication intermediary between the creator and the company. They examine and edit the stories and art produced for a particular project. They oversee its transit through the various company departments. Editors control the processing of the paperwork for contracts and payments to freelancers. They have a say in the promotion of the product via advertising advice, contact with the distributors and working at conventions. The editor advises which talent the company should rehire for future projects, and makes suggestions for new projects. Depending on the temperament and policies of the company, the editor may also be given creative opportunities as a writer.

Each company, depending on its size, offers a variety of editorial positions including editorial assistant, associate editor, specialized editors (eg., collections editor), managing editor and executive editor. As in any other business, unless you come into the company with extensive education, expertise or experience, you will be expected to work your way up from the bottom.

Legal Affairs

These individuals may be qualified attorneys in the full employ of the publisher, or on retainer in an on-demand capacity. For smaller publishers, they may simply be intermediaries between the company and its attorney, or an office administrator with legal/business acumen and experience.

Legal affairs are the people who prepare and execute contracts for the company. They can also oversee rights and permissions (both domestic and international) and licensing agreements. Any publishers worth pursuing make use of legal advisors.

Licensing and rights are complex issues often handled by a separate department. They arrange for use of company properties by outside parties. They arrange permission for reproduction in related mediums such

A Day In The Life of A Comic Book Editor with Archie Goodwin

Here is a very simplified view of the kinds of duties expected of an editor who works for one of the larger comic publishers. Archie Goodwin has been a comic professional since 1964, combining freelance writing work with editorial responsibilities. Editors have very full work days and frequently feel as if they are barely keeping up with their workload. Keep this in mind every time you send in an unsolicited submission sample, and it should help you understand why a response to your package may take some time.

6:00-7:00 am Get started on my day. I usually bring home some material from the office to read, so I spend some time reading solicited or contracted material: manuscripts, plots for some of the books I edit, or any other material that requires my attention.

10:00-10:30 am Arrive at the office. First thing I do is go through my voice mail. An interesting thing about being an editor is that you'll get calls on your voice mail from all hours of the night, often because freelancers live all over the world and also tend to work odd hours. Then I make a list of who has telephoned me and, depending on what part of the country they're in, spend some time returning calls. Generally 10:30-11:30 am is a good time to call people who work overseas. Since they're running five or six hours ahead of us I try to call them in the morning.

11:30 am - 12:30 pm All the Federal Express deliveries for the day have been opened and delivered to
the appropriate editors. At this time, with my associate editor Jim Spivey and assistant editor Chris Duffy, I'll go over what's come in. We'll go over scripts and artwork that have arrived, check how they adhere to our schedule: whether they sent in the pages, or number of pages, they promised. I then try to phone everyone who's sent in material, and at the very least let them know it has arrived. You can usually give an immediate response on artwork, but with a plot or script for ongoing projects it may take a day or two before we are able to read it. We do our best to give some sort of response to let the freelancer know it got here.

12:30-1:00 pm By this point in the day, chances are pretty good that a meeting will be scheduled. I have a number of weekly meetings I must attend as both editor and group editor. I'm much more involved in administrative and publishing responsibilities than a regular editor might be. I'm also involved in overseeing a couple of other editors, in addition to Jim Spivey and Chris Duffy, including Brian Augustyn and Dan Raspler. Meetings can be informal - with other editors, about things that are going on - or they might be more formal meetings. I also have to meet fairly regularly with the marketing or promotions department. We discuss the handling and promotion of books I'm editing and I provide input to help develop the sales strategy for a project. Unless I have a formal lunch appointment, I usually just run out and bring something back to my desk. I generally take the time while I'm eating lunch to go through complimentary comic books, of which there is a pretty constant flood. It's both a great perk, and a millstone. Part of my job is to look through these comics, and try to get an idea of what's going on not just with our books, but everybody's [other company's] books. I also make note of who's doing good-looking work, and who's stuff looks bad. And sometimes I read more material that has arrived during the day.

1:00-5:00 pm   By now, things are starting to get pretty frantic. This time of day is when you have your last shot at getting stuff ready to send along on the next step of the production of a book (like sending the script to the letterer, getting a plot ready for the penciller, or the lettered pages to the inker, etc.) I'm personally editing five regular monthly titles right now: *Legends of the Dark Knight, Hawkman, Manhunter, Starman, Fate.* Jim Spivey is personally editing the monthly titles *Damage* and *Primal Force.* Along with Chris Duffy, we try to keep those moving constantly since you need to be producing one issue of each, every four weeks. This time of day is when we're generally trying to get this material into production, or take care of proof-reading if it has not been completed. I'm also doing about nine other special projects like mini-series', one-shots, and annuals, that have to be kept moving.

Usually, in any given day, some kind of crisis occurs, so I will have one more responsibility in addition to trying to keep my books moving. It might be a freelancer becoming ill, and being unable to finish the job they're on. It could also be a freelancer who backs out on a project commitment at the last moment. Suddenly you find yourself running around looking for people who can jump in and help complete the book.

5:00-6 or 7:00 pm   I find this is a good time to make more calls. It is especially good for calling people on the west coast because of the time difference. At this time I also do some physical editing on scripts.

6:00-7 or 8:00 pm   I generally leave the office. However, I usually like to build in an hour or two, before I go home, where I just walk around. Sometimes I go to stores, but what I'm mostly doing is thinking. I consider where we're going with certain books or what I'd like to do with particular projects. I find that walking is a good time for me to think.

7 or 8:00 pm until . . . Arrive home. Usually use what's left of the evening to have dinner and spend some time with my wife. Sometimes, before going to bed, I'll read more material from the office.

On weekends, I generally come in for a while - usually on Saturday, occasionally on Sunday too - generally for three or four hours. That time is usually good if I have an extensive editing job to do, or for going through the tremendous ongoing accumulation of paperwork. I generally try to squeeze unsolicited submissions in wherever I can. Occasionally I try to go through those on a Saturday. Because of the significant accumulation of these submissions, there is generally a time lag before I can get to the material - anywhere from four weeks to six months, or longer - but if I possibly can make time to look at these, I do.

Additionally, there is a lot of travel involved with this job, in the form of conventions and various conferences. I have to arrange my daily work responsibilities to allow for the time I will be away, as the regular books must be attended to constantly. An editor working on their own couldn't handle as much as is possible without associate and assistant editors backing them up and following through for them.

There's also a certain degree of pressure to have specific materials ready for a given convention so it can be promoted properly. Many jobs have to be assigned and completed well before the convention season begins since many freelancers are less available in the summer, as they are also attending the conventions.

Conventions themselves are another form of work - manning the booth, meeting new talents, discussing project details with freelancers - but it's not the kind of work that really moves any of your books forward. They represent a pleasant form of work; it's great to meet the people who read your books, it's nice to talk with a lot of freelancers. But at the same time, the work you do won't necessarily pay off until a year or two later.

Also, every year there's generally some type of company-wide project. This year it's Zero Hour, a company-wide crossover. This requires more meetings, more coordination, and more material to read and keep up on so that my books are fitting in with all the other projects.

Every day you get between five and ten unsolicited submissions, and at least one or two queries from established professionals. For this reason, you can see how hard it can become to deal with submissions. It's almost a full time job, and at DC Comics this falls under the auspices of group editor, Neal Pozner, who handles finding and developing new talent, in between a schedule just as demanding as the one I've outlined for myself.

As you can see, there never seems to be enough time in the day.

as merchandise, media and games. They ensure that the company retains its rightful controls and profits appropriately from licenses. They also arrange for nonprofit usages of the company's products.

Short of those with legal training or specialized education, opportunities in the legal affairs area may be limited. However, as in any department, office personnel are required simply to keep the 'paperwork stream' flowing smoothly. In this capacity you probably can gain sufficient experience to move up in the company.

The Production Department

This area of the industry largely provides the closest position to being an art freelancer as you can get within a company's employ.

The production department is also the area most responsible for the look of the finished product. This department is composed of a multitude

ProFile

Professional: Bruce Bristow, Vice President of Sales and Marketing for DC Comics

Credits Include: BA from Brown University, MBA in Marketing from Northwestern, worked with Sales and Marketing at DC Comics for eleven years.

Question: Do you believe that individuals from other career fields have more to offer as industry professionals than people who gear their education specifically to the comics field?

Yes, I do. I think the industry benefits from receiving outside viewpoints for marketing, retailing and product development. Many people in the industry don't believe that, and are extremely skeptical of people who don't have comics as a personal background. But as the industry grows, and particularly as it grows outside the marketplace of the traditional, individual owner-operated stores, into specialty stores, chains of book stores, mass merchandisers, direct mail or anything else it's going to be more important that people understand the goals, problems and parameters of working in other areas.

My background is specialty retailing, and I have found many of those skills have been applicable to the comics business. To do certain things in the comics specialty market, and to make them work, we're going to have to deal with people from other industries, so we have to know their terminology, their preferences, and try to bring some of those things into this market. Any kind of advertising, marketing or business background ought to be applicable.

of positions, both general staff and management. Using the comic book as an example, let's look at how it might be handled by any given production department.

Once the editor has received the story and/or artwork and checked it over as the quality controller, the work is sent to the production department. The art director usually has a hand in quality controlling the artwork as well, and due to their familiarity with the project, can guide it through production.

If coloring must be done, it can be handled by a freelance colorist, an in-house colorist, or - as is happening more frequently in our industry - by a computer colorist. In addition to compiling, lettering and art, the production department will also design, typeset and assemble the cover, letters page, credits lists, and any interior advertising for the book. They also produce, and sometimes design, the advertising artwork to promote the book, point-of-purchase displays, convention promotion displays and general company advertising. They produce the camera-ready art and copy that enables a project to become a reality. Then it is shipped to the printer, where it is printed and ultimately distributed.

What I have described here is a very simplified view of a complex process. Depending on the size of the company, the production department may be only one individual, or composed of a vast army of people with very specialized responsibilities, working in concert. There are many creators in our industry who got their start doing production work.

Whatever your plans, this is an excellent source of experience and expertise while being gainfully employed in the comic industry. Plus, the insight provided by working within a company could help you become a better and more professional freelancer down the road.

Advertising and Marketing

The advertising and marketing areas of publishing comics also provide an excellent opportunity for creative expression.

Every publisher, regardless of size, must do advertising and marketing if it hopes to remain competitive and, at the very least, moderately successful. In many smaller companies, these jobs are also handled by the owner/publisher. However, in the larger and more established companies, many job opportunities are available.

Although advertising and marketing may be separate departments, they share similar responsibilities and job descriptions. They create and design the advertising and promotions that will help a company sell individual products, new product concepts, and the company itself. They utilize all ad media to promote their message: print, video, television, games, merchandising, and many industry crossovers (eg., gaming, trading cards, movies.) They are responsible for the concepts and gimmicks that excite fans, driving them to acquire the product or support the company.

An excellent example of advertising and marketing is the Ultraverse ad campaign employed by Malibu Comics to springboard their new superhero universe. The company took an aggressive and very creative tack, employing all possible avenues of promotion; wild postings (massive outdoor poster displays) in major cities, commercials on television stations popular with their target audiences, widespread print advertising in a variety of direct market and peripherally related publications, massive direct market campaigns, point-of-purchase promotions, free giveaways, extensive convention appearances, etc. Although carried out by many different company employees, all these ideas were the creation of the advertising and marketing minds.

Additionally, marketing and advertising positions are not restricted to publishing companies. Many publishers contract out to established firms - some who specialize in industry work - in conjunction with the efforts of their own staff.

Although education and experience are always a benefit, this is one area of employment where simple creativity and enthusiasm can get you work fairly easily without previous training. This is a fast-paced, demanding area of the industry that needs quick-thinking, enthusiastic and creative people.

ProFile

Professional: Del Stone Jr., Writer
Credits Include: *Hellraiser #20:"The Girl In The Peephole"*, Epic Comics; *Thumbscrew #1-3: "I'll Wait For You"*, Caliber Press; *Roadkill, December, Heat* and *Dakota* for Caliber Press; *Underground #4: "The Surviving Kind"*, Dark Horse Comics; "The Googleplex Comes and Goes" in *Full Spectrum 3*, Bantam Books; "Companions" in *The Year's Best Horror (1994)*, Donald A. Wolheim Pub.

Question: As a relative newcomer to the comic book industry, do you believe your experience in your daily job and your freelance prose work have been of some benefit to you as a comic professional?

I think that having worked for a newspaper taught me the importance of deadlines, discipline and that sort of thing. You encounter the same strictures in writing for the prose markets: You have deadlines, certain professional obligations, quality control considerations. The whole creative process is the same, regardless of the medium, but a lot of things about the comic industry came as totally new to me. Nothing can prepare you for that - you just have to do it.

You pick up skills from your other experiences that serve you well in the comics industry, and it gives you some familiarity, not only with the subject but, with the fantasy genre as a whole. Those skills and that knowledge are going to help you. If I had come into the comics industry totally cold, with no experience of having written for other books or a newspaper, I would have been lost. I wouldn't have known *where* to begin. It would have been like picking up a copy of *The Writer's Market* and trying to figure out how to be a professional writer simply by reading that book. It's a good source of information, but there's no exchanging that for real-world business experience.

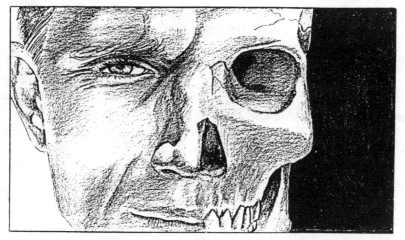

Art from Stone's *"I'll Wait For You"* **in** *Thumbscrew #1-3* **for Caliber Press**

Accounting and Royalties

Like any other business, there must always be people who ensure that the finances of a company run smoothly. This is where accounting and royalties come in. These are the people who process your payment for work on your project.

This department is responsible for managing the income and expenses of a publisher. Again, in smaller companies this position may also lie under the auspices of the publisher. However, in larger companies this department may be composed of many employees. Unless you love 'number-crunching,' you are unlikely to find much creative outlet in this particular job. These individuals are responsible for tracking monies paid to the company for sales, licensing, rights, etc. They also monitor expenditures such as employee and freelancer payments, operation costs, advertising and promotions budgets, and so on. It is their job to ensure that the company stays solvent and, hopefully, profitable by keeping the administrative personnel informed of the company's financial status and by adhering to the established budget.

Royalties are a percentage of the profits made by a project, paid to a freelancer as part of their financial compensation for work they have done. Royalties are defined by the word of the contract in terms of the size (percentage), when paid (at which point in sales of the product), frequency of payment (quarterly, annually, etc.), and geographical dictates (foreign versus domestic). Because of the complexity of the royalty issue, and the often significant variety of products created by a given company, royalties are often handled by a separate department or employee.

Again, despite the position existing within the comic industry, there is little artistically creative work involved, and the job basically encompasses many of the skills required of personnel in the accounting department.

Like legal affairs, accounting and royalties does require some business education or experience. Although there are office positions within this department that may not require much more than a willingness to learn office work, it is more likely that potential employees will be expected to possess basic bookkeeping skills, education and experience.

Administration

The administrative staff of a comic publisher are the top-level personnel who keep the company operating smoothly. This includes the publisher, editors, department managers and directors, business affairs, and office management. The company administrators do just that - administer the company. They keep company business rolling smoothly, handle employee matters, the budget, and the strategy for the company as a whole.

Administrative positions are generally filled through internal company promotion. They require knowledge about the company itself, in addition to specific business skills, which can only be acquired through experience working for that company.

Much like office help, administrative staff generally start at the bottom, although often with better education and work experience, and

ProFile

Professional: Dave Olbrich, Publisher of Malibu Comics
Credits Include: Co-founder of Malibu Comics; organizer and administrator of Will Eisner Awards 1988-89.
Question: Aside from creators, what other jobs do you feel are critical to the smooth operation of the comic industry?

As somebody who was once very interested in the creative side, but found far more interesting challenges - even creatively - in the process of promoting and advertising comic books, I would have to say the people who do the promotions and advertising are critical. It may be a personal prejudice, but I think the people who work on the sales side of publishing are probably the next linchpin of getting things done, as far as selling comics. The people in marketing and promotions, the people that work with the distributors and retailers to try to increase sales. It all comes down to communicating what's in the product to the customer.

Malibu has always been very strong in this area, and we've always put a high priority on it. We've certainly been able to sell more copies of any given product, than anybody else could have ever dreamt of, simply because we were able to get the news out to the retailers and distributors about what we were doing and how we were doing it. Ultimately, as a company philosophy, we like to let the creators create. We think that's their job. We think that the creative process should be left to the creative people. The job of the editor becomes working within the company to ensure quality control, and to communicate what's going on editorially to the people who are going to have to sell the product.

The creators depend very heavily, because of their cheques, on how well a book is promoted and how well the customers understand what they're buying. When you start falling down at that level, you've got a problem. You can't release a book and hope it'll sell in a vacuum! If you're

Cover for _Prime #1_ from Malibu Comics

publishing a book, you need to tell people you're publishing a book, so that the people who are interested in buying the book will even know it exists. To just do the creative side, to just do the printing side, to just do the editing side and then send it out there, is ultimately a self-defeating process. Also it's very valuable to understand the needs and desires of creative people when you're deciding how you're going to program your promotions and advertising. There's two things a company needs; the goodwill of the customers and the goodwill of the vendors. Ultimately, we're talking about pleasing the fans - which we work very hard to do - but also pleasing the creators, because without them we wouldn't have top quaility comic books.

I honestly believe that people who already understand and love comics, and who broaden their work experience, are far more useful to the industry than outside people that start to dabble in comics. The comic book industry, at least for the last fifteen years, has been quite dependent on product knowledge. So if you're not already familiar with the product, or familiar with the subtleties of the product, it's much more difficult for the company you represent. It's hard to train somebody about the subtleties of the product. I think people who are interested in comics shouldn't be afraid to take jobs outside the comic industry as part of their training process for a career in comics. But people who have long-standing jobs in other industries that are considering work in comics as a nine-to-five job, and have had no real interest in comic books, will have a little tougher time.

work their way up to the more established and lucrative career positions.

Office Help

Office help is the glue that keeps the company together and allows the specialized professionals to concentrate on their jobs.

This small army of critical help includes receptionists, secretaries, administrative assistants, mailroom staff, typists, shippers, filing clerks, transportation staff, couriers and general office help or, as they are popularly called, 'gophers.'

For inexperienced individuals eager to gain access to a publishing company position, this is often an excellent place to start, and can provide invaluable insight into company operations and professionalism.

One thing to keep in mind, however, is that these positions rarely command a high salary, and are often the first to be eliminated under company budget constraints.

Other Comic Industry Positions

Within the comic industry, but outside the publisher/freelancer realm, are a few jobs that can also be excellent sources of creative expression and employ. The three most noteworthy of these are distributors, retailers and convention organizers.

Although working for a distributor, in a retail outlet or at a convention may not seem an ideal career choice for you, rest assured that the benefits and experience can go a long way in helping you gain the business skills you need to ensure your professionalism.

Distributors

These are the companies that handle the ordering and distribution of the products produced by our industry. These organizations act as the central 'go-between' for publishers and retailers. They are supplied with information about new products to be released by the publishers, list them in catalogues they make available to store owners, take orders for the products from those same retailers, and ship the product received from the publisher to the individual retailers.

Distributors make their revenues by buying product in bulk, at a discount, from the publisher, and supplying it to the retailer at a slightly higher - although still discounted - price. The benefit of this system is a centralized supplier, which minimizes shipping and advertising/solicitation costs for both the publisher and the retailer. The problem with the distributor system is the influence and control these companies can exert over less prominent products or publishers. The distributor's motivation is to make money, so they tend to advertise and promote established, lower risk, moneymaking products, often neglecting the smaller, less-known works. Much like organized work unions, the distributors have their strengths and weaknesses depending on your viewpoint.

Due to the large size and geographically widespread nature of distributors - they often have warehouses all over the country - there are many job positions available, from basic office help and heavy labor all the way to top administration. Many industry professionals (including a few publishers!) have had valuable experience working for distributors. It is an excellent source of industry experience and insight.

Retailers

Believe it or not, the owner of your local comic book store is one of the most critical members of the comic industry. Without the retailer, it would be next to impossible for comics to reach the readers. The retailer exerts considerable influence over the face of the market, as well. Increased retail sales of a particular type of product (eg. more superhero sales versus horror sales) can easily skew the types of material produced by the industry (just look at the onslaught of Image anti-heros, and the multitude of 'clones' that followed from every other publisher!) Although readers do buy the books, the retailers control what is available for sale. A knowledgeable retailer is a successful businessman. Staying apprised of product, industry trends, marketing and advertising - not to mention small-business practices - are all critical facets to being a successful store owner. It is also an excellent source of industry education for individuals interested in pursuing other comic business work.

If you're the entrepreneurial type with a love of comics, this aspect of the industry may be most suited for you. Many employee positions also

157

ProFile

Professional: Frank Kurtz, Editor for Hero Illustrated Magazine/Artist/Writer
Credits Include: *Creepsville* and *Creepsville Resurective*, GoGo Comics; *Tor Love Betty* and *Cheapskin*, Fantagraphics; *Monster Scene Journal*.
Question: Aside from creators, what other jobs do you feel are critical to the smooth operation of the comic industry?

Besides the creators, I think you've got to have the business people. Now, I hate to get into that too much, but what it comes down to is, as a business, you've got to keep your head above water. The creative side is great, but a lot of times the guys who are doing comics don't account for getting the stuff printed, and all this other editorial and production stuff you have to do. I'm always thinking about the editorial side, but you've also got to have the guys who know how to do the promotional material. I think you've got to have a certain amount of business acumen, or have somebody who knows business, who you can really trust, to help you out. For example, Jeff Smith [creator of Bone] has his wife helping him, and Dave Sim has his very loyal staff. In those cases, there's a taskmaster on the editorial side, because if you don't have the ability, you've got to have somebody who gets your butt going, gets you in gear, pushes you along.

Question: As a self-published comic professional, what advice would you offer to creators who also want to self-publish ?

If you're self-publishing, do your homework! Investigate the industry. Check out all the options in printing. Shop around - the nickel-and-dime stuff is a pain in the butt, but it's important. You don't want to screw yourself, because the distributors are going to wait as long as they can to pay you. They're going to take thirty to sixty days to pay you, when you've taken the self-publishing route. So, be prepared to be broke.

Also, know your bookkeeping! This is the stuff nobody wants to talk about, but when it comes down to the end of the year, the IRS is going to want to know what you did. You've got to be able to show them that you either lost money or made money, and how much. So, even though it's the stuff you hate to do, be conscious of the business or you'll get screwed!

exist, although generally the pay level is low.

Convention Organizers

Conventions are one of the most effective and beneficial tools for promotion in the industry. They benefit the publisher, the freelancer, the distributor, special markets, and the fans. Convention organizers must put together a complete event catering to every aspect of the industry, and take into consideration all the special needs of the various industry participants, the whole time keeping the event entertaining and economically reasonable for the general public. To that end, organizers must be well versed in a multitude of business skills and acumen (much like a publisher) besides being knowledgeable about the comic industry in general. Organizers must be able to handle planning and strategy, work with community businesspeople, manage advertising, ensure proper promotion, make travel arrangements for guests, act as manager for the convention site, do crowd control, handle attendee satisfaction, and troubleshooting, just to name a few responsibilities.

Diversify yourself. Don't restrict yourself to the comic industry alone, pursue work in related businesses, like the animation industry or the book publishing industry, for survival as a freelancer. I've been involved as a professional in the comic book industry since the early '80's, and it's been in one state of flux after another. Black and white boom, color boom, it's just the most amazing thing I've ever seen. There are a lot of freelancers out there, newcomers, that I would suggest try to get involved with multi-media - a great new industry - or to get involved with storyboards and video scripting. Also, don't ignore fine art or commercial art which pays a lot more. The freelancer should be very well-rounded. Don't just limit yourself to working for the comic industry.

Rod Underhill, Attorney/Computer Fine Artist/Writer
(Nutopian Digital Pin-ups, CompuServe)

Organizing a convention is a complex, time-consuming, demanding and creative task. Due to its intricate role in the comic industry, it is also an ideal place to gain industry education. Although many positions in running a convention are generally volunteer, if you are looking for hands-on experience and connections in the comic industry, it is an excellent place to start.

Industries Related to Comics

If your first love is comics, but your are having trouble establishing yourself in the industry or are simply looking to broaden your horizons, you should seriously consider the jobs available in the many diverse markets

159

ProFile

Professional: Dan Danko, Senior Editor at Malibu Comics/Writer
Credits Include: *Gigantor* (writer), *Man Of War* (writer), *Lord Pumpkin* (writer), *Wrath* (editor), *Warstrike* (writing), Malibu Comics; editing *Skybox Ultraverse Card Series II* and *Ultraverse Masterworks Card Series.*
Question: Do you believe that individuals from other career fields have more to offer as industry professionals than people who gear their education specifically to the comics field?

I would say no. I really believe that with the exception of, maybe, a cover artist, I think you need to be a fan of the industry to understand how it works, and understand what a fan would want. You have to be a fan in order to write or draw for the fans. For anything that has to do with the creator side, it's helpful to be a fan.

With Malibu, our marketing department has people that were not comic fans when they came in. I think that when you get right down to it, marketing is marketing is marketing. You're pushing a product and you're trying to get people to buy the product. It helps to understand the audience, but you can research that. But you cannot research what it takes to be on the creator side or the production side. Your common editor or art director - if he doesn't understand that the way Todd MacFarlane draws Spiderman's leg behind his head is the coolest thing in the world (even though it's physically impossible) he'll likely sit there going, "It's terrible, terrible, terrible!" In my opinion, that's what makes Todd's art so dynamic. It's beautiful, and it's great to look at. I think that's where comic books are different, in that we shouldn't really place the importance on physics, but instead on what works, and what's visually appealing. What makes the reader excited about the book. So people who have a comic background are going to be better at making those judgements than people who come from outside the industry.

I think that, like any industry, if you didn't grow up with the working knowledge of how things operate, then you're always going to be a foreigner to it - or at least not as in tune as someone who grew up loving Jack Kirby and reading Spiderman, and thinking that Superman was the greatest thing in the world. I think that one of the things that does help drive the people in the industry, especially since it's really just another business, is that final fall-back on "I love comics." I don't think somebody coming in from outside the industry could appreciate that.

Warstrike **character design from Malibu Comics**

related to the comic industry. Comics are not the only products actively pursued by the growing collector and fan market. There are many related products and merchandising that are also available, and an equal number of careers associated with them.

Some of the more recognized products include T-shirts, lithographs, trading cards, books, posters, print collections, postcards, sportswear (IE., hats, ties, etc.), glassware, accessories (IE., pins, jewelry, etc.), novelty items, games (both computer and role playing), and videos, The list is extensive

---

Approach comics as a business, not as a recreational activity, dream fulfillment or some kind of ego-satisfying experience. It may turn out to be all those things, but above everything else it's a business. You have to treat it as a business, and have a business sense about it.

The fun part, of course, is writing the story and afterwards seeing your name in print, signing books, that sort of thing. That's all fun, and you'll enjoy it. But it's work, more than anything else. You have to be organized, you have to have resources, you have to have information, you have to conduct yourself as a professional, and you have to treat the people with whom you work as professionals.

*Del Stone Jr., Writer (**Roadkill**, Caliber Press)*

---

and is continually growing and changing. Each of these products represents a sub-industry within, or connected to, the comics business. And each represents a host of jobs and careers that demand creativity and business skills. If you want to enter the comic industry, any one of these fields is a viable doorway.

Unrelated Fields

Many professionals within our business have come from other industries, independent of the comic market. Although many of these individuals lacked the experience or a wealth of knowledge about comics, their skills developed in other fields have aided them in this industry. A love of comics - an interest in the product of our business - in combination with their education and professional experience has helped their success within the comic business.

The music industry and book publishing are two of the fields from which many comic professionals have come bringing their own special viewpoint and insights. The gaming industry and computer business have also provided us with individuals who have a wealth of knowledge and skills. Despite the source, individuals with non-comic industry expertise have served to enrich and broaden our industry, and make the comics business one of the new market forces to which the public is paying renewed attention.

ProFile

__Professional:__ Tim Bradstreet, Creator/Freelance Illustrator
__Credits Include:__ *Dragon Chiang* (inker), Semick Press and Eclipse Comics;
Red Sky Diaries (creator and artist), *Aliens: Music of the Spheres* (inker/cover
artist) and *X*, Dark Horse Comics; *Age of Desire* (artist) graphic novel
__Question:__ How have the independent publishers affected your comic career?

Really, they haven't affected my career as much as the game industry.
Basically, I leapt into comics from my work there. When I first started out,
I knew I wasn't good enough for comics, even though I knew that's what I
wanted to do. But I knew I could do game illustrations. And even though
I was really bad at first, I worked in that business for five years before I even
got into comics. It gave me a chance to reach my stride and I knew
eventually I was doing good work, and was getting regular jobs. All of a
sudden I was at the top of the industry. I was *the* guy in games to go to if
you wanted to sell a book. I still work in the game industry to this day.

They don't pay as well as comics, though some companies do. If you
can get a lot of work from TSR, *then* you're paying your bills. I supported
myself for five years doing game work, but it can be a real test of your
patience. A lot of the game companies are small, so unless you're working for

Art from one of Bradstreet's
***Vampire* print portfolios**

the "big's" you're not going to
be getting that paycheck in
thirty days. There can be a lot
of hair-pulling in trying to get
your money. And trying to
get rights for yourself.
They're five or ten years
behind the comic industry as
far as rights, but they are
catching up quickly. They're
not as organized or as
business-like as the comic
industry; and they don't
respect their creators the way
comics do. Comics has a
fandom, that kind of a thing.
With games, it's more like the
artists are the last guy on the
totem pole. As far as the
publisher is concerned, they
pay the printer, they pay this
person, they pay that person,
and then the artist is probably
the last guy to get paid. And
that could be months down

the line if they're low on cash or they're not selling books. I think they have a little more respect for the writers because, essentially, they're designing the games. That's what gaming is; this is the adventure, and this is how you play the game. Basically, writers are the people who are treated the best. For a writer, the game industry is a reasonable alternative if you're interested in that sort of thing.

I think the trick is to diversify. You can make a name for yourself in a lot more places and cover a lot more bases, and it'll always be better for you in the long run. If you can't get a job doing this, then look at what else is going on. You have to examine all facets of the genre, whether it be games, electronic games, computer games, comics or whatever. There are a lot of venues for the genre, and you don't have to limit yourself to comics!

The independents are a very valuable starting point for a newcomer. I recommend it to a lot of people who are busting their heads trying to get

into Marvel and DC [Comics]. I ask them, "Well, do you know Caliber? Are you familiar with their books?" They say, "Kind of, I see them around." So I tell them, "You know, if you've got an idea and you ever want to do a comic story - something personal, something that you want to do - then just do it! You're not going to get paid up front, but they'll publish it for you!" They [Caliber Press] are good people. If they think it's good material, then they'll publish it. That's a good way to start. I also recommend that people get a hold of gaming companies and try illustration for a while, just to get their feet wet. It'll also help you understand how the publishing business works.

So many people have started with independent companies that I can't believe more people who are trying to break into comics don't see this. Guy Davis, Jim O'Barr - that's how they got their start. That's all Caliber right there! It goes beyond that, too. Mike Mignola started doing fanzine drawings for Amazing Heroes [from Fantagraphics] and First Comics, and now he's a superstar. So you can see how it can help you.

I guess the bottom line is, if you're not making money off your artwork - you might have a part-time job but you'd like to make your full-time job comic illustrating or writing - try the independents. Unless you're "God" you're not going to get work from DC or Marvel. Especially if you don't have any connections. Sometimes even if you're "God" it doesn't help!

Summary

In this final chapter, I have described the various areas of the comic industry and related businesses, where career and job opportunities exist outside the freelancer arena. I've described the general structure of publishing houses, and the various positions that offer an exciting and stable alternative to work as a freelancer. We discussed various positions including *editor* and *publisher*, the *legal affairs department, production* jobs, *advertising and marketing, accounting and royalties, administration*, and *office help*. We've looked at the responsibilities each position holds and its role in creating the final product. I've also covered other comic industry positions and their role in the business, including *distributors, retailers* and *convention organizers*. I've also discussed the *industries related to comics* and some *unrelated fields*, where you might find creative careers more to your interest.

If after taking your initial plunge into the comic profession you find that this career is not quite what you had in mind, then perhaps some of these other positions might be of greater interest and enjoyment for you.

If you do find that being a comic professional is everything you hoped it would be, then at the very least, this chapter should have helped you gain a better understanding of how the industry operates. This understanding, in conjunction with your other business skills, will help you be a more effective and successful comic professional.

Conclusion

Thank you for joining me in a look at the important aspects of *Getting Into The Business Of Comics.* I hope you found some useful tips and insights to help you establish yourself as a business professional. This book was not intended to tell you how to develop the 'talent' you need to get work, but simply endeavored to shed some light on a variety of the areas crucial for doing business in the comic industry. Much of the information is also applicable to **any** industry or business. Much of this information was basic common sense.

Comics is an exciting and varied industry with many opportunities for enthusiastic and talented people. But don't be fooled by that word talent! Despite dictionary definitions and parental encouragement, talent is *not* something you are simply born with, that will guide you confidently through your life and career.

Talent = Hard Work. It's a simple and honest formula that you should never forget.

Leave behind all your ill-founded notions about the glamour of the comics business. Forget all the hype about sales, celebrity and big bucks. Start with a solid foundation of hard work, common sense, realistic goals, personal reliability and professionalism, and you'll find yourself secure in that career position you dream about.

Start with the basics outlined in this manual, including the many appendices that follow. These contain vital information about publishers, distributors, business forms, legal information, reading lists, company submissions guidelines and much more.

But don't stop there! Read, learn, ask questions and practice. Make yourself a better creator, a better businessman. Make yourself a better person. When you do, others will recognize your expertise and abilities, and you won't have to work quite so hard at getting "your big break."

Until that time, I hope that the information I have provided here will give you a solid starting point. Read it carefully. Re-read it. Then put it into practice. And before you know it you'll find yourself Getting Into The Business Of Comics!

Good Luck!!

Appendix A: Glossary of Terms

alternative work - comic content that does not tend to follow the established and acceptable superhero format.

bill of sale - form stipulating to the buyer of an original work just what rights, if any, they are purchasing with the work.

billing invoice - similar to a payment invoice, although generally provided by the creator to bill the employer.

camera-ready - the final state of finished art and/or text as it is sent to the printer for production

con or **convention** - an event held by a local sponsor over one or more days, which features a display of industry-related material by retailers and publishers, guest creators, panel discussions and exhibits.

contract - a written instrument which outlines the agreement between creator and employer. Can take a multitude of forms, including work-for-hire and creator-owned rights.

convention circuit - the regularly - and often annual - schedule of conventions. In the comic industry, the majority of conventions are held during the spring and summer. Therefore, the comic industry 'convention circuit' could be said to run from May through August.

copyright - stipulates who holds ownership of a work for reproduction purposes.

copyright release - a form which should be provided to printers and copier shops to release the copyright of reproduced images back to the creator.

cover letter - the single page correspondence sent with a sample package to an editor. The cover letter serves to introduce the freelancer to the editor, by providing information about education and past work experience, skills and outlines the type of work in which they are interested.

creator rights - the right to control the reproduction or publication of a character/concept created by a professional. The degree of control by the publisher can vary, and should be outlined in the contract. Relinquished in all standard work-for-hire agreements.

creator-owned rights contract - contract where the creator maintains most, or all, of the reproduction rights on the work they produce for an employer. Most common contract form with the smaller, independent creator-supportive companies.

critique - a structured or more formal situation where you obtain opinions and comments on your work from industry professionals, including other creators, publishers and editors

critique - an assessment by an individual (can be from another creator, an editor, a publisher, or a fan) of the caliber and quality of your work. It should include comments about technical expertise, individual style and expression, dynamic qualities of the work, presentation and overall impression. Comments should be used to improve upon the work, and tailoring future work to publisher requirements.

feedback - a critique of your work samples provided by an editor or professional. This advice can be invaluable in the continued improvement of your skills.

feedback - the information you get during a critique

form response - a pre-printed card or letter with a variety of replies to a mail submission

genre - a class or category of artistic endeavor having a particular form, content or technique. Can mean superhero vs. horror vs. science fiction, or it can mean inked vs. painted, depending on the context of use.

indicia - block of publishing and copyright information that appears in fine print inside published matter. In comics, often found on the bottom portion of the inside cover, front, back or title page.

letter of intent - outline of the elements of a contract agreement in letter form.

licensing - formal, legal permission to reproduce an image or character owned by a particular company or individual

licensing - a formal agreement between the author of a work, and an individual or company which wishes to reproduce that particular work.

merchandising - reproduction of a work on materials other than publications. ie., prints, t-shirts, trading cards, buttons, pins, etc.

'Name' - an established or fan-favorite professional

negotiation- discussion between a creator and employer as to the pertinent items to be covered by a contract.

networking or **schmoozing** - the popular name for the act of making business introductions and connections with potential employers during social activities. Often can take a friendlier, less-businesslike approach.

originals - the original artwork or typed pages produced by a creator

ownership of original work - stipulates who holds ownership of the physical work

page rate - the price per page paid to a creator for their work. May be paid between ten and thirty days after publisher's receipt of work.

panel discussion - generally held during a convention, these feature a panel of 'authorities' on the topic of discussion. Topics range widely, and the panel duration can run anywhere from 30 minutes to an hour or more. They often provide a question and answer period for the audience.

payment invoice/chit - form filled out and signed by the creator, billing employer for work done. Often provided by the employer, but also can be provided by the creator. Often can include fine print contracts.

permission to reproduce work in publication - a simplified contract form that focuses on the right to reproduce the work.

point-of purchase - the place from which a comic industry product is purchased by the general public (IE., a comic book store counter, in the case of a display)

portfolio - an organized display of samples of work, published and/or unpublished. Used to display your work to potential employers and other creators.

portfolio review - a time structured by publishers and editors for review of the sample portfolios of newcomers and aspiring professionals.

portfolio review - generally held at a convention, though occasionally scheduled by major publishers at their offices, this is a more formalized critique of a number of aspiring artists. Sometimes these are done in an organized appointment fashion, and sometimes it's simply a big line, where it's first come-first served

PR - public relations

purchase order - a printed form from an employer requesting the completion of a particular work. Can sometimes act as a contract.

Quarterly Estimates - tax payment made four times in the year, based on income earned in the preceding year. Required by IRS from self-employed income earners. Also helps to defray the impact of the end of year tax payment.

reading - where established or newcomer writers read excerpts of their written work to an audience of peers and/or the public

reproduction rights - the rights, which can be bought and sold, to reproduce a work for publication , merchandising or licensing.

response card - a quick and easy alternative to the self-addressed, stamped envelope. Preprinted with stock responses an editor can check off, this card can help supplement your mail-out log information. Can help save on postage costs if formatted as a postcard.

retailers - these are the business people who own and operate your local comic store. They are responsible for ordering the books that are purchased by the readers. Technically, they could also be considered your potential employers, because their orders determine which books sell well, and frequently shape the editorial choices of the publishers. At a convention, they are also called 'dealers'.

rights and permissions - an area of publishing that handles reproduction of a company's property by both businesses and nonprofit organizations

royalties - a percentage of the profits made by a project paid a freelancer as part of their financial compensation for work they have done

royalties - a percentage of the profits after all expenses have been paid, including company expenses and page rate (generally considered an advance against royalties to come). Generally expressed in percentage form, and usually smaller than share of profits.

royalty - small percentage payment made on each book sold, based on numbers of books sold. Can be made in advance form, or in addition to a flat -fee payment. On comics the royalty is usually divided between the creators who work on a particular book.

S.A.S.E. - a self-addressed, stamped envelope (usually a #14 - legal size), provided with a sample submission to facilitate a response and/or return of samples, by the editor.

sample - A sample of work produced by an artist or writer. Generally used to interest a publisher in employing a professional.

sample tearsheets - copies of published work

SASE - self-addressed, stamped envelope that should accompany every mail submission you send to a publisher.

share of profits - a portion of the total profits from publication of a book, after production costs have been paid. Generally expressed as a percentage, and in place of an advance page rate.

solicitation - copy used to 'advertise' a new book from a publisher. Usually found in a distributor catalogue, or a publisher flyer.

spec, 'on spec' - short for speculation or on speculation. Sometimes jobs are obtained based on the 'speculation' of the publisher. Ie., they speculate that taking on the project or creator will be profitable in the future.

standard forms - preprinted or typeset form which can be used as a type of contract. Can take the form of a letter of intent, bill of sale, permission for reproduction form or a billing invoice.

submission's guidelines - written rules provided by publishers to act as a guide for new talent submissions of artwork or writing. These guidelines stipulate the form and method that unsolicited submissions should take when sent to that publisher. Aspiring pros should strictly follow these guidelines for serious consideration of their work.

submissions guidelines - written rules provided by publishers to act as a guide for new talent submissions of artwork or writing. These guidelines stipulate the form and method that unsolicited submissions should take when turned in to that publisher. Aspiring pro's should strictly adhere to these guidelines for serious consideration of their work.

taxes - a crucial part of the business end of being a freelancer, self-employed taxes and social security taxes are required in addition to federal income tax. Freelancers are frequently required to make Quarterly Estimate payments to the IRS.

tearsheet - a copy of published work

unsolicited submission - a submission of work samples sent without invitation to a publisher.

unsolicited submissions - mail submissions sent to a publisher, without their invitation, with the hopes you will be considered for future work.

wild posting - multiple postings of an advertising image at public locations such as construction sites, building walls, fences and billboards. Often considered illegal depending on the legislation of individual communities.

work-for-hire contract - contract where reproductions of the work produced becomes the sole property of the employer. Most common contract form with major comic publishers and on licensed characters (such as movie characters).

Appendix B: Business and Legal Forms

Phoenix Rising Studio

Lurene Haines
Illustrations

YOUR NAME AND ADDRESS INFORMATION
SHOULD GO HERE, ALONG WITH
YOUR TELEPHONE NUMBER.
INCLUDE FAX NUMBER IF YOU HAVE ONE.

INVOICE

		Invoice no		Date	
Quantity	Description			Unit price	Amount

YOUR SOCIAL SECURITY NUMBER GOES HERE   TOTAL

Example of a *Billing Invoice*

☐ CORRECTED (if checked)

PAYER'S name, street address, city, state, and ZIP code		1 Rents $	OMB No. 1545-0115 **19**93	**Miscellaneous Income**
MARVEL ENTERTAINMENT GROUP INC. 387 PARK AVENUE SOUTH NEW YORK NY. 10016		2 Royalties $		
		3 Prizes, awards, etc. $		
PAYER'S Federal identification number 94-3024816	RECIPIENT'S identification number	4 Federal income tax withheld $	5 Fishing boat proceeds $	**Copy B For Recipient**
RECIPIENT'S name (first, middle, last) street address, city, state, and ZIP code		6 Medical and health care payments $	7 Nonemployee compensation $ 11800. 00	This is important tax information and is being furnished to the Internal Revenue Service. If you are required to file a return, a negligence penalty or other sanction may be imposed on you if this income is taxable and the IRS determines that it has not been reported.
		8 Substitute payments in lieu of dividends or interest $	9 Payer made direct sales of $5,000 or more of consumer products to a buyer (recipient) for resale ▶ ☐	
		10 Crop insurance proceeds $	11 State income tax withheld $	
Account number (optional)		12 State/Payer's state number		

Form **1099-MISC**   (keep for your records)   Department of the Treasury - Internal Revenue Service

Example of a *1099 Form - Statement of Earnings* for Income Tax

DC COMICS TALENT INVOICE

DC FORM #E-105 (Rev 6/92)

Date: _____   Expense Code: _____

Talent: _____
(Insert name of company if contracting party is incorporated)

Employee: _____
(Insert name of individual who will be performing services for contracting party if contracting party is incorporated)

Address: _____

TALENT INVOICE for work produced for DC Comics pursuant to the Agreement dated as of the above date between Talent and DC Comics with respect to the following (the "Work") :

Services: ☐ Script   000 1200 1010   ☐ Cover   ☐ Layouts   000 1200 2030

        ☐ Text   000 1200 1010   ☐ Painted Cover   ☐ Finishes over layouts 000 1200 2040

        ☐ Plot / Breakdown 000 1200 1020   ☐ Sketch 000 1200 2010   ☐ Logo 000 1200 1040

        ☐ Dialogue 000 1200 1030   ☐ Pencils 000 1200 2000   ☐ Graphic Services _____
                                                       (specify)

        ☐ Synopsis 000 1200 1040   ☐ Inks 000 1200 2020   ☐ Other _____
                                                        (specify)

Project Title: _____

Pages: _____ x Page / Cover Rate: $ _____ = Total: $ _____ [OR] Flat Fee $ _____

☐ Federal ID No. or S.S. No. _____
                                        (If contracting party is incorporated, insert Federal I.D. no. of company)

REQUESTED BY: _____   APPROVED BY: _____

SHADED AREAS FOR CORPORATIONS ONLY

(see reverse side for continuation)

ACCEPTED AND AGREED

By: ✗ _____   By: _____
    Talent's Signature (or Corporate Officer's Signature and Title if Talent is incorporated)   DC COMICS

I hereby acknowledge that I am familiar with and approve of the terms of the foregoing Agreement. I further acknowledge that I have entered into an employment agreement with Talent in accordance with the applicable provisions of the Agreement including, without limitation, the applicable provisions of Paragraph 8 thereof. If Talent shall fail to fulfill any of its obligations under the Agreement for any reason, then, in addition to any other remedies that may be available, DC may require that I render my personal services and fulfill all of Talent's obligations directly to DC upon the same terms and conditions set forth in the Agreement. I shall look solely to Talent for the payment of any and all compensation or other payment that may be required to be made as a result of any rendition of services arising under this Agreement.

_____   _____
(Employer's Signature if Talent is Incorporated)   (Employee's S.S. No.)

DC Comics' Agreement

MARVEL ENTERTAINMENT GROUP, INC.
WORK FOR HIRE VOUCHER AGREEMENT
SUBJECT TO THE TERMS ON THE REVERSE SIDE HEREOF

In consideration of Marvel Entertainment Group, Inc. ("MARVEL") commissioning and ordering from SUPPLIER the written material, artwork or services referred to in this Voucher (the "Work") and paying therefor, SUPPLIER acknowledges, agrees and confirms that the Work was created, prepared or performed by SUPPLIER under commission from MARVEL for use as a contribution to a collective work (known as "Marvel Comics") and that as such the Work was and is expressly agreed to be considered a work made for hire for purposes of all copyright laws.

In addition to the foregoing, SUPPLIER expressly conveys and grants to MARVEL forever all rights of any kind and nature which SUPPLIER may have in and to the Work (including but not limited to the unrestricted right to make modifications, adaptations and revisions to the Work), and the right to use SUPPLIER's name in connection therewith and agrees that MARVEL is the sole and exclusive copyright proprietor thereof having all rights of ownership therein. SUPPLIER agrees never to contest MARVEL's exclusive, complete and unrestricted ownership in and to the Work (including all copyright rights therein), or to claim adverse rights therein.

This agreement shall be binding upon and inure to the benefit of the parties hereto and their respective heirs, successors, administrators and assigns.

By signature on the face hereof, SUPPLIER acknowledges acceptance of the terms herein specified and by tendering payment to SUPPLIER, MARVEL acknowledges receipt of the Work and acceptance of the terms herein specified.

SUPPLIER'S NAME _____

NAME OF MAGAZINE _____

TITLE OF STORY _____

JOB NUMBER _____

NUMBER OF PGS (HRS) _____

SUPPLIER'S SIGNATURE _____

TYPE OF WORK _____
(Penciling, Script, Inking, Etc.)

PRICE PER PAGE (HR.) _____

794058
VOUCHER NUMBER

DATE VOUCHERED & DELIVERED _____

ISSUE NUMBER _____

TOTAL PAYMENT _____

EDITORIAL APPROVAL _____

SUPPLIER KEEP LAST COPY

DO NOT WRITE BELOW THIS LINE

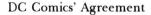

SUPPLIER'S NUMBER	VOUCHER NUMBER	INVOICE DATE M M D D Y Y	GROSS INVOICE AMOUNT
	794058		
ACCOUNT NO	CENTER NO	PROJECT NO	SUB NO	DISTRIBUTION AMOUNT

Marvel Comics' Agreement

Examples of *Work For Hire Contract/Payment Invoice*

This agreement is entered into between **Insert Publisher Name** (hereinafter Publisher) having a publishing address of **Insert Publisher Address**, and **Insert Artist/Writer Name** (hereinafter Artist/Writer) having an address of **Insert Artist/Writer Address**.

Effective **Insert Date of Agreement**, the Publisher agrees to employ the Artist/Writer to produce **Insert Name and Description of Work and Publication** (hereinafter Work).

The Publisher agrees to pay the Artist/Writer the sum of **Insert Amount of Payment** as compensation for First Printing Rights of the Work. Payment will be made within 30 days of receipt of the finished Work. If the Publisher does not pay the full amount within 30 days of receipt of Work, a late charge of **Insert Amount of Late Charge** will be added to the cost of the work, up to a maximum late charge of **Insert Max. Charge**. Execution of the Work will begin upon verbal and/or written approval from the Publisher, and will be delivered no later than **Insert Deadline Date** provided that approval is given no later than **Insert Approval Deadline**. If Work is not delivered by this date, a late charge of **Insert Penalty Charge** will be deducted from the cost of the work, up to a maximum of **Insert Max. Penalty** in late charges.

In the event that the Publisher decides not to use the finished Work, they will be required to pay the Artist/Writer a "kill fee" payment of **Insert Kill Fee (generally 50% of the proposed payment)**.

The finished Work is copyrighted by **Insert Artist/Writer Name**, and the Publisher is entitled to First Printing Rights only, for **Insert Name and Description of Publication**. All other rights will be negotiated separately.

The Publisher will provide the Artist/Writer with **Insert Number (usually anywhere from 15 to 25)** free copies each of the printed cover from **Insert Name and Description of Publication**.

Insert Name of Publisher   Artist/Writer

_____   _____

By: **Insert Agents Name**   By: **Artist/Writer Name**

Example of a *Creator-Owned Rights Agreement*

Your Comic Publisher
12345 Big Time Boulevard, Metropolitan City, Publishers State 54321

Below is an accounting for your *Big Muscled Hero* royalties for period ending June 01, 1993.

		ISSUE #1
ISSUES SOLD		19, 843
COVER PRICE		$4.95
SALES		$98,222.55
ROYALTY %	3.00 %	$2,946.68
ADVANCES PAID		$2,400.00
ROYALTIES DUE		$546.68

Example of a *Royalty Statement*

LICENSE AGREEMENT between:

_____ ("Licensor") and _____ ("Licensee")

_____   _____

_____   _____

_____   _____

                                          _____

Date of Agreement _____

The parties agree as follows:

A. **GRANT OF LICENSE.** Subject to the terms and conditions set forth herein, Licensor grants to Licensee non-exclusive license to the Property for the manufacture, distribution and sale of the Licensed Products throughout the Territory during the Term, as provided in this Agreement.

B. **PROPERTY.** Property means the original creative elements (including original designs, characters, artwork, names, words, symbols, likenesses, logographics and other indica) which appear in and have become associated with the motion pictures entitled _____ (collectively the "Pictures"). The Property also includes all Trademarks specified in Exhibit A attached hereto. The Property does not include any on-screen credits from the Pictures.

C. **LICENSED PRODUCTS.** The Licensed Products are   limited edition signed and numbered lithographs utilizing two

    images of cover art from _____ comic magazine series _____

    Lithographs to retail for approximately $40 and to number

    1,000 to 1,500 each image.

D. **TERRITORY.** The territory is   United States, its territories and possessions

E. **TERM.** The Term of this Agreement begins on _____ and ends _____

F. **MINIMUM GUARANTEE.** Licensee agrees to pay Licensor a minimum guarantee during the Term in the amounts and in the manner specified below.

    Advance Payment (due upon signing): $5,000.00

    Minimum Guarantee (due by end of term): $5,000.00

    Advance Payment shall be credited against the Minimum Guarantee due. Advance Payment and the Minimum Guarantee are non-refundable.

G. **ROYALTIES.** Licensee agrees to pay to Licensor Royalties equal to   Ten   Percent

    (10%)   of One Hundred Percent (100%) of Net Sales (as defined in Paragraph 6 of Standard Conditions). Royalty

    payments shall be paid as specified in Paragraphs 6 and 7 of the Standard Conditions and shall be credited against the Minimum Guarantee due.

H. **MARKETING DATE/OBLIGATIONS.** In order to achieve the best marketing of the Licensed Products, Licensee

    agrees that it will begin distributing substantial quantities of the Licensed Products no later than

    _____

I. **STANDARD CONDITIONS.** The Standard Conditions attached to this Agreement are a part of the agreement and are binding on the parties.

J. **ENTIRE AGREEMENT.** This Agreement (including the Standard Conditions attached hereto and incorporated herein by this reference) contains the entire agreement of the parties with respect to the subject matter hereof and supersedes all prior oral and written agreements, negotiations, understandings and communications regarding such subject matter.

Example of a *Licensing Agreement*

Appendix C: Art Schools

There are a variety of good art schools which offer some degree of instruction applicable to the comic book industry. You can look into these if you would like to refine your art education.

Here is a listing of a few of the more prominent educational institutes, and some of their requirements. Write for complete details and an admissions package.

The Art Center School of Design
1700 Lida St., P.O. Box 7197, Pasadena, CA 91109-7197
(818) 584-5000
Tuition (subject to change): For 1993 - avg. $6,500/semester, no room & board.
Requirements:
- A fully completed application for admission.
- A $35 non-refundable application fee.
- Official high school and college transcripts, sent directly to the Admissions Office. GED is accepted. SAT or ACT scores for students currently in high school.
- A compact portfolio of original work. You must submit your best, most recent work. It should represent your personal itnerests and abilities. It should contain a min. of twelve and max. of twenty original samples, including work related to applicant's proposed major. A portfolio of slides only is not acceptable. Slides or photos of 3-D or oversized pieces are acceptable but do not replace the twelve required original works. Sketchbooks may also be included.
- Portfolios will not be reviewed until other application materials have been submitted.
- An interview is not required, but is advisory and considered beneficial.

The Joe Kubert School of Cartooning
37 Myrtle Avenue, Dover, NJ 07801
(201) 361-1327
Tuition (subject to change): For 1993 - $7,700.00, not including room and board.
Requirements:
- High school diploma or equivalent degree.
- Complete and mail application form with non-refundable $25.00 fee.
- Respond to two essay questions.
- Suggest three possible interview dates. These cannot be guaranteed by the school, but they will try to accommodate you. For the first interview, in person is best, but if you live a distance away the school will permit a telephone interview. Make sure you get written verification of the interview date. The second interview, which will follow one week after the first, is always conducted over the telephone. At this point they wish to determine if you are sincere in your desire to attend the school.
- A portfolio containing a variety of your work. Minimum of fifteen pieces and a maximum of twenty-five. Variety is emphasized in both

mediums and subject matter. Submit your most recent finished or unfinished work. If you are doing a personal interview, bring the portfolio with you. Submit photocopies or slides if you live at a distance and are doing a telephone interview, but the portfolio must be received at least one week prior to the interview date. Your portfolio will be returned approximately one month following the interview.

Ringling School of Art and Design

2700 North Tamiami Trail, Sarasota, FL 34234
1-800-255-7695
Tuition (Subject to change): $9,000.00 per year, not including room and board. Financial assistance and scholarships are available
Requirements:
> - Submit a completed application form with non-refundable $30.00 application fee.
> - Official copy of transcripts from last high school or college attended, submitted by those institutions, not the student. (GED is accepted)
> - Prepare a visual presentation. Freshmen: Ten color slides or photographs of recent work. May also ask for a formal portfolio review, but this does not negate the photo requirement. DO NOT send original pieces of work, as portfolios are NOT returned. Photos will be returned if an S.A.S.E. is included. In lieu of prepared work, the school will accept submission of art exercises outlined in their admissions guidelines. Requirements vary for transfer students, foreign students, veterans, experimental learning students, part-time students and non-degree -seeking students attending part-time.
> - Two letters of recommendation, at least one from a current art instructor, if possible.

The School of Visual Arts

209 E. 23rd St., New York, NY 10010
(212) 592-2100
Tuition costs are available by mail inquiry only.
Requirements:
> - High school transcript
> - Two hundred and fifty word essay on reason for wanting to attend the school, including goals and interests.
> - A portfolio containing ten to twenty pieces, with emphasis on creativity and original work - nothing copied from someone or somewhere else.
> - Personal interview and portfolio review if you live within 250 miles of New York City
> - Complete application form with non-refundable $25.00 application fee.

Appendix D: Conventions

Here is a listing of the more established comic conventions and trade shows in North America. I have tried to include conventions representing major geographical areas (ie., Northwest, East Coast, South, Midwest.) This list includes the approximate month that the convention takes place. The contact information where you can get additional data about the particular convention is also included.   Conventions with an (**) are highly recommended for newcomers trying to get exposure with the publishers.

Center Con
Time: April & September
Location: Seattle, WA
Center Con
Box 2043
Kirkland, WA 98083

**Chicago Comicon
Time: July
Location: Rosemont, IL
Chicago Comicon
6830 Camden Road
Downers Grove, IL 60516
Attn: Nancy Ford

Dallas Fantasy Fair
Time: July
Location: Dallas, TX
Bulldog Productions Inc.
P.O. Box 820488
Dallas, TX 75382

Dragon Con/
Atlanta Comics Expo
Time: July
Location: Atlanta, GA
Atlanta Comics Expo/
Dragon Con
P.O. Box 47696
Atlanta, GA 30362
(404) 925-0115

Heroes Con
Time: June
Location: Charlotte, NC
P.O. Box 9181
Charlotte, NC 28299-9181
(800) 321-4370

Mid Ohio Con
Time: November
Location: Columbus, OH
R.A.P. Productions
P.O. Box 3831
Mansfield, OH 44907
Attn: Roger Price

Motor City Comic Con
Time: March
Location: Novi, MI
Time: October
Location: Dearborn, MI
Motor City Comic Con
19785 W. 12 Mile Rd., Suite 231
Southfield, MI 48076
Attn: Michael Goldman

**NY Comic Book Spectacular
Time: February
Location: New York City, NY
Great Eastern Conventions
225 Everitts Rd.,
Ringoes, NJ 08551
Attn: F. Greenberg

**San Diego Comic Con
Time: August
Location: Sand Diego, CA
San Diego Comic Con
P.O. Box 128458
San Diego, CA 92112

Sun Con
Time: August
Location: Tampa, FL
Borderline Productions
P.O. Box 82254
Tampa, FL 33682
(813) 932-0494

Wonder Con
Time: April
Location: Oakland, CA
WonderCon
P.O. Box 2328
Berkeley, CA 94702
Attn: Bob Borden

World Convention
Time: April
Location: Toronto, Ontario
341 4th St.,
Midland, ON L4R 3V1 Canada
Attn: Maggie Hamilton
(705) 526-6699

Appendix E: Reading List

Reference Books

To follow is a partial list of reference books, available to artists and writers, on the business and legal aspects of your career. Take the time to check out at least one or two of these publications. Many are available in your local library, or through your local bookstore. These are invaluable tools in conducting business with some authority. I have noted with an asterisk (*) the publications I have found most useful as a professional.

*Beverly Hills Bar Association Barristers Committee for the Arts. *The Visual Artist's Manual: A Practical Guide to Your Career*. New York: Doubleday & Company, Inc.

* Crawford, Tad. *The Legal Guide for the Visual Artist: The Professional's Handbook*. New York: Madison Square Press, Inc.

Crawford, Tad. *The Writer's Legal Guide*. New York: Hawthorn/Dutton.

Davidson, Marion and Blue, Martha. *Making It Legal: A Law Primer for the Craftsmaker, Visual Artist and Writer*. New York: McGraw-Hill.

* Graphic Artists Guild. *Pricing and Ethical Guidelines*. New York: Graphic Artists Guild.

Klayman, Toby and Steinberg, Cobett. *The Artist's Survival Manual*. New York: Scribner's

Trade Publications

Below is an alphabetical list of a few established trade publications for the comic industry. As a professional, it is in your best interest to stay apprised of the status of our business. These publications can help provide you with the information you need to be an informed freelancer. Check out one or more of these regularly.

The Comic Buyer's Guide
700 E. State St.,
Iola, WI
54990-0001

Comic Scene
475 Park Ave. S.,
New York, NY 10016

The Comics Journal
7563 Lake City Way
Seattle, WA 98155

Hero Illustrated Magazine
1920 Highland Ave.,
Suite 222
Lombard, IL 60148

Wizard Magazine
151 Wells Ave.,
Congress, NY
10920-2064

Appendix F: Companies and Distributors

Company Contact Information

Here are a partial listing of some of the better known comic companies. If you wish to send a submission, contact the company, using an S.A.S.E., and request a copy of their submission guidelines. Keep this listing as a reference in your business files.

Archie Comic Publications
325 Fayette Ave.,
Mamaroneck, NY 10543
(914) 381-5155
Submissions Editor:
Victor Gorelick

Caliber Press/
Stabur Graphics
11904 Farmington Rd.,
Livonia, MI 48150
(313) 425-7930
Submissions Editor:
Gary Reed

DC Comics, Inc.
1325 Avenue of the
Americas
New York, NY 10019
(212) 636-5400
Call or write for
submissions guidelines

Dark Horse Comics
10956 SE Main St.,
Milwaukie, OR 97222
(503) 652-8815
Submissions Editor:
Edward Martin

Disney Comics
500 S. Buena Vista St.,
Burbank, CA 91521
(818) 567-5739
Write for
submissions guidelines

Eclipse Enterprises
P.O. Box 1099
Forestville, CA 95436
(707) 887-1521
Attn: Submissions Editor

Fantagraphic Books
7563 Lake City Way
Seattle, WA 98155
(206) 524-1967
Submissions Editor:
Tom Verre

Gladstone Publishing
P.O. Box 2079
Prescott, AZ 86302
(602) 776-1300
Submissions Editor:
John Clark

Harris Publications
1115 Broadway, 8th Floor
New York, NY 10010
(212) 807-7100
Submissions Editor:
Meloney Crawford
Chadwick

Harvey Comics
Entertainment
100 Wilshire Blvd.,
Santa Monica, CA 91401
(310) 451-3377
Attn: Submissions Editor

Kitchen Sink Press
320 Riverside Drv.,
Northampton, Ma 01060
(413) 586-9525
Submissions Editor:
Jim Vance

Malibu Entertainment
5321 Sterling Center Drv.,
Westlake Village, CA 9136
(818) 889-9800
Submissions Editor:
Chris Ulm

Marvel/Epic
387 Park Ave. S.,
New York, NY 10016
(212) 696-0808
Submissions Editor:
Glenn Greenberg

Mirage Publishing
P.O. Box 486
Northampton, MA 01061
(413) 586-7066
Submissions Editor:
Dorothy Sloan

Now Comics
60 Revere Drv.,
Northbrook, IL 60062
(708) 205-2950
Submissions Editor:
Barry Peterson

Topps Comics, Inc.
254 36th St.,
Brooklyn, NY 11232
(718) 768-8900
Write for submissions
guidelines

Voyager Comm./Valiant
275 Seventh Ave.,14th Floor
New York, NY 10001
(212) 366-4900
Submissions Editor:
Don Perlin

Viz Communications
P.O. Box 77010
San Francisco, CA 94107
(415) 546-7073
Attn: Submissions Editor

Distributors

Under the auspices of the **Independent Association of Direct Distributors (IADD)** there are a number of large distribution companies with wide ranging business locations. Here is a listing of some of the more noteworthy distributors.

IADD Andromeda Publications Ltd.
2113 Dundas St.W.,
Toronto, Ontario M6R 1X1, Canada
(416) 535-9100

Capital City Distribution, Inc.
2537 Daniels St.,
P.O. Box 8156, Madison, WI 53708
(608) 223-2000

Comics Hawaii Distributors
4420 Lawehana St., #3
Honolulu, HI 96818
(808) 423-0265

Comics Unlimited, Ltd.
101 Ellis Street
Staten Island, NY 10307
(718) 948-2223

Diamond Comic Distributors Inc.
1966 Greenspring Dr.,
Timonium, MD 21093
(410) 560-7100

Friendly Frank's Distribution, Inc.
26055 Dequindre
Madison Heights, MI 48071
(313) 542-2525

Heroes World Distribution Co.
961 Route 10 East
Randolph Business Campus, Bldg. L
Randolph, NJ 07869   (201) 927-4447

Multibook and Periodical, Inc.
4380 S. Service Rd., #117
Burlington, Ontario I7L 5Y6 Canada
(416) 632-5573

Styx International
#10-62 Scurfield Blvd.,
Winnipeg, Manitoba R3Y 1M5 Canada
(204) 489-0580

IADD Administrative Office
2319 California St.,
Berkeley, CA 94703
(510) 644-2038

Appendix G: Submissions Guidelines

To follow are the submissions guidelines from select companies (those who provided the information on request), in alphabetical order. These guidelines were current at press time, and were provided by the publisher or submissions editor.

Use these as a strict guide when sending samples of work to the company.

Caliber Press

At Caliber Press, we try to keep everything as simple as possible, hence this brief letter about our guidelines.

First off, all of our books are strictly paid on a royalty basis, after publication. No page rates, no guarantees, no advances. We have tried different methods and this is what works best for us and our creators. The amount earned is totally dependent on sales, If the book does real well, then the creators do,

All of our books are in black and white. We have done color in the past but are very reluctant to do so now.

Creators maintain complete ownership of their material right from the beginning. We allow creators a great deal of control of the production aspects as well. Our motto is "it's your book" and we truly feel that way.

We don't put together teams on books. We don't match up writers with artists, pencillers with inkers, etc. Proposals should come in with the writer and artist set already. We help you with the lettering, but that too comes from the creator's royalties. We allow creators to do their own covers if they want (virtually all of them do and most do fully painted covers.) We don't have a great need for colorists or cover artists because of this.

What we want to see on a proposal is a rough idea of what the series will look like, where it's going, etc. Art-wise, we need to see at least a few pages of finished continuity so we can have a feel for what it looks like. Scripts should include some dialogue.

Please do not plan on doing a thirty-eight issue epic. Most series will never get that far. Plan on one to six issues. I f you want to continue after that, you can always do another mini-series or continue past the original storyline.

The most important thing to realize is that when working in the independents, you're not likely to make a great deal of money. Some people can make a living from it, but most cannot. Over half of the over 400 comics that come out every month have sales of 3,000 or less. Be realistic in what you're expecting. The best way to approach it is to do the work for the love of it or think of it as a stepping stone to prove yourself, or to do a project that you really want to do regardless of sales. We're not trying to be overly pessimistic here, but comic work is hard and frustrating so be prepared.

To follow is a brief description of the types of material that we are looking for. Please remember that we get hundreds of submissions a month, and that sometimes we can't answer them as fast as we would like. Especially during busy times of the year such as the convention season and major holidays, like Christmas.

We hope that this letter is taken as an honest approach and does not discourage you from submitting to us and other companies. Always make sure that you check out titles from the company that you are submitting to so you are aware of what it is they do. Sometimes a proposal will be rejected because we're already doing something that is very similar. Other times, it is evident that the submitter has no idea about what the company he is submitting to does.

Be sure to enclose an SASE (self-addressed, stamped envelope) if you want a reply. If you want your work returned, send along an envelope large enough, with sufficient postage. If you do not send an SASE, more than likely you won't hear from anyone. After all, if you don't care about your work enough, why should we? Besides, the expense is enormous when added up over the course of a year, and all this for material we don't want to use!

Please don't call us a day or two after you have sent in your proposal. We probably haven't had a chance to look at it yet. We allot certain days for looking through submissions and sometimes our schedule just can't fit it in on a particular week. Do not send submissions Next Day or Federal Express. It's a needless waste of money.

The best way to show your stuff is to send letter sized photocopies. NEVER SEND ORIGINALS!! Do not send scraps of paper that are not connected. If you're sending out a lot of proposals, the best thing to do is invest in a rubber stamp and stamp your name, address and phone number on every page.

What We're Interested In

This may sound flippant, but what we're looking for is material that is good, regardless of subject matter. We do a lot of material that is different from what's out there, but we also do some of the more conventional stuff as well. Caliber is a very diverse company that has done zombies, westerns, war, punk detectives, horror, science fiction, superheroes, slice of life. . . you name it. We've probably done just about every genre.

Things to generally stay away from, unless it's something that's really different and/or good; the science fiction epic, Dungeons and Dragons, westerns (after seven issues, we've just about given up), and funny animals. That's not to say that we won't do something in those areas, but it is much harder to come up with something that is different or unique.

Many of our titles are more sophisticated, yet not adult. Though hard to categorize, titles in this line include Baker Street, Taken Under, Silencers, Warp-Walking, Fringe, Deadworld and Realm.

We also have a few anthologies that accept submissions. Again, these will be based on a pure royalty payment system. Most of the time we would prefer complete stand-alone stories, but we are willing to look at some serials if most of the work is complete.

Whatever route you choose, we wish you the best of luck!

❖

DC Comics Artists' Submissions Guidelines

How To Submit Art To DC Comics

Please send **COPIES** of your work (*never* send original art) along with a self-addressed stamped envelope (SASE) for a reply to: *Submissions Editor, DC Comics Inc., 1325 Avenue of the Americas, New York, NY 10019.* If you don't include a SASE, there's no guarantee you'll receive a reply. DC Comics is not responsible for the safety or return of any original material sent to us.

You'll receive an answer as soon as we evaluate your work. This may take several weeks. **DON'T PHONE** to discuss your submission. We receive dozens, often *hundreds* of submissions a week, and it's impossible for us to follow up on them over the phone.

You may send samples to a DC editor with whom you'd like to work. Some editors will look at work from new artists, but there's no guarantee you'll receive an answer from an editor whose main concern is getting out his or her books.

If your showing your samples to a DC editor at a convention, be sure your presentation is neat and that you follow these guidelines.

Focus your skills on one medium: *pencilling, inking, coloring,* or *lettering.* Bad inking may be misread as bad pencilling, and vice versa.

Pencils: Pencillers should submit 4-6 **COMIC BOOK PAGES** *in order,* showing the progression of a story through a series of pictures. Don't send pinups and paintings. They don't tell us you can tell a comics story.

You can make your own story sequence, visually advancing it from panel to panel and from page to page. Or you can work with a writer friend or rework an existing comics story (without copying the art). Your story should be easy to follow, moving along clearly and dynamically. It's better to draw well in traditional block panels than to try to impress us with sexy pin-ups, overly complex layouts or artistic gimmicks.

Your samples should also show basic drawing abilities. In addition to knowing how to draw heroic action figures and expressive faces, you must be able to draw the average guy on the street, buildings, cars, animals, aliens - **ANYTHING** you may find in a comic book. Your art should display an understanding of perspective and anatomy. You should be able to draw people in different types of clothing and in a variety of poses, from an old woman hunched in a chair to a muscular super-hero punching through a wall. It's best not to limit yourself only to comics as your reference and inspiration. Life-drawing and other general art classes and books are important parts of your education. The *dedicated artist* draws everything he sees, all the time.

Professional comics pencillers work in a 10" X 15" image area on a sheet of Strathmore bristol board that measures 11" X 17". They usually lay out their pages with a lead pencil or non-reproducing blue pencil, and finish their art with a regular pencil. Don't use too hard a pencil (3H or harder) or bear down too hard on the page. This will leave grooves in the paper.

Inks: Inkers should submit photocopies of both your inks *and* the pencils you have inked, so that we can compare the two. We would prefer to see your inks over more than one penciller. If you have noaccess to pencil samples from a friend or professional, write DC's Submissions Editor for photocopies - but you *must* include a self-addressed 9" X 12" envelope with about one dollar in postage. Inking on vellum over the photocopies or on bristol board with a lightbox is probably the easiest way for you to work.

A comic-book inker's job is to add **DEPTH** and **CLARITY** to the pencils without obscuring the penciller's work. This is done by spotting blacks and varying line weight to give the page variety and each panel a three-dimensional feel, *not* by adding unnecessary detail. Objects in the foreground must look and "weigh" differently from objects in the background. You must also know which pencil lines should be omitted in the inking. Storytelling is an important part of the inker's job, and knowing how to draw separates the best inkers from the rest.

Professional comics inkers use artists waterproof india ink, applied with a variety of brushes and pens. Corrections can be made by using one of several types of white paint. Remember, your ink line comes from your brain as much as from the tools you use.

Lettering: Comic-book letterers are responsible for captions, word and thought balloons, balloon shapes, panel borders, title lettering, credits and sound effects. Caption and balloon lettering have to be uniform and easy to read, with slight "breathing room" between letters, words and lines. Too tight letter spacing is hard to read. Story titles and sound effects are usually lettered in a bold, open style.

You can letter your samples onto full-size photocopies of pencilled pages (to secure copies of pencils, see the inking section above), or you may submit 3-4 pages of lettering without art, on 8 ½" X 11" paper. The first method is preferable, since it will show us how your lettering will look on an actual page. Show us *all* types of lettering, from word, thought, electric (jagged edge) and whisper (dotted line) balloons to sound effects.

Comic letterers use an **AMES LETTERING GUIDE** (set from 3 to 3½ on the bottom scale), available at many art supply stores, for spacing and guidelines, and one of a variety of pens - ranging from technical pens to fined-down calligraphy pens - for words. Balloons and ruled panel borders are usually done with a technical or ruling pen.

Coloring: Coloring is an essential part of comics storytelling. The colorist must interpret the art and tell the story through color, adding depth, dramatic effect, mood and most important, **CLARITY**.

The most important characters and objects in each scene and page must be clearly visible to the reader. This often requires coloring people and things differently than they would appear in real life. For example, if a panel features Guy Gardner standing amidst a crowd of dozens of people, Guy could be colored normally, while the others could be colored in a monotone (or a series of related muted tones) to ensure that Guy is clearly seen in the panel.

Colorists can create **MOOD** by taking further liberties with realism. For example, if an artist has drawn a sequence of panels in which Lobo gets angry, a variety of reds - a color often used to convey anger - could be used on both Lob himself and in the background. Blue and green, conversely, establish a placid feel.

Standard comics color guides are coded to match a chart of 124 colors available to us. marking up your guides is an essential part of coloring.

Colorists should submit 4-6 pages of fully colored and coded comic-art photocopies. Colorists work on reduced photocopies (art reduced 64% onto 8½" X 11" paper). If you need photocopies to color, or a copy of the DC coloring chart showing the available colors, send a self-addressed, stamped 9" X 12" envelope to DC's Submissions Editor with your request.

Professional comics colorists use **DR. MARTIN'S DYES**, although colored pencils or markers are also acceptable.

1. *Always send photocopies - never send originals!*
2. *Include your name, address, and phone number on each page of your submission.*
3. *Always include a self-addressed, stamped envelope with your submission, with enough postage for the return of your copies (if you want them back).*
4. *Please handle all submissions-related correspondence with DC through the mail. Don't call.*

❖

Dark Horse Comics

(Please Note: Due to the length of Dark Horse's submissions guidelines, and the space constraints in this book, what follows is a condensed version of their guidelines, highlighting the more important areas. Send directly to Dark Horse Comics for a complete copy.)

It is the policy of Dark Horse Comics to secure a signed Submission Agreement before reviewing series, story and/or character proposals. If your desire is to only submit art or script samples, signing this agreement will not be necessary. If, however, your intention is to submit any original series, story, and/or character material, it will be necessary to submit a signed Submissions Agreement before any Dark Horse personnel will receive your proposal. **Any submissions of original series, story, and/or character material that is not accompanied by a signed Submissions Agreement will be returned or destroyed without review.** A Submissions Agreement can be acquired from the submissions editor with an S.A.S.E. **Also, please note that Dark Horse will not review unsolicited story ideas or proposals pertaining to any licensed property currently published by Dark Horse (Aliens, Predator, Terminator, Indiana Jones, etc.) or any copyrighted or licensed property not owned by the submitter. Such material will be returned or destroyed without review.**

ARTIST GUIDELINES

■ **Never send original art in an unsolicited submissions!** Send photocopies only.

■ **Send full size photocopies.** Make sure they are clean and sharp and easy to "read". Send full size (11 X 17) copies rather than reduced pages.

■ **Put your name, address and phone number on the back of every page.**

■ **Include a self-addressed, stamped envelope.** If you want a response, send a letter sized S.A.S.E. If you want your samples returned - which we would prefer - be sure to enclose a 9 X 12 envelope with adequate postage.

■ **Do not make telephone follow-ups to unsolicited submissions!**

■ **Do not fax art submissions!** The Dark Horse fax machine is for business only!

■ **Think about what you're sending.** There's no need to send an entire twenty-four page story in order to show an editor that you can draw. Save yourself some postage - you can probably get by with sending four or five story pages, provided those pages show a variety of characters and actions.

■ **Pencillers:** If you're sending finished work (fully pencilled and inked), include copies of the original pencilled pages before they were inked. If you want to show full-color work, send color copies (preferred) or slides. You may also include tearsheets of previously printed work.

■ **Inkers:** Include copies of the original pencils before they were inked. Dark Horse will be happy to supply you with photocopies of pencilled pages that you can ink on vellum overlays. Send a 9 X 12 S.A.S.E. posted for three first-class ounces. Be sure to return the pencil copies with your sample inks so that the editor can compare the inks to the pencils.

■ **What to expect:** If an editor has work to offer you, you will get a phone call. If not, you will receive a form rejection letter (without an S.A.S.E., you will probably get no response.) Unfortunately, we don't have time to critique your work.

■ **Technical Specifications:** *Image Area/Original Art, Interior Pages* - 10" wide, 15" tall. Use paper no smaller than 11" wide, 17" tall (industry standard); no larger than 12" wide, 18" tall.

Image Area/Original Art, Double-Page Interior Spreads - 21 1/16" wide, 15" tall.

Image Area/Original Art, Covers - 10" wide, 15 1/8" tall. Allow 1/4" on all sides for trim. Wraparound cover (including front and back cover), 19 3/4" wide, 15 1/8" tall. Remember that on a wraparound cover, the front cover is on the right hand side of the art.

WRITER GUIDELINES

■ Signed Submission Agreement. Before Dark Horse will review an original proposal, a Submissions Agreement must be signed by the proposal's copyright holders and returned to Dark Horse.

■ Cover Letter/Brief Overview. Very important. This is the sales pitch for your proposal. If it doesn't "grab" the editor, the remainder of the proposal will likely not be read. Make sure it is neatly typed - hand-written proposals will not be reviewed - and proofread for spelling and grammar: spelling and grammar errors give the impression that you're not a professional. Be clear, succinct and cover all bases. Your cover letter must include -

    - current addresses and phone numbers of all collaborators, date of submission, working title of story or series you are submitting.

    - introduction with a brief list of published professional credits, if any, including those of any project collaborators.

    - brief story or series overview concentrating on central characters, themes, settings and story situations and including the project's desired format (how many pages, issues, etc.) and the acceptable format alternatives.

■ Complete Synopsis. Being as succinct as possible, this portion must include all important story elements. **Tell the entire story - beginning, middle, and end**. Avoid details that are absolutely not essential. A short-story synopsis should be not longer that one page. Synopsis for a series (limiteed or ongoing) or graphic novel should be no longer than five pages.

■ Full Script. If you are a current published professional, you need not include a script of your proposed project, but you should include published examples of your best recent work with sample script for same. If you are not an established professional, you **must** include a full script for any short story or single-issue submission, or the first issue of any series. There are no exceptions to this rule. **Proposals from unknown writers that do not include scripts will not be reviewed.**

■ Mailing and Packaging Requirements. Send proposals First Class Mail or Air Mail outside the U.S. Do not use Express Mail services. Include a self-addressed, stamped envelope with all submissions. **DO NOT FAX PROPOSALS! Faxed unsolicited submissions will not be reviewed!**

Eclipse Books

(Please Note: Due to the length of Eclipse's submissions guidelines, and the space constraints in this book, what follows is a condensed version of their guidelines, highlighting the more important areas. Send directly to Eclipse Comics for a complete copy.)

Because of the volume of submissions we receive, we may not reply to you for three months or more. Please be patient; we will look at your work and make comments if we can. Don't telephone to monitor the progress of your submissions: the works are reviewed by several of our editors, rather than any one particular person, and it is unlikely we will be able to help you over the phone.

Good Luck!

WHAT WE ARE BUYING

At the present time Eclipse is buying comic book artwork in three categories; pencils, inks and cover paintings. If you intend to both pencil *and* ink, please include samples of the same pages before and after inking.

Writers who send us elaborate plot treatments, lengthy stories or full scripts for series proposals are going to be disappointed by our response: we seldom have time to completely read these materials. Because Eclipse Comics are creator-owned, we do not hire "fill-in" or "guest" writers to script stories about our ongoing characters very often.

WHAT TO SEND US

Artists should send photocopies only, or transparencies of painted cover art, when mailing in submissions. **Never** send original art when applying for a job.

Writers should only send typewritten or computer-printed material. We do not read hand-written manuscripts or faint dot-matrix printouts. Script format should follow that for screenplays. Avoid the use of blocks of all upper-case typing.

A self-addressed, stamped reply envelope must be enclosed if you want a response - and it must bear enough postage for your artwork or manuscript if you want the material returned.

GUIDELINES

Pencil Art: Pencilling samples must be prepared in a size proportionate to the image in the printed comic book (6" X 9".) Originals can be drawn either "twice-up" or "one-and-a-half-up." Draw originals on whatever board or paper suits your needs. We want to see finished pencils, not roughs or thumbnails.

You must supply samples of your continuity work, at least five consecutive pages, to show how you handle movement through time and space in a story framework. We want to see these things in a sample continuity: Normal people of both sexes and several ages in street clothing; a hero or heroine; a villain or villainess; samples of one-point, two-point and three-point perspective; architectural and mechanical backgrounds; vegetation backgrounds; a quadruped (horse, cat, dog, rat, etc.); a room interior containing realistic furniture. No dialogue is necessary. Just let the action carry the story along. Try to show us your very best work. If you feel most comfortable drawing an existing character, we will not be hurt or offended if it's not an Eclipse character.

We would like to see variation in page format from the standard three tiered page of six panels. You should include such things as vertical panels, horizontal panels, inset panels, borderless panels, circular or irregular panels, and occasional two-page spreads to help convey information or stimulate an emotional response from the reader. We also look for variation in camera angle and point-of-view, including distance, mid-range and close-up shots as well as down-shots, up-shots, occasional silhouettes, or fancy lighting effects.

Ink Art: Trying out for a job as an inker can be frustrating if you have no good pencil samples upon which to demonstrate your talent. If you cannot secure full-size 10" X 15" photocopies of pencilled pages by a professional penciller, send us a self-addressed 9" X 12" manila envelope with a dollar postage on it and we will send you pages to work on..

Inkers should use India ink, not markers. Be sure to include before-and-after samples and label the pages clearly to indicate who pencilled them. If you are inking your own pencils, make copies of your continuity portfolio before inking.

Painting: We buy only a limited number of paintings per year, for use as covers. We rarely buy watercolors, however, as they reproduce too faintly to compete on the comics rack. Subject matter is limited at this time to depictions of the characters we publish and for which the regular series artist does not produce every cover.

Written Submissions: A fully scripted comic story should contain a complete panel by panel description (for the artist) of what is viewed, plus all the dialogue, sound effects, and descriptive captions. Think of it as a screenplay.

If you have had any success writing short stories, novels or plays, you should find it easy to adapt your techniques to comics.

❖

Fantagraphics Books

When submitting work to Fantagraphics and Eros, please remember that we are not responsible for unsolicited submissions, therefore we request that only photocopies (or some other cheap reproductions) be submitted. **Do not send originals!** For our convenience, please use standard size (8 1/2" by 11") paper for all copies sent. Please address all submissions to "Submission Editor" and include a self-addressed stamped envelope (or an international reply coupon.)

Please do not sent portfolios or other expensive packages. Likewise, it is unnecessary to send submissions by overnight mail, Federal Express or courier. We judge your work according to its aesthetic merits and our current needs, not according to attractive packaging that costs money.

We publish primarily black and white comics in standard comic format (6 5/8" by 10 1/4".) Submissions should be proportioned to fit this size. We publish 24-32 page one-shots as well as series.

We prefer to see submissions from creators who can supply us with a complete project. We don't have the time or facilities to bring together writers, pencilers, inkers, etc. Please send a script or a rough synopsis of your idea, along with three to five finished pages from the story. This will give us a more accurate idea of your storytelling, drawing and page layout skills than will unrelated drawings or sketches.

Please include a cover letter with your submission. We do not need to see a résumé.

189

It is quite difficult to generalize about the content of **Fantagraphics** comics. Briefly, I will say that we look for comics that are a product of a unique vision. We are not particularly interested in superheroes, sci-fi, fantasy or other well-worn genres. We look for art that is, to a large extent, self-defined or highly stylistic.

Eros submissions don't need to adhere to the thematic restrictions listed above. As a rule, there are no restrictions. We look for submissions of an "adult" nature which may range from soft-core erotica to hard-core pornography. The main consideration here is the quality of the artwork. While style remains a personal choice, sales indicate that realism is preferred by our audience. A consensual and/or humorous approach is encouraged.

❖

Harris Comics

General Tips

Harris publishes the horror titles, Creepy, Vampirella, and Eerie, among others, so we are more interested in material with a horror or suspense angle than traditional superhero fare. However, we will look at superhero material if that's all you have in your portfolio at the moment. Make sure your submissions are neat and legible. Always send copies, **never originals**! A stamped, self-addressed envelope is a good way to ensure a prompt response. However, remember that we get a large volume of submissions and it is not unusual for us to take up to a month to respond. Particularly during convention season. DO NOT CALL THE OFFICE.

Writers

Enclose a brief summary or "springboard" of your story idea. Keep it short - a page or two is ideal. Leave the reader wanting to see more of your story, and stress an angle or hook that will distinguish your story or series idea from any other. **Do not send full scripts.**

Artists

Keep in mind that Vampirella is an attractive female as well as an action heroine. Send examples of your storytelling ability - that is, pages of actual comic book work with panel breakdowns, in addition to pinups. You may write to us for a few pages of sample scripts to use for tryout pencils.

When inking, remember that an inkers job is to enhance rather than obscure the pencils, and to indicate depth and texture on the page.

❖

Harvey Comics

While we are not specifically seeking artists at this time, you are welcome to submit samples of your work.

The primary new comic book material we are currently working with is our Hanna-Barbera line (*Flinstones, Jetsons, Scooby-Doo, Yogi Bear*, and a host of other characters.) We also publish an action-adventure line, featuring *Ultraman*.

Please submit two or three samples of your best work (photocopies only - we cannot be responsible for the safe return of originals!) While we would prefer material similar to the lines we publish, please choose pieces that you feel best represents your talent.

Good Luck!

❖

Malibu Comics

- **A self-addressed stamped envelope is necessary for a response. (Outside U.S., enclose international reply coupons.) We do not respond to submissions without a S.A.S.E.**
- **Please make sure your name and address are on every page of your submission.**
- **No phone calls please**
- **If you would like your entire submission returned you must enclose an envelope large enough and sufficient postage or your submission will be regrettably discarded.**
- **Please allow 10 weeks for response.**

FOR WRITERS:
- All proposals should be no longer than five pages.
- Proposals should be typewritten and double-spaced on 8 1/2" X 11" paper.
- You may submit a comic script involving pre-existing characters or the ones that you have created, but most often our writers are given assignments based on their ability to tell a story in comic book format rather than the specific characters which they may have created or written about.
- New project proposals should include an outline of the series and a brief description of the characters and plot for subsequent issues, as well as the estimated number of issues of the project. Please include samples of any artwork that has been created for the project.

FOR ARTISTS (PENCILLERS, INKERS, LETTERERS AND COLORISTS):
- Please send photocopies of original illustrations, NEVER send originals.
- Include at least one multiple-panel story page and one splash page for consideration.
- Inkers should enclose a copy of the pencil artwork they have inked.
- Colorists/painters should enclose printed samples of their work, color photocopies, or 3" X 5" prints. Please no slides or transparencies because they are difficult to evaluate.
- Letterers, please only send samples of comic book style lettering (dialogue, italic, bold, sound effects, etc.) Do not send samples of any other type of lettering because it cannot show us how you would letter in comic book format. For examples of comic book lettering please look at some of our comics.

❖

Marvel Comics

(Please Note: Due to the length of Marvel's submissions guidelines, and the space constraints in this book, what follows is a condensed version of their guidelines, highlighting the more important areas. Send directly to Marvel Comics for a complete copy.)

WHO TO SUBMIT TO

Address your submissions to "Submissions Editor." You may submit work to any other editor, but due to their heavy workloads, we cannot guarantee when (or even if) you'll get a response from any of them. The Submissions Editor will send you a response within four to six weeks, and will see to it that the rest of the editorial staff sees your work if it meets Marvel's current editorial needs.

NEW CHARACTERS

Do not submit new character designs or proposals for new books to us. No one in the business makes a living just selling character ideas. Marvel characters are created and designed by the writers and artists of the books they appear in. Unless there is a contest, most editors won;t even look at new character submissions for fear it might be similar to something already in development.

IMPORTANT

Always enclose a self-addressed, stamped envelope large enough to return your submission and our S.A.S.E. response. Make certain your name and address are on every single page of your submission. Submissions without return postage will be regrettably discarded.

WRITERS

Before submitting material to a Marvel editor, call or write first to see if they are receptive to reading potential inventory material. The sheer volume of submissions Marvel gets these days has increased to the point that we can no longer devote any time to reading unsolicited material and will return all such material unread. Assuming an editor gives you the go-ahead, submit a synopsis of your plot idea no more than one page (or one paragraph) long. Editors have no time to read fully fleshed-out stories. If they like the synopsis, they give the go-ahead to submit the completed story and things proceed from there. Once you submit material, don't expect an immediate reply because editors usually give the lowest priority to submission answering (due to the fact that getting their books to the printer has to be the highest priority and takes most of their time.)

You can write a story about any Marvel character who has his or her own book, but if you want the story to be seriously considered for publication, you will write stories for titles that use inventory material on occasion. If a book has been written by the same person for several years, it is not likely that the editor of that title buys many inventory stories. Never submit stories featuring characters that do not have their own books. New books or limited series are never created just so we can buy a novice writer's story.

Submit short plot synopses only, double spaced, no more than one page in length; establish the characters and the situation, introduce the conflict, and show the resolution. You may submit more than one plot synopsis at a time, but a dozen may tax an editor's patience. Do not submit detailed plots or full scripts until you have an editor's approval of your premise or rough synopsis.

Plot submissions should feature Marvel characters. We cannot buy any stories about characters Marvel doesn't own, nor can we judge how well you handle

Marvel characters if you use characters that belong to someone else. Creating incidental characters or villains for your story is okay, but be aware that if we buy the story using them, Marvel will own those characters.

A regular monthly Marvel comic is 22 pages in length. Submit single-part stories that are self-contained. Never submit multi-part stories. Inventory stories requiring more than 22 pages or any other special format are never purchased from novice writers. Inventory plots for 8-page stories are viable as well.

ARTISTS

Please submit photocopies only - never originals. Submit comic book story pages only. No other kind of artwork will tell us how you work in the comic medium. Submit samples showing your ability at one discipline only. If you're trying to sell yourself as a penciller, and your pages are inked and lettered too, flaws in your inking or lettering may influence our opinion of your pencilling.

Pencillers: We are looking for three main things in all pencil art samples -

1) Your ability to tell a story through pictures

Your samples should demonstrate your ability to tell a story in a sequence of pictures. Draw four to six pages of a story, breaking down each scene into the optimal number of panels to tell the story visually. Do not send pin-up shots, since they do not show any storytelling ability.

2) Your ability to draw.

Your samples should demonstrate good drawing - a knowledge of anatomy, perspective, convincing environments and backgrounds. Beyond that, your samples should show your command of the human figure in a variety of activities, everything from a simple conversation to a frenetic fight scene. Concentrate on what's inside the panel borders, not the overall design of the page. Complicated page lay-outs, figures jutting through the borders, and other visual gimmicks usually hurt the storytelling.

3) Your ability to draw marvel characters who look and act right.

Your samples should show your visual understanding of Marvel heroes: not simply how they look, but how they stand or move, their size compared to their surroundings, how they force other characters to react or relate to them. Send samples of Marvel characters only, since we're experts on them and know how they should look and act.

Professional pencillers work on a 10" by 15" area floating within an 11" by 17" artboard.

Letterers: Send samples which demonstrate your skills at regular, bold and italic lettering, dialogue and thought balloon shapes, captions, sound effects, and panel bordering. We prefer balloon shapes that are rounded and regular, not scalloped and irregular and odd-shaped. We prefer sound effects that are open and not "hairy", illegible or overly obtrusive. Submit three to four pages of samples.

Inkers: We recommend that you submit samples of artwork inked over someone else's pencils rather than your own. (Otherwise, it is difficult to separate problems in your pencil drawing and problems in your ink rendering.)

Pencilled art should be enhanced, not diminished. Be sure to submit a photocopy of the pencil art you worked from so that we can see what your had to work with. Submit four to six pages of inked artwork, preferably from several different pencillers so we can see how you handle a variety of pencil styles. Avoid using zip-a-tone in your samples since it will only obscure your linework.

Colorists: There are only 64 colors that can be used in standard newsprint comics. Keep your color schemes simple. Submit six to ten colored pages, preferably in sequence. Color over photocopies of inked pages at the same size as the printed comic page: 5 7/8" by 9" (This is a 60% reduction from the original artwork size of 10" by 15 1/4".)

SAMPLES

If you can find no one else's pencils to ink, or you need samples to color, write to the Submissions Editor for photocopies or professional work. Include return postage of at least $1.00 for pencil photocopies or 60 cents for photocopies to color. You must also include a self-addressed, stamped envelope large enough to hold the photocopies (9" X 12".) Canadian and foreign - send international postal reply coupons only. We annot use foreign stamps, money or postal orders!

We hope this answers all your questions. Good luck in future endeavors!

❖

Mirage Publishing

At this time, Mirage Publishing does not have a formal set of written submission guidelines. Additionally, there are no work assignments available at this time. While not actively seeking unsolicited submissions, they will accept material to place on file.

Guideline

Following industry standards we usually require three to four pages of your work.

· If you are a *writer*, then a brief story breakdown and sample of your writing.

· If you are a *penciller*, examples of your art in comic book layout form.

· If you are an *inker*, pencil pages plus the same pencilled pages with your inks.

· As always, **please send photocopies only**. We cannot be responsible for any original art and/or manuscripts sent to us.

❖

Now Comics

Three things for everyone to remember are : One, please do not call to inquire about your submission. As soon as it can be reviewed thoroughly we will either write or phone you. Two, send no originals. Send copies only, as submissions are not returnable. Three, please include copies of any published samples you may have when you send your materials.

WRITERS

No more T*wilight Zone*s are needed! If you have an idea for another Now title, send a one- or two-page typed synopsis explaining the plot development and the conclusion. Although we have regular writers for all our series and miniseries, we occasionally need a "fill in" issue to give the regulars a break.

For a new series idea, I need to see a one-page, typed explanation of the concept, descriptions of the characters, and any plot outlines you have developed.

All writers, please send a short, non-returnable script sample as well, so that I may familiarize myself with your style of writing. This also ensures that I have a good example of your work on file when considering writers for upcoming projects.

LETTERERS

Please send full-sized copies of your hand-written samples done on two-ply Bristol with alphabets and numbers in regular, italic, and boldface; sample captions; sample word, electric, and whisper balloons; and a variety of sound effects. Also, include any published samples you may have.

PENCILLERS

Send full-sized copies of at least two pencilled pages done on two-ply Bristol with a 10" X 15" live area. Include copies of the script pages from which you worked.

We are looking for good anatomy, realistic human figures, and dramatic story-telling with a good sense of action. The ability to render cars and detailed backgrounds is also a plus. Very tight, finished pencils are preferred. Any published samples are also welcome.

INKERS

Please send full-sized copies of at least two inked pages along with copies of the pencils from which you worked. Don't ink your own pencils; we can best judge your work by inks done on another artist's pencils. Photocopies of pencilled pages can be obtained from artists at comic conventions.

We are looking for a strong, confident line with variance in the line weight. Don't be afraid to lay down a lot of ink. Include any published samples you have as well.

PAINTERS

Please send color copies, slides or photos of your work. Specify if you do covers, interiors or both. Also include any other samples that you feel are good examples of your work. Remember that submissions are not returnable.

COLORISTS

As with painters, please send color copies, slides, or photos of your original colored pages. Also, let us know if these are airbrushed, hand painted or both. If you have extra copies of any comics that you have worked on, send them along as non-returnable samples.

EVERYONE: Writers and letterers, send your samples to Geoff White. Pencillers, inkers, painters and colorists address your samples to Barry Petersen.

Along with the specific samples as outlined, send any published or other samples that may aid in our decision. Also, write a cover letter outlining any pertinent background information and additional information you would like to bring to our attention. Artists should mention how much time was spent on each page. Keep in mind that submissions are not returnable, so send copies only.

Remember to put your name, address and phone number on all pages of your submission package. We receive many samples, but we will try to respond in a timely manner. Include a self-addressed, stamped envelope for a quicker reply. No calls, please. We look forward to receiving your samples.

Valiant Comics

Artist and Writer's Submission Guidelines

■ Inlcude a self-addressed, stamped envelope. This allows us to respond in a timely fashion - within one to two months of receipt of your submission. Work will not be returned nor will a reply be given if a self-addressed, stamped envelope is not enclosed.

■ Please do not submit creator-owned properties. We are concentrating on our existing universe. At this time we are NOT looking for original work. Please submit material that pertains directly to the Valiant universe.

■ Direct your writing submissions to the attention of Kevin VanHook, Submissions Editor. We will look at only typed or printed material. Make sure what you submit is as professional as your intentions. Grammar and spelling errors distract the reader from the content of your work.

■ Art submissions should be directed to Don Perlin, Art Submissions Editor.

■ Do not send original work; photocopies are fine. Please make sure to put your name and address on every page.

■ Please don't telephone to monitor the progress of your submission. *All* work will be evaluated.

Thank you for thinking of *Valiant.*

❖

Appendix H: Agents

To follow are answers to basic questions about agent representation in the comic industry, provided by Mike Friedrich of *Star*Reach Productions*. If you want more information send your request, and a self-addressed, stamped envelope, to *Star*Reach Productions, P.O. Box 2328, Berkeley, CA 94702.*

Question: What are the responsibilities of a comic agent?

As comic agents, the way we approach it is that we consider ourselves a marketing firm. This involves keeping our eye on the long-term goals of our clients. We build networks and relationships with their fellow professionals and editors, from which interesting work, and a good life, flows. It's important for them to recognize where they want to be in the future so that they can do the kinds of work they're interested in and get the kinds of rewards they wish to have. We feel our primary responsibility is to *know* our clients. We work with them to get to know their goals, come up with a plan to help them achieve those goals and then help to execute that plan.

We also help newcomers learn who to avoid. A newcomer needs to know which editors will say one thing, then change their minds later without telling you. They need to know which publisher will hire you one day, then refuse to pay you the next day. You can avoid a lot of heartache by having someone with that knowledge and experience guiding you through those pitfalls.

Question: Would you say that agent representation was more beneficial than self-representation?

I don't think we'd be in business if we didn't believe we were of value to our clients. Where that value comes in is in acting as an objective voice. Also, in the broadest sense, being a time-saver.

It can take a long time for anyone who's trying to break into the business to know everybody to whom you could submit your work. We are currently in regular contact with over a hundred editors. For an established professional, it's getting to know who the right person is to submit your work to at this time - or the right artist or writer to hook up with to do a project. So it's the quality of networking that we help with for an established professional. And all of that is time-saving.

It's not that we do magic here. Anyone can spend time to learn who the one hundred editors are, but why? Anyone could spend the time calling dozens and dozens of people to find the best person with whom to work, but why? Why do that when someone else can use their expertise and knowledge to do it. We also get into the more complicated business issues of negotiating contracts and structuring deals before there are even contracts. A lot of professionals choose not to even get involved in that.

Question: Would any type of agent be suitable for representation in comics?

I think that representation, in general, is an idea that all professionals should consider. There are agents that are specifically book and film agents who have represented their clients in the comic market. But there are some benefits to working with an agent that has specific industry knowledge - they don't need to spend your time learning what this particular field is all about. There are different requirements editors in comics than there are in other fields. Comics also has a different rhythm of production and marketing than other fields. This affects the position of the talent in the comic market. It's useful to have someone with knowledge of the industry to help out the writer or artist.

Question: How would a professional go about locating an agent?

Almost all the people who come to us have come through referral by our clients. On this end, we screen the people who call us requesting representation, because we know what kinds of clients we are going to be best able to serve. So, we're not in a position to help out everyone who requests representation.

We also meet people when we attend major conventions, where we usually set up a booth. Other agents may just wander the floor. But our booth serves a multitude of purposes, an important one of which is to create interactivity between our clients.

Question: What does a comic agent receive as compensation for their services?

The way we operate is that we work on a commission basis. It will range between ten and fifteen percent of what someone is earning, depending on the circumstances. We exclusively represent all our clients' work within the comics field. Work flows from the relationships that you have. Our job is to help energize those relationships which lead to work. For that reason, we represent our clients' work whether it is actively secured by us, or indirectly affected by our advice and activity.

Question: Would you recommend a comic agent for a newcomer trying to 'break into' the comic business?

'Newcomer' has a very broad definition. We have not been very successful in representing new writers. We have been quite successful representing new artists - specifically pencillers. We have also been moderately successful representing new inkers.

The problem with new writers, is that since this is a visual medium, no editor seems to have time to do anything but look at the pictures, and few editors have any time to read a new writer's ideas. The advice we usually give to writers is, "Find an artist." The best way to get your writing read is to find somebody to draw it. In the past, we have matched new writers we represent with an artist. We currently represent a couple of new writers, but we have to be a lot more selective in making that choice than we do with a new artist in the field.

Writers we have been able to best represent are those that already have their 'foot in the door' (have some published credit) but need our help to open it further. We can also better represent people who already have some editorial or artist connections, as this gives us something to build on.

As a writer, the trick is to get an editor to spend time on, and pay attention to, your story pitches. Getting their time is always tough. The best way for that to happen is to use anything you might already have in print, or take advantage of a recommendation by an artist already working with that editor. In that respect, we connect our clients with each other. We spend a lot of time networking our clients with each other.

Appendix J: A Guide To Self-Publishing

The following is a brief guide to self publishing compiled by Gary Reed, Publisher of Caliber Press. This is meant to be an introduction to self-publishing, and is not intended to be a complete guide. The author assumes no obligations, liabilities, etc.

In talking with creators about self-publishing, the primary factor for not having self-published seems to be intimidation by the process. However, the only secret involved is knowing what is required. Hopefully this guide will answer most of your basic questions about the process. I will address these as generalities, but remember to keep in mind, exceptions do occur.

The Big Picture

When you decide to publish a comic, you must remember to plan ahead, usually at least four months prior to when the book actually comes out. The process of offering your book to the comic marketplace is generally called soliciting orders. You will inform the distributors of your title, they in turn will put it in their ordering catalog and distribute these catalogs to the comic retailers around the country. The retailers will place their orders with the distributor who will then total all the orders. Once a total has been determined, the distributor will send you a purchase order which details the number of copies of your book they want, where to ship them, and confirmation of the price they will pay. This will indicate how many copies you have pre-sold and you can use this information to set your print run. Although first impressions make this seem an efficient system, there are problems. The retailer is taking a risk when ordering your book, because they must essentially guess how well the comic will sell, four months ahead of time. Remember, in the direct market the retailer is bound to accept all copies he orders and cannot return them. If he doesn't sell them, he's stuck with them. This is why many retailers don't bother with smaller press titles.

The Basics

Your comic should be traditional comic size (6 3/4" X 10") as deviations from this size will hurt your potential sales quite a bit. Most stores have display space designed for comic size and odd sizes will not fit. Many stores will not even carry digest or magazine size, especially small press titles. There is no rule, but it can be a strike against you if your book is not comic size.

The average black and white comic runs 32 pages and has a cover price of $2.50. Some publishers feel a reduced cover price will encourage sales but in small press comics this is not, typically, the case. Retailers are either interested, or they're not. Over-pricing, however, will turn-off many interested retailers. You can increase the cover price as your page count increases. Most publishers also include the Canadian price on their titles. This runs anywhere from 20-30% more. Check some other titles on the stand or find out what the current exchange rate is prior to establishing a Canadian price.

On all correspondence and advertising, make sure everything is typeset. Hand-written ads flash a warning sign to retailers that the comic itself is likely to be low quality. Make sure you have someone proof read everything, including your comic. Although the handwritten aspect is sometimes part of the appeal, try to make your comic look as professional as possible.

Production

Original art can be any size, but should be proportional to 6 3/4" X 10". Most artists use 10" X 15" or 11" X 17". There are some suppliers who solicit comic art paper in the distributor catalogs or advertise in the Comic Buyer's Guide. The type of paper is mostly a matter of personal choice, but quality will dictate how well the work reproduces or holds ink.

Having a printer cut in half tones (B&W shots of color work) or screens into your line work can be time consuming and costly. It's best to do it yourself. If you have a lot of half-tones to be cut in, get them all shot separately and then cut them into your line work. If you use zip-a-tone, be sure to watch how you lay it over other zip to avoid moray patterns.

Printers use comic flats in pagenations of 8 or 16, so your book should always be in those increments (16,24,32,40,48, etc.) Some printers who use 16 page plates will charge your for the 16 plate even if you only use 8 pages, so sometimes it can cost the same to print a 40 or 48 page book. Covers (inside and outside) are printed separately, and are not part of the page count. Sometimes to save money, a publisher will print no additional cover and use the first page as the cover piece (called self cover) but reproduction and quality are usually terrible. It is best to run a separate cover.

A full color cover will have to be separated. This is a process where colored art is separated into four negatives; red, yellow, blue and black. Some printers will cut flat colors onto black and white art, but if your art requires a lot of colors cut in, it may end up costing the same as a separation. These can run from $100-$200. Most printers can handle the separations for you and then they will also cut in the logo, prices and any additional type on the cover for a flat fee of about $125-$200. For full color covers that need separations (99% of covers), the printer can use almost any type of art. If it is done on inflexible board, a transparency will be required first. This can add up to $100 to the cost. But, if the board can be "peeled" - the top layer removed - the printer will be able to wrap it around the scanner drum for separation. Don't forget that although a separate piece of color art for the back cover will make the comic look even better, it will cause an additional separation charge.

Logos and other cover type are usually sent separately from the cover and just have to be in black and white. Most people typeset it but your printer can also do it (you indicate the color) for a small charge. Most printers have no trouble following the general guidelines for color percentages. For instance, the popular deep red color is 100% Red with 100% Yellow. Note that 100% Red is actually magenta, which is vastly different from your typical red. Pick up a color guide book or see if your printer has a chart or uses other color processes.

The most important thing about dealing with printers is to remember that they aren't mind-readers. Also, although your book may be a labor of love to you, to the printer it is simply one more production job they must fit into their schedule. Most printers who print small print runs have a great deal of other work, and to them comics are a low priority. If you impose on them too much, they may decide the job isn't worth the trouble. Always give them a full mock-up copy of both the book and the cover. Remember, for a printer there is no "typical" comic book. Spell everything out!

Printers

At the end of this guide are a list of printers. You can call or write for prices, but in general the approximate costs are as follows: 3,000 = 23 cents, 2,000 = 40-45 cents, 1,000 = 60-75 cents. You will also have to pay for separations, additional camera work, and any shipping costs if the printer ships your books. This can amount to another couple hundred dollars. So, if you have orders for 1,600 copies and you print 2,000, here's a rough breakdown of your costs at 45 cents each: Adding shipping ($150.00) and separations ($150.00) to the actual printing cost ($900.00) will give you a grand total of $1,200.00. If you sold 1,600 copies (cost to distributor at .875) then you have $1,400.00 in sales, less the cost of printing, for a profit of $200.00.

When you get your orders from the distributors, they will tell you exactly where to send the books. If the orders are too low to a specific warehouse (under 25 copies), it is probably cheaper for you to ship them direct yourself. Check with your printer as they may have specific arrangements with certain distributors.

Solicitations

When your comic is basically finished, you are ready to solicit the title with the distributors (see Appendix G for a list of distributors.) They should all be sent the same information; cover price, number of pages, content rating (ie., Mature), number of issues planned, black&white v. color, creators involved, exact title and issue number. and a one paragraph general description. Also list your company name (if different), and an address and phone number where they can contact you. Also include a fax number if you have one.

You must also tell the distributors the price at which they are buying the book. The general rule is a publisher gives the distributor a 60-65% discount off the cover price. Therefore, at a 65% discount, the distributor pays .875 of the cover price for each copy. They in turn offer it to retailers at a discount of 30-55% depending on the retailer order volume. So, the retailer makes a profit of 30-55%, the distributor makes a profit of 10-35% and you as publisher make a profit of 35%, which has to go to talent, production, advertising and printing of the comic. Remember though, that as the "front man," the retailer is taking the largest chance because he is the only one that has no idea how many copies he should sell. The distributor will usually make the lower end, as most of the accounts that carry smaller press are large retail outlets who will get the distributors top discount of 50-55%. A store has to sell at least half of their order just to break even on the title and if they discount, they will have to sell up to 75% of the order to break even.

A full mock-up of the comic is required by many distributors. It should be a comic or letter size copy. At the very least, you should include some art examples, especially the cover. Do not send originals or color. A black & white stat or half-tone in a 2" X 3" (or proportional) size is recommended.

Starting The Process

It is important to note that you have to work far in advance to allow for the distributors to solicit the book, and orders to be returned. Here is an example of a rough schedule for an *August* release book:

April 15 - Send all information, mock-up, discount structure, etc. to distributors.
May 8 - Solicitation flyers due to distributors (see Advertising section and Distributor Flyer Count below)
June 1 - Retailers receive catalogs from distributors
June 20 - Retailers place orders with distributors
July 15 - Distributors send out purchase orders to publishers.

As you can see, orders don't come in until about two weeks before the comic is due to ship - and those are the early ones. Some distributors don't get their orders in until the same month that the book is shipping. Since most smaller press printers take 4-8 weeks to print, it is very hard for small publishers to get their books out in the exact month. Distributors recognize this problem, and in many cases allow some leeway. But, if it is too late, they will only take the book on a returnable basis or not at all. Capital City has instituted a new policy of charging $500 for a title that is solicited then cancelled, and $750 for a re-solicitation. On comics taken on a returnable basis, they will take 20% of the retail price.

Advertising

Advertising is an aid, not a guarantee. Everyone wants to advertise and it's hard to argue that it won't help your book. Conversely, it may not help as much as you would expect. If you have a book that will appeal to a lot of people, advertising makes them aware of it. If your book will have only limited appeal, it won't matter how much you spend in advertising. At the very least, you should send out solicitation flyers to the distributors. They will send one to each retailer who receives their catalog. Currently, publishers must provide about 12,000 flyers to distributors. (see the list on numbers to send to each distributor, at the end of this guide.) Flyers should be roughly letter sized. Diamond and Capital City currently charge $150.00 for each flyer, to distribute the flyers. The other distributors do not charge.

One avenue available to all publishers is advertising in the distribution catalogs. This can be very effective as retailers will be looking at your ad as they are getting ready to order titles. Here's an example of this type of advertising (I'll use Diamond Distribution for this example): A full page ad costs about $900.00 and must be camera-ready. If you are selling your book wholesale for 87 cents, and you deduct printing/shipping costs of 50 cents, the cleared profit on your book will be 37 cents. You must sell 2,432 comics just to cover the cost of the Diamond catalog ad alone. If you believe that by advertising, that comic will generate sales in excess of 2,432 copies then, go for it. Other distributors do charge less, but your return is also lesser, as they do not have the same degree of exposure as Diamond. Your solicitation flyers will run about 4 cents each if you run 10,000 copies, one-sided - that equals $400.00. Add on the $300.00 flyer charge for Diamond and Capital, plus about $20.00 for shipping the flyers, and your total cost for flyers will be about $720.00. That means, after deducting the cost of printing/shipping/separations and such, you have to sell about 1,000-1,900 copies just to cover the bare minimum.

Other sources of advertising include magazines and periodicals. Their rates range from $180.00 (Comic Journal) to over $3,000.00 for a full page ad. Gear your advertising to the audience who follows the various periodicals - you probably shouldn't send a superhero title ad to the Comics Journal. But be sure to follow their shipping dates.

Some people follow the philosophy that you should advertise right before the title comes out, as it will generate interest. This may be true, but if it does work, it won't help retailers who ordered your book a couple of months back. Now they will have to re-order the title to get additional copies, and unfortunately this appears to be one of the weakest areas of the distribution system. Also, did you print enough copies to cover re-orders? If not, you may have to go back to print. If you do, you cannot send out second printings in lieu of first printings. You will have to solicit the title all over again, as a new (second printing) title.

Most publishers feel the best time to advertise is when the retailers are ordering the comics. You must sell to the retailers first!

Some Harsh Realities

This information is not intended to scare or intimidate you, but to apprise you of the realities of the situation before you get involved. Comics is a tough business, and you must approach it with your eyes open.

There are reportedly between 5,000 and 7,000 comic stores in North America. Of those, only 800 to 1,500 will likely even consider carrying a small-press independent. Of those, 300-400 will probably account for 80-90% of your orders. If you know who those stores are, target them specifically!

Each month there are 500-600 titles offered to retailers. Marvel, DC Comics, valiant, Image, Dark Horse and Malibu account for about 200 titles. This means you are competing with another 300-400 comics every month but retailers only spend 15-20% of their money on the more than 100 other smaller publishers. These include Topps, Caliber, Fantagraphics, Kitchen Sink, Millenium, Archie, Harvey, Eclipse, Viz, and Revolutionary. That's a lot of scrambling for that 15-20%!

Distributors and the fan press will not give you a lot of attention until you prove that you will produce a good book, and can deliver it on time. No one is going to spend any energy on "maybe's."

It may seem like a good idea to offer your comics directly to the retailers, but many distributors will not carry your title if you do that. They usually have no problem with this practice on re-orders, but it is frowned on for initial solicitations.

Remember that in addition to soliciting your title, you have other office time involved in invoicing your comic, arranging for re-orders, dealing with shortages and damaged shipments, fulfilling mail orders (if you take them), filling the copyright papers, shipping, etc.

Don't count too much on re-orders for small-press books. That's not to say that it won't happen, it's just rare. Also, watch out for over-printing. That's how most independent publishers go out of business - by over-estimating the demand for their comic

Your primary purpose as a self-publisher should be to get your book out on time, not generate large amounts of money. It may happen, but if you don't go in expecting it, you won't be disappointed. many people have launched successful books and are doing well, so it is not impossible - just difficult.

Self-publishing will guarantee you total control in presentation, printing and promotion. But it has to be satisfying in its own right if you want to do it. Good luck!

Printers

ASSOCIATED PRINTERS
402 Hill Ave.,
Grafton, ND 58237
(701) 352-0640
Print many independents, higher print minimums and very good quality

BRENNER PRINTING
106 Braniff
San Antonio, TX 78216
(512) 349-4024
Print majority of independents, including Caliber books. Good prices.

PRENEY PRINT & LITHO
2714 Dougall Ave.,
Windsor, Ontario
N9E 1R9 Canada
Printer of Cerebus, some Caliber books and many independents.

Distribution Flyer Requirements

(See Appendix G for complete distributor contact information)

Andromeda Publishing
200 flyers

Friendly Frank's
600 flyers

Capital City Distribution
4000 flyers

Heroes World
800 flyers

Comics Hawaii
100 flyers

Multibook and Periodical
200 flyers

Comics Unlimited
600 flyers

Styx International
200 flyers

Diamond Distribution
4500 flyers

Appendix K: Legal Guide to Getting Your Money

The Eclectus Ltd. Guide To
Getting Your Money From A Publisher
by Rod Underhill, Attorney at Law and Protem Small Claims Court Judge

STEP ONE: THE DEMAND LETTER

Send a polite, but clear, letter demanding that you be paid at once the money that is owed to you. Do not threaten in any manner, other than to state that you will proceed to Court by a specified date if payment is not received.

STEP TWO: SMALL CLAIMS COURT

If your demand letter hasn't resulted in payment, this is where you should probably head. Designed to allow laymen to proceed without an attorney, Small Claims Court has the ability to hear cases concerning up to $5,000.00 in value, in California. Check your local court for the money limits in your area. If you are owed more than the jurisdictional limit of your Small Claims Court, you should probably consult an attorney.

STEP THREE: IS THE BUSINESS THAT YOU WISH TO SUE A CORPORATION?

Special rules apply if your 'target' is a corporation. Call the "SECRETARY OF CORPORATIONS", a State Agency usually, and ask them if "Acme" (or whatever) is registered as a corporation. If so, ask them: "Who is named to receive service of process?" That's who you serve your Small Claims Court lawsuit on!

What if the Secretary of Corporations says "Never heard of them."?

1. They may be listed under a different name. For example, the now defunct Pacific Comics was actually the unofficial name of 'Blue Dolphin, Inc.' Here's a suggestion: call or write the FICTITIOUS NAME STATEMENT division of the municipal government of the area that the Business operates out of. They will usually have the real name of the Business listed along with their DBA (doing business as) name. Armed with the real Corporation name, you can call the Secretary of Corporations and get the data you need so you can sue the right guy.

2. The Business may not be a Corporation, after all. If not, sue the 'owner.' You might have to ask around, if you're not sure. Somebody will probably know. Most Businesses that you will deal with will be Corporations, however.

STEP FOUR: ONCE YOU ARE AT SMALL CLAIMS COURT

It is advisable to write a short, typed, statement explaining the basic facts of the dispute. Tell the Judge that you want to "file a trial brief in lieu of an opening statement." This will allow you to get all the facts to the Judge without him cutting you off, or you getting too nervous. Be polite, no matter how much of a jerk the other guy is. Show the Judge any documents (contracts and so on) that you might have to support your claim.

STEP FIVE: ONCE YOU WIN YOUR CASE

The Court will give you a paper called the "Judgment." If you're lucky, the Business will pay you at once. If not, you will have to "collect" upon the Judgment. Go and see your local Marshal, who can help you attach bank accounts, or seek out further collection advice from your local Law Library. You can even assign the debt to Collection Agencies, although they will take a hefty piece.

WARNING!

BE VERY CAREFUL REGARDING DOING BUSINESS WITH PEOPLE OUTSIDE OF YOUR OWN STATE. IT MAKES SUING THEM ALMOST IMPOSSIBLE. ALSO, A BUSINESS MAY BE REGISTERED AS A CORPORATION IN ONE STATE, BUT NOT ANOTHER, SO CALL THE SECRETARY OF CORPORATIONS IN THE STATE THE BUSINESS OPERATES OUT OF. TRY TO SUE IN YOUR OWN STATE IF THE BUSINESS OPERATES IN ANY WAY IN YOUR OWN STATE (FOR EXAMPLE, IF THE BUSINESS DISTRIBUTES IT'S PRODUCT IN YOUR STATE, YOU MAY HAVE ENOUGH OF A 'NEXUS' TO SUE.)

SOME MORE TIPS

1. Try and get at least 50% of your money "up front." You'll do a lot better, that way. After all, you can't buy food on promises, can you?

2. Make sure you have some type of written agreement. It doesn't have to be a formal contract, but a letter signed by you and the business should suffice, if the basic terms are included; how much, when it will be paid, how much up front, and other specifics. Think it out carefully. Remember to consider who will own the copyright, who will own the character, etc. A written agreement will keep everyone a bit more honest.

3. Don't be bullied. Stand your ground, and sue if you don't get paid. Most bad guys will fold in Court. If they show up in Court, that's a good sign, as it usually means that they will pay you if they lose.

4. Don't be afraid to go to your local Law Library. Ask the Law Librarian to point out any books on Small Claims Court Procedure. Also, some Small Claims Courts have attorneys who will help you file your case, for free. Ask!

GOOD LUCK!

Contributor Biographies

Terry Beatty has been a writer, penciller and inker in comics since 1979. Terry is recognized for his work on **Ms. Tree**, **Wild Dog**, and **Guy Gardner** (inker) all (most recently) from DC Comics, **Elfquest: New Blood** stories (writer) from Warp Graphics, **Johnny Dynamite: Underworld** (artist) from Dark Horse, and **Scary Monsters Magazine** (cover artist) from Dennis Druktenis Publishing. Terry lives in Muscatine, Iowa with his wife, talented writer Wendi Lee, and exclaims with panic in his voice, "I need more toys!"

Tim Bradstreet has been an inker in comics since 1990. Prior to that he spent five years establishing himself as an illustrator in the gaming industry. Tim says, "I'm like the Dave Dorman of the gaming industry for interior art!" His comic credits include **Dragon Chiang** for Eclipse Comics, **Red Sky Diaries**, **Aliens: Music of the Spheres** and **X** for Dark Horse Comics, in addition to his **Age of Desire** graphic novel. Tim lives in his new house in Bloomington, Illinois.

Bruce Bristow has been in the comic business since 1983. He is currently the Vice President of Sales and Marketing for DC Comics, and has built up the DC Comics Sales and Marketing Department over the last eleven years. "I'm probably most proud of the things we've done that have professionalized the industry, brought comics into other distribution channels and increased the audience." Bruce is a dedicated - if occasionally injured - runner who always tries to make time during his convention travel to run with a few other industry professionals. Bruce lives in Princeton, New Jersey and commutes daily to Manhattan.

Mike Carlin has been involved with comics as a professional since 1980, writing and drawing for **Crazy Magazine**. He started out at the High School of Art and Design and was an intern at DC Comics in 1974 as part of the high school program. He then went to the School of Visual Arts, where he studied with Harvey Kurtzman and Will Eisner. "Eisner gave me my first paying work - a dollar a joke for some joke books he was illustrating and putting together. I made up a lot of jokes - I made a lot of money on that. Thank you, Will!" In 1982 Mike became an assistant editor at Marvel comics where he also did some writing. Shortly thereafter he joined the ranks of DC Comics, where he is currently an executive editor overseeing most of the superhero titles. Mike is also the editor for all the **Superman** books. "My advice to everyone is: Shave it off!" Mike lives in the New York area, where his shoe size remains a 9 1/2 but his waist size is always changing.

Richard Case has worked in comics since 1987. Richard's work includes an extended run as penciller on the popular **Doom Patrol** series from DC Comics, **Dr. Strange** and **Dark Hold** from Marvel Comics, pencilling and inking **Ghost Dancing** for DC Comic's Vertigo line, and a turn at writing, in addition to drawing, **Annie Ammo** for Axis. He says happily, "Remember, there is no more glamorous job than a career in comics." Richard lives in Mebane, North Carolina.

Paul Chadwick began his professional comic career in 1985. He earned a BFA from the Art Center College of Design in 1979, and then spent the next six years as a storyboard artist for Disney and other studios. He has also done freelance illustration for movie posters, book covers and advertising. Paul's creation, **Concrete**, for Dark Horse Comics, took the comic industry by storm, inspiring a whole new generation of alternative comics. His other comic credits include pencilling **Dazzler** and various anthology stories and pinups for DC Comics, and painted covers for **Stalkers** and **Open Space** for Marvel Comics. Paul says, "Keep in mind you're telling a story. Be clear, and give enough information to make the reader care. Comics are more like literature than they are like movies." Paul lives in Connecticut with his wife, Elizabeth.

Dan Danko has been working in comics since 1987 and is currently a writer and senior editor at Malibu Comics. Some of his work includes writing on **Gigantor**, **Man Of War**, **Lord Pumpkin**, and **Warstrike** - all from Malibu Comics. He is also editing **Wrath**, the second **Skybox Ultraverse Card Series** and the **Ultraverse Masterworks Card Series**. Dan proudly states, "I think that I would achieve the pinnacle of my life if one day somebody was filling out one of those things for CBG [Comic Buyer's Guide] that asks "Who's your influence?" and they listed me." Additionally, Dan believes that ". . . we all owe our futures to Tim Boo Bah." Dan is hiding out in Southern California.

Guy Davis started working as a professional in 1986. Guy got his start with the independents, and really established himself as co-creator and artist on Caliber Press' award-winning series, **Baker Street**. He has since gone on to do work with DC Comics on the acclaimed **Sandman Mystery Theater**. Guy says that many fans don't recognize him at conventions these days since he underwent a radical hairstyle change. "The thing I remember most, is my mohawk hitting the floor, " he says. Guy lives and works in the south Michigan area, and that's all he's saying.

Les Dorscheid has worked since 1982 as a comic professional. He attended the Madison Area Technical College and The Art Center College of Design. He started his professional career by painting products for advertising - food mostly; cheese salad dressing, crackers and something called Flavor Fry. His comic career began with his work on **Nexus** for Capitol Publishing, and his hand-painted color work has helped influence the look of comic coloring. Les has worked on more than twenty titles, including **Batman:Red Rain** and **Deadman** for D.C. Comics, and **Aliens:Hive** and **Nexus** for Dark Horse Comics. He also has self-published two art prints,"Discretion" and "See, I Told You" (for more information write: **Moonlit Graphics**, 1415 Andaman, Sun Prairie, WI 53590). Les says, "Keep practicing, working and struggling. Most big shots were just little shots that kept shooting." He lives in the sunniest part of Wisconsin with his wife, Susan, and their two sons, Kyle and Andrew.

Dave Dorman has worked as an illustrator in the comic and related industries since 1978. Some of his work includes cover art for **The Batman** for DC Comics, the **Indiana Jones** and **Star Wars** series for Dark Horse Comics, and a large variety of paperback novels. He is also note for his illustration work in **Aliens:Tribes**, a graphic story album for Dark Horse Comics, the **Roadkill** series (which he also co-created) for Caliber Press, and the ninety-eight piece painted trading card set for **Skybox's Malibu Ultraverse Masterworks**. Dorman says laughingly, "Comics!?! Blah, blah, blah, blah, blah!" He currently lives and works in Northwest Florida with his writer/artist wife, Lurene Haines.

Dave Elliott has been a comic professional since 1984. He started out as the publisher of *Atomika*, producing a wide variety of books for both the US and European markets including the very popular **A-1**. He also ran, very successfully, *Tundra UK* again responsible for producing an eclectic mixture of cutting-edge material. He is currently the publisher of the hot up-and-coming company *Blackball Comics*, based in London. He lives in England with his wife, Helen and beautiful new daughter, Amy.

Matt Feazell has been a professional freelancer since 1980 when his first published comics work appeared in **Anarchy Comics #3** from Last Gasp. From 1987 to 1991 he did a back-up feature in **Zot!** for Eclipse Comics. He continues to publish his own work in minicomic form under the name Not Available Comics, which have become quite successful for him. (To get more information, or order Matt's comics write to: Not Available Comics, 3867 Bristow, Detroit, MI 48212.) Matt works as a production artist for The Metro Times, a weekly newspaper in Detroit. He states happily, "It seemed like a good idea at the time!" Matt lives in Detroit with his understanding wife, Karen Majewski, who is working on her doctoral thesis.

Mike Friedrich began his professional comic career in 1967. He worked as a freelancer for DC Comics and Marvel Comics until 1975. Some of his writing credits include **Robin**, **Justice League**, **Batman**, and **Green Lantern** for DC Comics as well as **Iron Man**, **Ka-Zar**, and **Ant-Man** for Marvel Comics. In 1974, Mike launched Star*Reach as the first independent comic publisher, which he ran until 1979. In 1980 he returned to Marvel where he set up their direct sales department. In 1982 he revived Star*Reach Productions as a talent agency for artists and writers. Some of the clients he represents include Paul Chadwick, Steve Englehart, Norm Breyfogle, Howard Cruse, and P. Craig Russell. He says, reflectively, "To be an agent in the comic business meant re-defining the position, because there was nothing like this in other fields." Mike is the President of the Board of Directors for the non-profit Pro/Con held annually in Oakland California. His agency is located in Berkeley, California.

Archie Goodwin started his professional comic career in 1964. He began by writing for Warren Publishing, and then eventually took over as an editor. He then moved on to Marvel Comics as a writer, and followed that up with freelance work for a variety of publishers. From 1973-74 he worked for DC Comics as an editor and writer and, after being editor-in-chief of Epic Comics at Marvel, most recently returned in 1989 where he is now a group editor. Although he went to art school in New York, and even worked for a while in the art department of Redbook Magazine, Archie feels his real strengths lie in writing. "The art training certainly helps me as a comic book writer and editor," he says. Some of his writing credits include **Creepy**, **Eerie** and **Blazing Combat** for Warren Publishing, the award-winning **Manhunter** (with Walt Simonson) for DC Comics, newspaper cartoon strips **Secret Agent X-9** and **Star Wars** with art by Al Williamson, and most recently the graphic novel, **Barman: Nightcries** with Scott Hampton. At DC Comics Archie currently oversees a large variety of regular monthly books, including **Legends of the Dark Knight**, as well as a number of special projects. He lives - and works very hard! - in New York.

Lurene Haines has been working as a comic professional since 1986. She moved to the U.S.A. from her home of Victoria, British Columbia, after completing a Bachelor of Science degree, to work as as art assistant and business manager for comic artist Mike Grell. She left Seattle, Washington in 1988 to begin working as a freelance writer and artist. Some of her credits include **Green Arrow: The Longbow Hunters** for DC Comics, **Hellraiser** for Epic Comics, **Indian Jones and The Fate Of Atlantis** for Dark Horse Comics, **Ms. Fury** and **Star Trek: Deep Space Nine** for Malibu Entertainment, and **Thumbscrew**, **Femina**, and **Femina Two** for Caliber Press. She is currently branching out to do work as a children's book writer and illustrator. Lurene maintains, "There's no substitute for professionalism; act like a businessperson, and you'll always be treated like one." She shares a home and studio with her husband, artist David Dorman, in Northwest Florida.

Scott Hampton has been a professional comic illustrator since 1982. Scott's credits include the **Silverheels** and **Pigeons From Hell** graphic novels from Eclipse Enterprises, **Batman:Nightcries** from DC Comics, and **The Upturned Stone** painted graphic novel from Kitchen Sink Press. Scott lives in Durham, North Carolina with his wife Letitia Glozer. Scott says, "I hope a lot of *professionals* read this book, so that their behavior will live up to the standards described herein."

Marc Hempel has been a comic professional since 1978. He earned a BFA in Painting from Northern Illinois University. Marc's credits include **Breathtaker** and **Sandman:The Kindly Ones** for DC Comics/Vertigo, **Gregory I-IV** for DC Comics/Piranha Press, and stories for **Hellraiser, Marvel Fanfare** and **Epic Illustrated** for Epic Comics. **Gregory** has been nominated for two Eisner Awards and two Harvey Awards. Marc says, "Express the character! Express the emotion!" He shares a studio with artist/writer Mark Wheatley, in the Baltimore area.

Kelley Jones has worked as a comic professional since 1985. He majored in historical anthropology at Sierra College before beginning work as a freelance artist. Kelley's credits include **Batman: Red Rain**, **Dark Joker** (graphic novel), and **Batman: Bloodstorm (Red Rain II)** for DC Comics, in addition to their new **Batman: Haunted Gotham** monthly series. He also worked on **Aliens:Hive** for Dark Horse Comics. Kelley says his most recent favorite quote is by Charles Fort, "I think we're someone else's property." He believes in being a nice guy, and treating the fans fairly, and with respect. Kelley lives and works in northern California.

Michael Kaluta has been a comic professional since 1969. He is a self-described fantasy illustrator whose delicate and expressive artwork has influenced a whole generation of illustrators. His work includes the infamous and ongoing creation, **Starstruck** seen from a variety of publishers and most recently from Dark Horse Comics. His work on **The Shadow** began with DC Comics, and continues with writing and art on the Dark Horse Comics series and now some production design work for the movie. His **1994 J.R.R.Tolkien Calendar** is a self-proclaimed labor of love. He says, mysteriously, "It's a big universe. Somebody's got to live in it and it might as well be you." Michael lives and works in his Manhattan apartment which is frequently crowded with guests.

Barbara Kesel sold her first professional comic story in 1981. In 1984 she began working as an editor at DC comics, where she stayed for about five years. After working two years as a full-time comic freelancer, she joined the ranks of Dark Horse Comics in 1991. She is currently the Managing Editor at Dark Horse, but still fits in some freelance writing projects. Her credits include writing **Hawk and Dove** for DC Comics, as well as editing their **New Teen Titans** and **The Watchmen** books. She has edited **Aliens: Genocide, Aliens: Hive, Star Wars: Dark Empire**, and Rick Geary's **Blanche Goes To. . .** books for Dark Horse Comics. She also traffics **John Byrne's NextMen** & **Danger Unlimited**, in addition to Mike Mignola's **Hellboy**. Her freelance work also includes writing the **Golden City** segments, and it's sequel **Will To Power**, for Dark Horse Comics' *Comics Greatest World*. Barb says defiantly, "No, I *don't* draw the words into the little balloons." She lives in Oregon with her husband, writer/artist Karl Kesel.

Karl Kesel started his professional comic career in 1984. He is an alumni of The Joe Kubert School of Cartooning, where he spent a year over the 1977-78 semesters. His credits include inking Steve Rude for **The World's Finest** series and John Byrne for **Superman** at DC Comics. He is also currently writing the **Adventures of Superman** and **Superboy**. His writing, pencilling and inking skills will be showcased in the mini-series, **Indiana Jones and The Sargasso Pirates**, for Dark Horse Comics. Karl's 'cartooning idol' is Milt Caniff, who he happily paraphrased, "My job is to sell the *next* issue of the comic I'm working on!" Karl lives in Oregon with his wife, writer Barb Kesel.

Frank Kurtz has been connected with the comic industry in various capacities since 1985. He got is start in the industry on the retail end of the business, and is now the editor for **Hero Illustrated Magazine**. Frank is the creator, artist and writer of **Creepsville** and **Creepsville Resurected** from GoGo Comics, and **Tor Love Betty** and **Cheapskin** from Fantagraphics. He is also a writer and contributing editor for **Monster Scene Journal**. Frank has said "It may sound arrogant, but of course I want to be called The Greatest Man Alive!" One of Franks favorite quotes is from the film **Plan Nine From Outer Space**; "We are all interested in the future, because that's where you and I are going to live the rest of our lives." Frank lives in the Chicago area, but wouldn't be more specific than that.

Wendi Lee has been a writer and comic professional since 1983. After a stint as the press liaison for Renegade Press Wendi began work as a freelancer. Her work credits include co-writer on **Elf Quest #7** and **#10** and a story for **Elfquest: New Blood Summer Special** from Warp Graphics, six **Jefferson Birch** western novels for Walker & Co., and **The Good Daughter**, a lady P.I. crime novel from St. Martin's Press. "Brevity is everything," she says. Wendi shares a home with her husband, well-known artistTerry Beatty, in Muscatine, Iowa.

Mark A. Nelson has been a comic professional since 1983. He is also a professor at Northern Illinois University, where he has been teaching art for the last fifteen years. Some of his credits include **Aliens: Book One** for Dark Horse Comics, **Nightbreed #11** & **#12** and **Feud** for Marvel Comics, interior illustrations for **Dragon Magazine**, and **Blood and Shadows** for DC Comics. He also does a feature, "Pencils and Inks" for **Hero Illustrated Magazine**. "You're only as good as your last drawing, "says Mark. Mark and his artist wife, Anita, live in the northern Illinois area with their dog, Maya, and their two cats, Ziffel and Zoe.

Mart Nodell is considered one of the founding fathers of comics. He began his professional comic career in 1938, and is responsible for the creation of the ever-popular **Green Lantern** from DC Comics. Mart worked in comics until 1950, then left to work as an art director in advertising. During that time he was responsible for accounts with **Stouffers, Kellogs, Proctor and Gamble, Wheeling Steel** and **Sara Lee**. His team also created the infamous **Pillsbury Doughboy**, which Mart designed. Mart returned to comics in 1975, and he and his wife, Carrie are popular convention guests all around the world. Mart is currently working on a "top-secret" project with Dark Horse Comics. Mart says, "Comic book fans are alive and well!" He and Carrie live in sunny south Florida.

Mitch O'Connell got his first professional comic job with Charlton Comics in 1981. His professional credits include illustration and advertising art for **Spy Magazine, Playboy Magazine, National Lampoon, Seven-11, Burger King, MacDonalds Restaurant , Coca-Cola**, and **Kelloggs**. His comic work includes **The World of Ginger Fox** graphic novel for Comico, and a wide variety of comic covers and back-up stories for many different publishers. Mitch says, "You're going to be judged by your worst piece, so if you only have seven good pieces, only show seven pieces." (To order Mitch's hot new book, **Good Taste Gone Bad: The Art Of Mitch O'Connell** send $15.00 (post paid) to **Good Taste Products**, P.O. Box 267869, Chicago, IL 60626.) Mitch lives in Chicago with a wide variety of inspirational, yet tasteless, art objects.

Dave Olbrich is one of the four founders of Malibu Comics and currently holds the position of Publisher. He has worked in the comic industry since 1981 in a variety of jobs including managing a retail comic store, working at a comic book distributor, and for a short time was the circulation and advertising director at Fantagraphics and the managing editor of **Amazing Heroes Magazine**. His latest pet project is setting up the new **Bravura** line of creator-owned books. Dave says one of Malibu's philosophies is, "We think the comic book industry can run more smoothly if we all pull in the same direction." Dave also said, " I firmly believe that the retailers and creators are probably the most important pieces in the comic industry because, in the end, the rest of us are just middlemen." Dave leads the Malibu pack in Southern California.

Jerry Ordway started working as a comic professional in 1980. While working as commercial artist, he attended the Chicago Comicon where he got his first small job from a DC Comics Talent Search. In 1981 he took the plunge, and became a full-time comic freelancer. Jerry has worked on **All Star Squadron**, **Infinity Incorporated**, **Power of Shazam**, and **Zero Hour** for DC Comics, and on **The Fantastic Four** for Marvel Comics. He also co-created **Wildstar** with Al Gordon, for Image. Jerry is very well-known for his long, popular run working on the **Superman** series for DC. "Hey, I subscribe to that Work Ethic," he says. Jerry says one of the most pleasurable experiences in his life was being involved with the **Time Magazine** cover for Superman's 50th anniversary. Jerry lives in Connecticut with his wife, Peggy and his lovely daughter Rachel.

Gary Reed is the publisher of Caliber Press and has been a comic professional in a variety of capacities since 1983 when he started his first retail store. He currently owns two comic shops, **Reader's Exchange** and **Comics Plus**. He started his comic publishing company, Caliber Pess, in 1989. Some of his work includes writing **Mechanoids**, and co-creator/co-writer of the popular series **Baker Street**, with Guy Davis. He also has published **Realm of the Dead**, the **Roadkill** series, **Deadworld**, **Sinergy**, **Realm**, **Negative Burn** and **Joe Sinn**. "The limiting factor in the growth of comics is the reliance on the superhero story," he says. He lives with his wife, Jennifer, and their children in Canton, MI.

Joe Rubinstein has been a well-respected inker in the comic industry since 1975. "Eighteen years without a single day off!", Joe says, "If I died, seven other people could have a career." Some of Joe's work includes the **Wolverine** mini-series and **Captain America** for Marvel, as well as **Superman** and **Batman** for DC Comics. He is also recognized for his beautiful oil paintings, and has studied under the guidance of noted painter, Burt Silverman. He resides in Brooklyn, New York and exclaims "Editors; a cowardly and superstitious lot."

Walter Simonson has been a professional artist and writer in comics since 1972. In his auspicious career, Walt has worked on **Thor** for Marvel Comics and **Manhunter** for DC Comics. His latest projects include writing the **Legends of The World's Finest** series for DC Comics, and his own creation, **Star Slammers** for Malibu's Bravura line. Walt says, quite happily, "If I were you, I'd read the Superman books!" Although he is originally from College Park, Maryland, Walt and his wife, renowned writer Louise Simonson, now live in the state of New York.

Del Stone Jr. had his first professional comic sale in 1991. He is a journalist, currently working as the Assistant Managing Editor for The Northwest Florida Daily News, in addition to writing freelance for the speculative fiction market. His comics credits include "The Girl In The Peephole" in **Hellraiser #20** from Epic Comics, "I'll Wait For You" in **Thumbscrew #1-3**, **Roadkill**, **December**, **Heat** and **Dakota** for Caliber Press, "The Surviving Kind" in **Underground #4** for Dark Horse Comics. His prose work has appeared in small press, trade and mainstream venues. His prose story "The Googleplex Comes and Goes" in **Full Spectrum 3** from Bantam Books has been nominated for a Nebula Award. His story "Companions" appears in **The Year's Best Horror (1994)** from Donald A. Wolheim Pub. "The best piece of advice I ever got was, 'Wear clean underwear'" Del is single ". . . not by choice!" and lives in Northwest Florida with his two cats, Pavlov and Maggie.

Sean Taggart has been working in the mainstream comic industry since 1991. Prior to that he worked as a freelance illustrator in the music industry for about six years. After working as the Special Projects Manager for The Topps Trading Card Company, Sean took a position with DC Comics as their Trading Card Editor where he is handling the **Batman: Saga Of The Dark Night** and the **DC Comics Masterseries** trading cards. Sean is frequently heard to exclaim, "Where's my piece!?!" Sean lives with his wife, Bronwyn in Brooklyn, New York.

Chris Ulm has worked in comics as an editor and writer since 1986. He has worked on **Dead Clown** for Malibu Comics, **Robotech** for Eternity Comics, **Rune** (co-writer with Barry Windsor Smith) for Malibu Comics, and is the editor on Malibu's Ultraverse line. Chris says, "Just call me Frogboy!" Chris lives and works in Southern California.

Rod Underhill has been working as a comic professional since 1981. He also works full time in the legal profession as an attorney and protem Small Claims Court Judge. His comic credits include **Airlock #1-3**, **The Forbidden Airlock #1**, **Wonderwall #1** and a variety of fine art prints all published by his own company, Eclectus. He has also written the story for a graphic novel, **Caligula** with art by Topper Helmers, and created a series of fine art pin-ups - done in conjunction with Homage artist, Brian Haverlin - called **Nutopian Digital Pin-ups** for CompuServe. He says, "There's nothing wrong with working in the comic industry, as long as you wash your hands when you're done." Rod resides, and practices law, in Southern California.

Mark Verheiden has worked as professional comic writer since 1986. Before coming to comics, Mark worked for five years in "bad" advertising at the Los Angeles Times. He claims, "It was a job. I was glad I had it." While he was working there, he wrote a couple of low-budget films - one of which actually "kinda" got made. Mark says he banged around for a while before he found his niche in comics and movie work. Mark's comic work includes **Aliens**, **Predator**, **The American**, and **Timecop** for Dark Horse Comics. His film credits include the film **Timecop** and re-writes for the films **The Mask** and **Darkman Two**. Mark says his household philosophy is, "Life's too short to be angry all the time." He lives and writes in California with his lovely wife, Sonya and their son, Ben.

Charles Vess has worked as an illustrator in the comic field since 1978. His very first professional comic job was the cover for **Amazing Spiderman #261** from Marvel Comics. His other credits include the graphic novel **Spiderman: Spirits of the Earth** (writer and painter) plus many stories, covers, posters and pin-ups for Marvel Comics. He has also done the illustrated book **A Midsummer Night's Dream** for Donning, **Sandman #19**, **Books Of Magic**, and **Swamp Thing** covers for DC Comics, and the "Ballad" series in **Dark Horse Presents** for Dark Horse Comics. He says "Your eraser is the best artistic tool you'll ever have . . . and remember, it's only lines on paper folks!" The award-winning Charlie lives in a southwest corner of Virginia and has a sleeping dragon on his black-and-white business card.

Mark Wheatley has been involved in the comic business since 1977. Mark says the rallying cry for **Radical Dreamer** is "Dreams cannot die!" Mark's work includes **Breathtaker** and a two-part **Batman: Legends Of The Dark Knight** for DC Comics, **Radical Dreamer** from Blackball and Mark's Giant Economy Size Comics, writing the **Flash 1994 Annual** and creating a new **2099** series for Marvel Comics, and developing **Argus**, a new series, for DC Comics. Mark lives in the Baltimore area with his wife, Carole, and shares a studio with artist/writer Marc Hempel.

George White has been associated with the comic industry since 1990, before which he spent five years as the chief of staff for a U.S Congressman on Capital Hill.. He is currently the president of Top Dog Marketing, a marketing and public relations firm that works with a number of companies and creators in the comic industry, including **Skybox Comic Cards**, **Blackball Comics**, the **Heroes Convention** in Charlotte, NC, the **Heroes Aren't Hard to Find** comic store chain and **Wildstorm Production**. George is quite excited about his pet project, the **Skybox Master Series: Creator's Edition Cards**. He says, "Comic cards are the elixir of life!" George lives with his wife Anne and his two comic- and card- chewing Labradors in Chapel Hill, North Carolina.

Chuck Wojtkiewicz (pronounced Voyt-kev-itch) began working as a comic freelancer in 1983. He worked for eleven years as a graphic artist, while trying to get into comics. His comic work includes a brief stint working on the short-lived TSR Comics line, **Mecca** for Dark Horse, as well as **Superman: Man of Steel** and **Justice League International** for DC Comics. Chuck says, impassioned, "There is no legendary, happy comic-company bull pen. This is a real job." Chuck shares a studio with six other artists, and lives with his beautiful wife, Marc, in the artistic heart of North Carolina.

Index